CONNECTIVE

BRANDING

CONNECTIVE BRANDING

Building Brand Equity in a Demanding World

Dr Claudia Fisher-Buttinger

and

Dr Christine Vallaster

A John Wiley & Sons, Ltd., Publication

Copyright © 2008 John Wiley & Sons Ltd, The Atrium, Southern Gate, Chichester,
West Sussex PO19 8SQ, England
Telephone (+44) 1243 779777

Email (for orders and customer service enquiries): cs-books@wiley.co.uk
Visit our Home Page on www.wiley.com

All Rights Reserved. No part of this publication may be reproduced, stored in a retrieval system or transmitted in any form or by any means, electronic, mechanical, photocopying, recording, scanning or otherwise, except under the terms of the Copyright, Designs and Patents Act 1988 or under the terms of a licence issued by the Copyright Licensing Agency Ltd, Saffron House, 6-10 Kirby Street, London, EC1N 8TS, UK, without the permission in writing of the Publisher. Requests to the Publisher should be addressed to the Permissions Department, John Wiley & Sons Ltd, The Atrium, Southern Gate, Chichester, West Sussex PO19 8SQ, England, or emailed to permreq@wiley.co.uk, or faxed to (+44) 1243 770620.

Designations used by companies to distinguish their products are often claimed as trademarks. All brand names and product names used in this book are trade names, service marks, trademarks or registered trademarks of their respective owners. The Publisher is not associated with any product or vendor mentioned in this book.

This publication is designed to provide accurate and authoritative information in regard to the subject matter covered. It is sold on the understanding that the Publisher is not engaged in rendering professional services. If professional advice or other expert assistance is required, the services of a competent professional should be sought.

Other Wiley Editorial Offices

John Wiley & Sons Inc., 111 River Street, Hoboken, NJ 07030, USA

Jossey-Bass, 989 Market Street, San Francisco, CA 94103-1741, USA

Wiley-VCH Verlag GmbH, Boschstr. 12, D-69469 Weinheim, Germany

John Wiley & Sons Australia Ltd, 42 McDougall Street, Milton, Queensland 4064, Australia

John Wiley & Sons (Asia) Pte Ltd, 2 Clementi Loop #02-01, Jin Xing Distripark, Singapore 129809

John Wiley & Sons Canada Ltd, 6045 Freemont Blvd, Mississauga, ONT, L5R 4J3, Canada

Wiley also publishes its books in a variety of electronic formats. Some content that appears in print may not be available in electronic books.

Library of Congress Cataloging-in-Publication Data

Fisher-Buttinger, Claudia.
  Connective branding : building brand equity in a demanding world / Claudia Fisher-Buttinger and Christine Vallaster.
     p. cm.
  Includes bibliographical references and index.
  ISBN 978-0-470-51240-1 (alk. paper)
  1. Brand name products—Management. 2. Brand name products—Valuation—Management. 3. Branding (Marketing) 4. Corporate image. I. Vallaster, Christine, 1971– II. Title.
  HD69.B7F57 2008
  658.8′27—dc22   2008040265

British Library Cataloguing in Publication Data

A catalogue record for this book is available from the British Library

ISBN 978-0-470-51240-1 (HB)

Typeset in 11.5/15 pt Bembo by SNP Best-set Typesetter Ltd, Hong Kong
Printed and bound in Great Britain by TJ International Ltd, Padstow, Cornwall, UK

To Jason and Julian
To Gert and Hannah

CONTENTS

PROLOGUE ix

INTRODUCTION xiii

PART I   SETTING THE STAGE   1

1   MARKET FORCES   3

2   EMERGING STRATEGIES TO ADDRESS MARKET FORCES   31

PART II   A FRAMEWORK FOR COPING   121

3   BRAND FRAMEWORK FOR BUILDING CONNECTIVE BRANDS   123

PART III   CRITICAL SUCCESS FACTORS FOR MAKING IT HAPPEN   211

4   PRACTICAL APPLICATIONS – STAKEHOLDER ENGAGEMENT   213

5 PRACTICAL APPLICATIONS – THE PROCESS
   OF ALIGNMENT   279

**EPILOGUE – THE LAW OF THE SEVENTH
             GENERATION?**   349

INDEX   351

PROLOGUE

When studying the history of branding, there are two key themes that systematically emerge as the primary drivers of brand success:

- Differentiation
- Consistency

As product markets have evolved, so has the notion of what differentiation and consistency mean. Initially, when brands were still equated with logos, differentiation was mostly limited to identification of origin, and consistency meant consistent quality.

With the arrival of life-changing inventions, differentiation could be achieved through unique product features and their functional benefits, while consistency found a home more in the visual application – product design and visual corporate identity.

As genuine functional differences started to erode, differentiation shifted into communications, placing a new emphasis on advertising and creativity. In parallel, consistency came to mean a certain degree of uniformity in communications, across media and channels.

But what about today?

New forces have entered the branding environment; they necessitate fundamental changes and paradigm shifts:

- The Internet has created a world where uncensored information spreads rapidly through social networks, shifting control from companies and established institutions towards the customer and employee.
- An environment of eroding trust has emerged as one scandal is chasing the next in our global economy. Recent research found that nearly eight out of ten of the world's most admired companies in their respective industries lost their crowns over the past five years.[1]
- Sustainability has evolved from a mere buzz-word into a business imperative. Unprecedented attention is given to issues around the environment and ethical and social issues. Increasingly, companies are called upon to save our planet.

In this complex world, differentiation is no longer possible through functional benefits or creative communications alone. More and more, companies are bringing the organisation into branding as a new source of differentiation, making employee engagement and employee willingness to enact the brand promise a key concern of brand building.

Oscar Wilde exclaimed that "Consistency is the last resort of the unimaginative." However, in today's world consistency no longer means the literal compliance with manuals and guidelines, but rather the alignment of expectations created with experiences actually had.

---

[1] Ross, L.-G., Communicate until your tonsils bleed, Ethical Corporation, 6 March 2008, accessed: http://www.ethicalcorp.com/content.asp?ContentID=5754

As a result, branding has become more complex. This book is our attempt at penetrating this complexity. We have interviewed 120 brand experts across the globe to discuss the state of branding as well as their approach to mastering the challenges they face. Our book is the product of our own thinking and experience enriched by interesting insights shared by our interview partners. We try to offer interesting angles that might not have been considered before and to draw lateral connections that might not have been made before. Our goal is to ask the right questions, not to provide all the answers. Our book encourages readers to see branding for what it is, namely creative thinking, combined with a strong business sense, a knack for opportunities, clarity of thought, focus and the courage to be true to a set of chosen values and beliefs.

We would like to thank all our interview partners for sharing their wisdom and our families for their continued support and encouragement. In particular, thank you Jason for all your invaluable input and feedback.

Munich, May 2008
Claudia and Christine

INTRODUCTION

As the business and branding environment is changing, brand management has to respond with adequate tools and frameworks. When the brand's main job was to make the customer happy and to drive sales, branding focused naturally first on creating a favourable image with customers (e.g. through advertising) and later on creating a positive customer experience (through the management of customer interactions, also called "touchpoints" or "moments of truth"[1]).

The commonly used definition of brands as "the sum of all associations customers have with a certain product or service" perfectly suited this environment and brand paradigm; but today, brands are expected to deliver on a much broader range of

---

[1] Schmitt, B., *Customer Experience Management*, Hoboken, New Jersey: John Wiley & Sons, Inc. 2003.

xiv INTRODUCTION

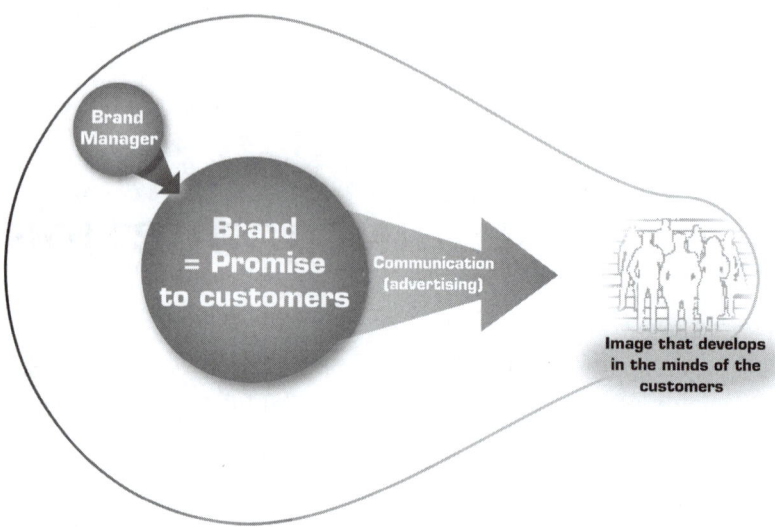

Figure 0.1 Traditional understanding of brands

objectives beyond protecting premium prices, some of which they are not (yet) particularly well equipped to master:

- *Attract and retain talent.* During recruitment drives, brands are now supposed to position the company behind the brand as an attractive employer.
- *Increase employee commitment.* Through positive identification brands are responsible for increasing employee motivation, commitment and satisfaction, thereby reducing attrition, sick leave and accidents, and improving productivity.
- *Drive the share price.* Via volatility reduction platforms such as customer loyalty and growth platforms such as geographical expansion and product extensions, brands are appealing to analysts, shareholders, potential investors, and the financial media, ultimately helping to drive the share price.
- *Address CSR (corporate social responsibility).* More and more, brands are also used for corporate reputation management, to

address media, activists, government and non-government lobby groups, as well as to manage crisis situations.

In order to address this new environment and the much broader role that brands now play, the definition of "brand" has to change in a number of ways.

BRANDS MUST ADDRESS MULTIPLE AUDIENCES

Inside the company, greater emphasis needs to be placed on employees' willingness and ability to enact the brand; more collaboration is required from a number of functions that regularly interact with key stakeholders and touch the brand (in particular, corporate reputation, human resources and sustainability functions), and brand ownership no longer rests with middle management, but with the CEO.

With regards to external stakeholders, customers are still the single most important brand audience, but no longer the only one. Other external stakeholders like suppliers, shareholders, governments, the press, NGOs, etc., will increasingly come into contact with the brand; however, segregation of audiences and "stories" told is no longer possible because the Internet allows for an instant spread of information worldwide. Therefore, a coherent brand message and approach are required.

BRAND VALUES MUST BE LIVED FROM WITHIN

The brand evolves around a small set of values that are experienced by the entire organisation and radiate outwards to all key stakeholders (see Figure 0.2). This goes far beyond the creation

INTRODUCTION

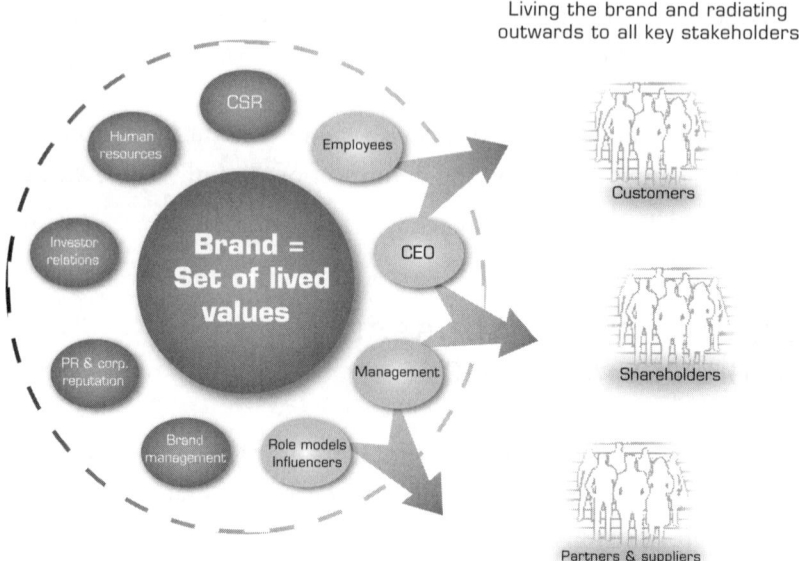

Figure 0.2 Broadening audiences addressed

of a favourable image through communications activities and requires the anchoring of brand values in every part of the organisation.

BRANDS ARE BUILT ON INTERACTIVE RELATIONSHIPS

The other important shift is the move away from a paradigm that is built on disseminating information from the company to the target audience(s). The new paradigm is built on interactive relationships between the company and all key stakeholders (as well as *between* stakeholders in some cases). This also translates into a power shift – companies are no longer the sole creators of brands.

Figure 0.3 New understanding of brands

Given these shifts, a more appropriate definition of brand is as follows:

> A brand is the sum total of relationships among stakeholders, or the medium through which stakeholders interact and exchange with each other.[2]

---

[2] Myers, D., Whose brand is it anyway?, in Ind, N. (ed.), *Beyond Branding*, Philadelphia: Kogan Page, 2003, pp. 21–35.

CONNECTIVE BRANDING

We believe that integrating all aspects of branding in this complex, new environment is the appropriate response to the new demands made of brands. This can be achieved through two major mechanisms – engagement and alignment. The result is a well-coordinated brand where all elements operate in synchronicity.

Connective branding is a framework intended to guide branding and marketing strategists through the treacherous waters of today's branding environment.

We have organised the book into three main parts:

- *Part One: Setting the Stage.* A number of market forces are playing together to create an environment that calls for a new shift in branding. While companies find themselves more and more incapable of controlling all aspects of their business, and therefore more vulnerable and prone to making mistakes, the Internet acts like a giant megaphone into a "socially networked" world, exposing and magnifying any mistakes. All this is happening against a backdrop of two opposing movements – eroding trust and an increasing CSR imperative. Companies have partially started to address these market forces.
- *Part Two: A Framework for Coping.* We have developed a framework that helps companies to build and maintain strong brands even in the current challenging environment. The two key drivers of brand equity are engagement and alignment.
- *Part Three: Critical Success Factors for Making it Happen.* We discuss the critical success factors for meaningful stakeholder engagement and alignment of brand promise and brand experience. We draw on a rich body of original case studies from around the globe, with a particular focus on European brands.

SNEAK PREVIEW – DIFFERENCES BETWEEN TRADITIONAL BRANDING CONCEPTS AND CONNECTIVE BRANDING

Table 0.1 summarises how *connective branding* is different from traditional branding approaches.

From external image to lived values

While traditional branding concepts focus on the creation of an external image primarily through advertising based on a one-way, often manipulative communication paradigm, connective branding is based on living the brand and radiating the brand promise outwards. This necessitates a more engaging communications paradigm where the brand is delivered through every point of interaction between brand and stakeholder, shifting the branding focus from the product towards the company behind the product.

From insular to networked

Traditionally, a brand manager was responsible for both creating and maintaining the brand, with limited interaction with other departments and functions. In the connective branding model, the brand is owned by the CEO, with a CMO or top level manage having brand responsibility. As audiences are converging, it becomes increasingly important for all functions to interact with key stakeholders and touch the brand to collaborate. As a result, the brand is no longer the *sole* responsibility of the marketing department but of all internal functions and processes, necessitating a networked approach towards fulfilling the brand promise.

Table 0.1 Overview connective branding

	Traditional branding concepts	Connective branding model
From external image to lived values		
Focus	External image	Embedded values
Key point of reference	Product	Company behind product
Primarily delivered through	Advertising	Every interaction
Communication paradigm	Manipulative	Engaging
Information flow	One way	Interactive
From insular to networked		
Brand creation	Brand manager	Co-creation
Brand ownership	Brand manager	CEO
Brand responsibility	Mid-level management	CMO or top-level manager
Collaboration	Minimal – isolated	Networked
Delivered by	Brand/marketing team	Every employee
Processes involved	Direct impact only	All enabling processes
From targeting customers to all key stakeholders		
Target	Primarily customers	Customers, employees and all other key stakeholders
Objectives	• Drive sales and loyalty (customers) • Differentiate against key competitors • Protect premium pricing	• Drive sales and loyalty (customers) • Differentiate against key competitors • Recruit and retain talent (employees) • Motivate employees • Support share price and protect premium pricing (financial community) • Build relationships with partners, suppliers, NGOs, distributors, retailers, special interest groups, etc.

From targeting customers to addressing all key stakeholders

While traditional branding concepts have primarily targeted customers, connective branding expands the role of the brand beyond the customer to include all stakeholders. With this comes the need to satisfy different, in some cases conflicting, expectations. The brand now also needs to inspire employees and keep engagement high, appeal to the financial community as well as build relationships with partners, suppliers, NGOs, distributors, retailers and special interest groups.

PART I

SETTING THE STAGE

Chapter 1 Market forces

We discuss the four key market forces that have created the necessity to adopt new paradigms for successful and strong brands – an environment of distrust; the Internet "megaphone"; control issues caused by an increasingly global economy and the outsourcing of critical processes; the growing sustainability imperative.

Chapter 2 Emerging strategies to address market forces

We describe how companies have started to react to these market forces. We discuss emerging sustainability strategies, emerging online strategies, emerging corporate branding strategies and a new focus on authenticity, providing examples and analysing perils and benefits.

CHAPTER 1

MARKET FORCES

*I*n this chapter we will discuss which changes and dynamics define the brand environment and how they impact on brand building.

Branding has evolved through a number of stages over its relatively short history, each reflecting the economic, social and political environment at the time. In the late 1890s with the advent of railways and long-distance product distribution, branding emerged as a way to identify the manufacturer and was largely limited to the use of logos. For the first time, consumers were able to choose from a wider selection of goods from companies outside of their local economy. To cope with this greater choice (and risk), logos were used not only to indicate the manufacturer, but also to signal quality. The industrialisation that followed brought an extraordinary wave of life-changing innovation, introducing new products like the car, the vacuum cleaner, and the electric iron. At this point, it was widely believed that good products sold themselves and advertising's primary role was to make sure everyone knew the product existed. In contrast, the proliferation of consumer goods in post-war USA brought an explosion in consumer choice, but with only incremental innovation. This led to the need to differentiate products, and the focus of branding shifted again, to the communication of superior features, unique ingredients, and their functional benefits.

As real product differences increasingly eroded, companies started to shift their focus from what a product could *do* towards how a brand made the consumer *feel* (emotional benefits), attempting to build emotional bonds with customers primarily through advertising. This sparked a creative revolution in advertising which itself became synonymous with branding. But, with the proliferation of media in the 1950s and 1960s, advertising became ubiquitous, turning consumer excitement into consumer fatigue. Companies had to find new ways to engage with the customer. With the arrival of the Internet, a new possibility emerged: a shift from a one-way communication (company to consumer) towards an interactive dialogue *with* the consumer and *between* consumers.

Branding is about to shift again, and again this is being driven by economic, social and political trends. An unprecedented wave of corporate scandals from Enron to Parmalat, the current credit crisis that is engulfing the financial services sector on a global basis, combined with the difficulties surrounding the current Bush administration in the US, and political and economic repercussions of the 9/11 terrorist attacks have created an environment of distrust. Meanwhile, the globalisation of the economy has led to increasing pressures to outsource business processes in order to take advantage of lower labour and manufacturing costs, particularly in emerging markets. The resulting complex and global supply chains have proven difficult to control, causing more scandals like the massive product recall of Mattel toys manufactured in China, and the exposure of child labour in connection with Gap Inc. in

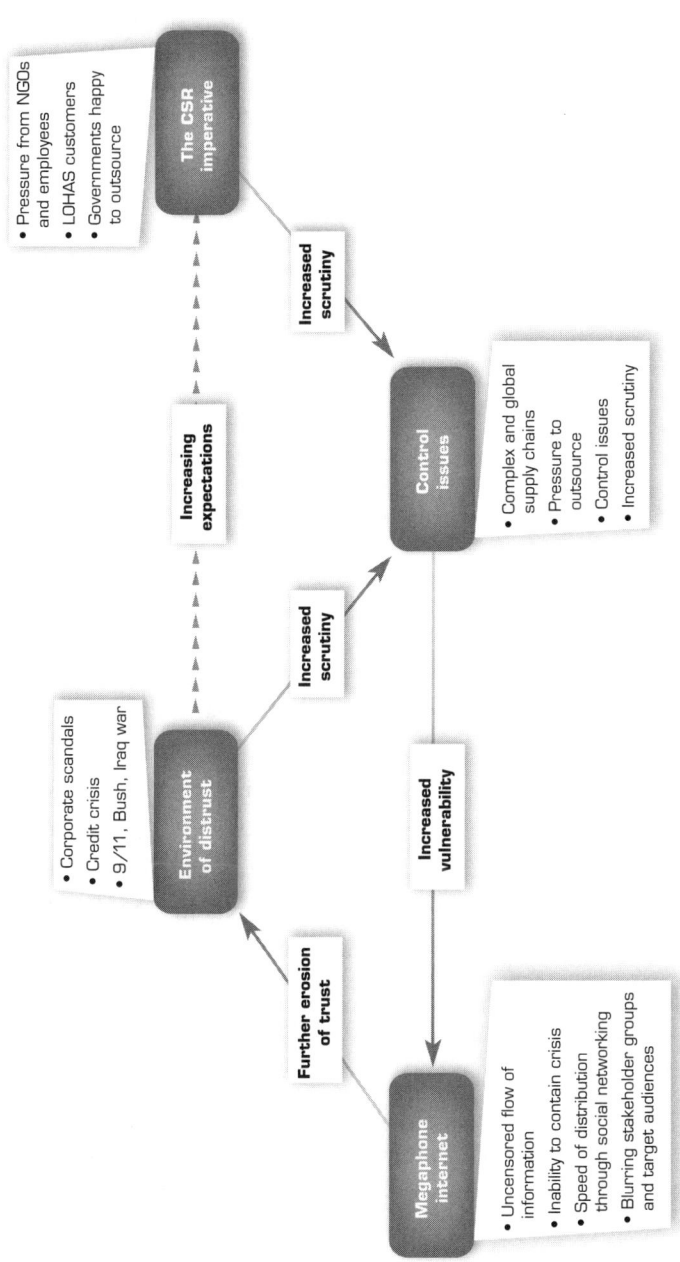

Figure 1.1 Economic, social and political trends calling for the next shift in branding

India. To add further pressure to this dynamic, Web 2.0 has turned the Internet into a giant megaphone that makes it impossible for companies to control information or contain a crisis, further amplifying both distrust and vulnerability. Increasing expectations towards businesses to be environmentally, socially, and ethically responsible create further pressure points and additional control issues, feeding into the cycle (see Figure 1.1).

How can companies build, protect and nourish strong brands in this environment? To answer this, we will explore each of these trends in more detail.

AN ENVIRONMENT OF DISTRUST

An erosion of trust over the past decade has been documented by many research studies.[1] This erosion of trust is most pronounced with institutions that traditionally carried a lot of authority, like governments, politicians, organised religion, and also the media. In the USA, for example, the disputed election of President Bush, the weapons of mass destruction fiasco leading to the war in Iraq, the less than objective behaviour of the media and the profiteering of Halliburton and other insider groups have created an environment of suspicion and cynicism. This has resulted in heightened scrutiny of and lowered expectations towards the integrity and credibility of the political system.

This breakdown of trust also extends into the corporate world, where an unprecedented wave of big corporate scandals like Enron, WorldCom, Parmalat, Tyco, etc. has and still is shaking up the trust of consumers and employees alike. To make things worse, the recent subprime mortgage crisis has demonstrated the

---

[1] See, for example, the Edelman Trust Barometer, conducted on an annual basis with worldwide opinion leaders, or the World Economic Forum: www.weforum.org

negative effects of our networked global economy, discrediting an entire industry in a matter of days. It did not help that the crisis involves all major financial services brands, from Citigroup to UBS to Deutsche Bank, nor did it help that the prevalent communication strategy seemed to be one of attempted cover-ups where banks were slow to admit to the actual size of their exposure.[2] Unfortunately, this is just another blow to the already eroding trust of customers and employees, leaving them equally disappointed and scared.

Large and global companies seem to evoke particular distrust at the moment. While their dealings and activities have become quite complex and somewhat impenetrable, they have risen to an entirely new echelon of transnational status and power. As their influence has increased to a point where it is perceived as unstoppable, these companies have become the target of the wrath of anti-corporation and anti-globalisation interest groups, who exert pressure to counter the impact of their size and political powers. Through books like Klein's *No Logo*[3] or movies like Joel Bakan's *The Corporation* (which tries to prove that a corporation has the personality traits of a psychopath), this sentiment has entered the mainstream. Today, heightened suspicion and scrutiny of (large) corporations is no longer limited to far-left activists; large global companies have become distrusted by *mainstream* consumers. Books, movies, articles, and blogs that point their fingers to companies like Adidas, Bayer, Nike, Donna Karan or Shell demonstrate – sometimes in a rather sensationalist way – how these popular and well-known brands are involved in exploitative practice – be it child labour, environmental destruction or cruelty to animals.[4] This has further contributed to

---

[2] Bell, M., Eine Branche verspielt ihren Kredit, *W&V*, 5, 31 Jan. 2008: 12–16.
[3] Klein, N., *No Logo*, Canada: Alfred Kopf, 2000.
[4] Klaus, W. and Weiss, H., *Das neue Schwarzbuch Markenfirmen – Die Machenschaften der Weltkonzerne*, Berlin: Ullstein Buchverlage GmbH, 2006.

this collective distrust. As a result, consumers now want to know which company stands behind the brands they love and whether they are indeed worthy of their affection and patronage. They start to absorb information about companies that goes far beyond the usual PR and advertising messages. Exposed unethical practice is often the work of subcontractors and other business partners, but it calls to account the entire supply chain.

As far as corporate functions or departments are concerned, finance and accounting are not the only ones that suffer from eroding trust. A particular lack of trust has plagued marketing for a long time, fed by empty promises, exaggerated claims, and wrong information. It is only natural that as a result, people have become more suspicious, more alert and more aware. For example, people have started to scrutinise products for suspicious ingredients (e.g. food is searched for E-numbers and carcinogenic agents) and country of origin tags (e.g. "Made in China" has developed a bad, if not feared, reputation for toys due to the Mattel/Fisher-Price scandal, or "Made in India" labels on clothes have developed unpleasant associations with unethical labour standards). Companies are examined with a fine-tooth comb for their business practices (e.g. Walmart has a bad reputation for paying low wages, having no health insurance and putting small shops out of business), media for their hidden agenda (e.g. Michael Moore, in his movie *Fahrenheit 9/11*, paints an interesting picture of how the relations between the Bush family and FOX media might have played a pivotal role in George W.'s election), political parties for their integrity (e.g. Hillary Clinton has been exposed to increasing amounts of criticism for accepting donations from the pharmaceutical lobby), and so on.

So who do we trust at this point in time? One group that has been able to steadily build trust over the past decade or so in most countries is NGOs. They seem to carry many characteristics of what is considered trustworthy in the current environment. They are deemed to be highly authentic, based on a strong belief system, directed at solving pressing issues of public concern or related to a good cause, and they are seen as truly independent from the "system", thereby willing and able to do what is right and to expose what is not. Interestingly enough, the latest Trust Barometer[5] shows some signs that trust in businesses (but not governments) is starting very slowly to reverse the negative trend. At the same time, NGOs for the first time are showing a slight decline in trust. One can't help but wonder if these two movements are the result of the latest trends in CSR – namely, the increasingly common practice of corporations to partner with NGOs, thereby improving the trustworthiness of businesses and decreasing that of NGOs.

Companies that are most likely to thrive in an environment of distrust are companies that are built on a strong ethos, like the old Body Shop, Ben & Jerry's, and Green & Blacks. However, many of these trustworthy companies have been bought up by large global corporations, leaving consumers and employees even more concerned: will they all sell out eventually?

> **Why is this universal breakdown of trust significant?**
>
> This universal breakdown of trust in the many authorities we assumed infallible is attacking one of the fundamental principles of branding. Brands are built on trust, without trust they cannot operate and survive. However, if trust is no longer a given, brands need to go back to the basics and start to rebuild this trust. Rebuilding trust is not possible through advertising or any other means of image creation alone, but requires that the brand is lived *inside out*. This means that a small set of values that drive the brand are embedded into every action and decision the company takes.

---

[5] Edelman Trust Barometer, 2008, accessed: http://www.edelman.co.uk/trustbarometer/

CONTROL ISSUES

Pressures to leverage cost advantages through outsourcing and moving production to countries with lower cost structures have become proliferate and intense. However, companies are finding it difficult to develop operational models that allow them to adequately control all aspects of the resulting complex and geographically dispersed supply chains. On the one hand, they now have to deal with a multitude of different cultures in terms of work ethics, skills, languages, and business conduct, as well as a patchwork of different rules and regulations. On the other hand, they struggle to impose a multitude of standards and guidelines on their employees, contractors, and subcontractors, which are impossible to enforce despite all good intentions.

Not surprisingly, identifying and addressing supply chain risk has become an issue of high priority not only for big global corporations, but also for medium-sized companies that have decided to take advantage of international opportunities. A 2006 research study on risk management conducted by Accenture[6] found that 73% of companies experienced supply chain disruptions in the past five years and 94% indicated that the disruption affected profitability and their company's ability to meet customer expectations. But things can get much, much worse. For example, in August 2007 Mattel, the American toy company, decided to recall a large number of their Fisher-Price toys because of dangerous lead paint found on their toys made in China. A couple of weeks later, hazardous lead paint was found on their Sarge toy cars, and potentially lethal magnets were discovered in the dolls of their Barbie line, all made in China, resulting in more product recalls. Yet by the end of the month, more lead paint was found on further toy lines (GeoTrax, It's a Big World, and Barbie), making a third

---

[6] Malone, R., Risk is Top Priority, *Forbes* magazine, 15 Nov. 2006, accessed: http://www.forbes.com/2006/11/15/risk-accenture-management-biz-logistics-cx_rm_1114accenture.html

recall necessary in the course of only one month. In total, almost 20 million toys were recalled, giving the company a huge wave of negative publicity and emotions. As Mattel found out, there are few things that outrage the consuming public more than those presenting danger to its children.

Mattel responded in a way that is often chosen by large companies in such situations – they put a face to the issue by making their CEO, Bob Eckert, the focal point of all communications. Eckert apologised in a personal video featured on the Mattel website, he gave numerous interviews, and he publicly discussed the problem and outlined key steps taken towards solving it. While these activities will hardly offset the damage done to the Mattel brand, they will at least provide damage control. Admitting mistakes, taking responsibility and, most importantly, demonstrating that the company will do whatever it takes to rectify the situation are all part of the hard work required to regain trust; but there is also another part that is about transparency and accessibility. Since the recalls, Mattel has been inundated not only with questions from parents and retailers, but also with requests for interviews and additional information from academics, journalists, researchers, etc. While this is creating additional stress points in already turbulent times, it is nearly impossible for Mattel to deny those interested a peek behind the curtains without raising further suspicions or creating a feeling of alienation. After all, the *way* a crisis is handled is often an equally decisive factor in how a company is judged as the crisis itself.

The reaction of leadership to the crisis is the ultimate acid test of what a company is all about and which key values they subscribe to. Eckert is quoted as saying: "How you achieve success is just as important as success itself"[7] – his motto for running Mattel. Therefore, Eckert did not hesitate to make the decision

---

[7] Yang, J.L., Mattel's CEO recalls a rough summer, *Fortune* magazine, 22 Jan. 2008, accessed: http://money.cnn.com/2008/01/21/news/companies/mattel.fortune/index.htm

to call back the flawed toys when in fact there might have been options resulting in less reputational damage for Mattel but higher risks for the children playing with Mattel toys. His focus on doing the *right* thing as opposed to the easy thing is a brave endeavour to position Mattel as a responsible company; unfortunately, not one that is typically rewarded by mass media more interested in sensationalist headlines than a balanced view.

It is important to note that the ultimate responsibility and blame seems to rest with the corporation behind the faulty toys – Mattel – and not the various product brands – Barbie, Sarge or Fisher-Price. This demonstrates that consumers increasingly are trying to get to the bottom of things and hold the company behind the brand accountable.

This case demonstrates the basic dilemma faced by many companies today. Outsourcing production to China or other countries with lower cost structures is often a competitive necessity, but this business practice creates huge risks in terms of quality standards, safety, and of course reputation.

Outsourcing is dangerous for brands because it reduces transparency from the company's perspective and increases the risk of things going wrong. It also places potentially highly important interaction points between the company and key stakeholders in the hands of someone who is not directly part of the company and therefore probably not privy to the same information with regards to company culture, brand promise and expected behaviour. New directions in outsourcing such as bundled services and end-to-end, fully managed supply chains may further amplify these issues.

Lack of control can also come from complex financial transactions or an over-reliance on electronic systems. For example, the latest case of a rogue trader with Société Général has called into question the reliability and transparency not only of their quality assurance programme, but also of their entire high-tech derivatives system. The incident makes experts wonder how one junior trader could have bypassed the entire system and single-handedly caused financial damage of 4.9 billion euros.[8] Of course, the reputational damage is also severe. Not only is the Société Général brand suffering enormously, but there is a negative halo affecting the entire French derivatives industry. The scandal has left many observers wondering how, in an age of alleged financial transparency, an institution of the magnitude and repute of Société Générale could allow such a failure in checks and balances.

> **Why is this lack of control significant for branding?**
>
> Brands represent a promise to their stakeholders and can only thrive when this promise is kept, every time. If companies lose control over parts of their supply chain, they also lose the ability to consistently deliver on this promise, thereby exposing the brand to huge potential for damage or even failure.

CORPORATE SOCIAL RESPONSIBILITY (CSR[9]) – TREND OR REMEDY?

CSR has come to include a vast array of activities, which is probably in part responsible for the confusion and lack of focus that

---

[8] FT Reporters, The rogue trader who cost SocGen 5bn €, Financial Times, 24 Jan. 2008, accessed: http://search.ft.com/ftArticle?queryText =Societe+general+4.9bn+rogue+trader&y=6&aje=true&x=9&id= 080124000758&ct=0

[9] CSR is not a term that seems to be much liked by anyone today. Alternative suggestions have been made from "Social Innovation", to "Good Corporate Citizenship" to "Sustainability" or simply "Good Business". Since an accepted new label has not yet emerged, we will stick with the term CSR for now.

pervades in this area at the moment. The CSR umbrella covers ethical business conduct and governance (labour standards, corruption, product safety); social responsibility and corporate giving (to the local community, the poor in general, addressing the social divide, helping the underprivileged); and currently the concern for our planet and the environment (climate change, water conservation, and "green" in general have topped the CSR agenda). Al Gore certainly has given new energy to the "green" movement, helping to make it a concern for the mainstream and not just that of special interest groups. In summary, CSR embodies ethical and respectful business practices and conduct towards the consumer, suppliers, employees, society, the community, the law, the environment and any other stakeholders.

In order to fully appreciate the spectrum of CSR alternatives, we will briefly discuss its development.[10] Initially, CSR was the strategy of quirky small companies that used their strong belief system as a means of competitive differentiation upon market entry. The early Body Shop and Ben & Jerry's are older examples of this; Patagonia, innocent and Aveda would be their modern-day counterparts. Then CSR was discovered as a tool for companies in certain industries that attracted a lot of negative attention ("stigma" industries); they saw CSR as a systematic way to offset the public's anger and counter any potential reputational damage caused by disasters through good deeds. These industries include, for example, energy and oil companies as well as companies producing toxic waste (due to their environmental impact), the clothing industry (due to exposed unethical manufacturing practices such as child labour or sweatshops), the pharmaceutical industry (due to their failure to supply developing countries with free or cheap medication against highly contagious diseases like HIV/

---

[10] This section is heavily based on the Special Report on CSR by *The Economist*, Just good business, 19 Jan. 2008.

AIDS), and recently, fast food and packaged food companies (due to their alleged contribution to obesity).

As the various "scandals" fed a growing need for information and transparency, the public started to take a closer look at corporate activities and corporate misbehaviour. Corporations reacted with a defensive strategy and started to produce glossy CSR reports that were meant to demonstrate their good deeds, contribution to society and the environment, and their sensitivity to pertinent related issues. However, the problem with these reports is and was that they are based entirely on corporate self-descriptions and lack a strategic and holistic evaluation of the corporation overall. Not only do these reports focus primarily on the positive social impact, neglecting the negative side, but they also pick and choose which parts of the company to focus on, pointing out, for instance, how the carbon footprint was reduced for one particular business unit.

As it became clearer that CSR could be a new means for the public to gain transparency of corporate actions and behaviour, the pressure to take CSR seriously increased. Special interest groups and activists quickly picked up on this opportunity, becoming more aggressive and also effective in drawing attention to issues by targeting large and well-known companies, some of which might not even have been a primary "culprit" (for example, Nestlé in the global debate for water conservation). The emergence of a flurry of ratings and rankings created further momentum for the CSR boom, playing on peer pressure and competitive comparisons. In parallel, employees started to get excited about the idea of CSR, turning it into a new tool for recruiting and retaining top talent. On the consumer side, the importance of CSR is fuelled by the fast growing LOHAS (Lifestyles of Health and Sustainability) movement which has created a market for goods and services that appeal to consumers who value health, the environment, social justices, personal development and sustainable living. The LOHAS market is said to have grown to $230 billion in the USA alone[11] and the current boom of "green" products ranging from cars (the star being the Toyota Prius) to investments (socially responsible investments are increasing in popularity; most big banks have started to integrate "ESG" – environmental, social and governance issues – into their equity research) speaks for itself. Finally, governments have started to address CSR in legislation, as can be seen, for example, in the UK. The Companies Act 2006 has been designed to bring the regulatory framework for businesses up to date to better reflect the modern business environment. The related UK government site explains: "It enshrines in statute the concept of Enlightened Shareholder value which recognises that directors will be more likely to achieve long term sustainable success for the benefit of their shareholders if their companies pay appropriate regard to wider matters such as the environment and their employees."[12] Since October 2007, quoted companies must disclose information on environmental, employee, social and community matters.

Business schools create the business leaders of the next generation. They have to have their finger firmly on the pulse of time and think ahead how to best prepare their students for the challenges they will face. Recognising the demand for CSR and the associated shift towards a new set of underlying values, they have been adding classes to equip their students for a changing environment with new standards around the positive and negative social and environmental impacts of corporate action. One of the pioneers in this effort is Yale School of Management (SOM) which is taking a fundamentally new approach to teaching the MBA programme, both to better align with the school's distinct mission of educating leaders for business and society, and to become more

---

[11] Everage, L., Understanding the LOHAS Lifestyle, *Gourmet Retailer*, 1 Oct. 2002, accessed: http://www.allbusiness.com/retail-trade/food-stores/4216653-1.html

[12] www.csr.gov.uk/ukpolicy

relevant to the needs of contemporary managment. Dean Podolny, who arrived at Yale from Harvard Business School in July 2005, with the unanimous support of the Yale SOM senior faculty, decided to retire the traditional curriculum with courses like marketing, finance, and organisational behaviour in favour of an interdisciplinary approach that better reflects the need for complex decision making and multidisciplinary management. The new curriculum trains future managers and leaders to focus on managing external stakeholder groups like state and society, customers, investors, and competitors, as well as internal stakeholders like innovators, operating executives, fund managers, and employees in general. In addition to this major shift towards a multifaceted view of the commercial world, a reinvigorated focus on value-based management was introduced in order to create awareness and sensitivity of expectations and responsibilities among the leaders to be. Dean Podolny explains:

> The focus on values at Yale SOM is not new; it is part of the mission, history, and traditions of the school, demonstrated for example by the fact that SOM is consistently ranked at the top of "most ethical" business schools. But what is new is that business leaders need to have the ability to lead across boundaries. They are operating in an incredibly complex environment that not only requires a disciplined approach to problem solving, but also the courage to take their own personal values into the business. Our leadership development program, for example, helps students to explore and articulate their values and their commitments in small groups of twenty. They get a chance to understand the impact a particular set of values can have on business decisions made.

The new curriculum has been very well received by the MBA students. Not only did SOM experience significantly higher application rates, but also recruiters are rewarding the new programme with heightened interest in Yale SOM graduates. One student explains:[13]

---

[13] mba.yale.edu

A lot [of people] would ask me about what was happening at Yale. They'd heard about the changes and were curious. It was through talking with them that I realized how much I've been shaped by SOM's mission to educate leaders for business and society. And I was proud to be a Yale student. I realized that at a table of MBAs from around the world, SOM students will be the voice that seeks to find the balance between what's profitable and what's right.

Today, there is no doubt that CSR is booming; contrary to the prophecy of hard core free marketeers like the late Milton Friedman, who in 1970 wrote an article with a title giving away the main point: "The social responsibility of business is to increase its profit".[14] Clearly, society's expectations towards companies taking on public responsibilities have shifted since then, to the point that virtually no (large) company can afford to ignore CSR any longer. There is very little ambiguity about what the public does see as part of a company's social responsibility – namely, the entire social and environmental impact along its value and supply chain, bringing elements that used to be peripheral or secondary to a brand right into their core. This has not always been the case. Quite famously, Nike was one of the first companies who had to wake up to the fact that the public might care about their work standards when they faced huge public outrage over their alleged connection to child labour in the 1990s.

Today, the exposure of non-compliance with CSR standards can have significant financial and reputational repercussions. For example, the tragic child labour scandal that is engulfing Gap Inc. is deeply disturbing on a human level and confronts the company with a need to address the issue at a fundamental level. Britain's *Observer* newspaper reported in October 2007 that it had found children making clothes with Gap labels in a squalid factory in New Delhi. The undercover investigation exposed how, despite Gap's rigorous social audit systems launched in 2004 to weed out child labour in its production processes, the system is being abused by

---

[14] Friedman, M., The social responsibility of business is to increase its profit, *The New York Times Magazine*, 13 Sep. 1970.

unscrupulous subcontractors and quoted the children as saying they were from poor parts of India and had been sold to the sweatshop by their impoverished families. Some said they were not paid for their work.[15] Gap responded quickly, saying the factory was being run by a subcontractor who was hired in violation of Gap's policies, and none of the products made there will be sold in its stores. In fact, they thanked the newspaper for exposing the situation so that they could react swiftly. Gap North America President Martha Hansen was repeatedly quoted saying: "This is completely unacceptable and we do not ever, ever condone any child laborer making our garments. We act swiftly, and quite honestly, I'm very grateful that this was brought to our attention."[16] The fact that there was not even an attempt to blame this on anyone else demonstrates the nature of the current sentiment. Of course, such a reaction also creates expectations. And Gap Inc. – in what appears to be the biggest commitment to ending child labour ever undertaken by a major retailer – is now drawing up plans to label its products "Sweatshop Free". According to *The Observer*, Gap Inc. is working with the anti-sweatshop charity the Global March Against Child Labour to hammer out proposals to tackle child labour in India. The system would closely mirror the highly successful RugMark programme which has largely eradicated child labour in India's carpet industry. As an organisation operating independently of the carpet industry, RugMark certifies that carpets bearing its label are free of illegal child labour, monitoring looms and factories through surprise and random inspections.[17]

---

[15] McDougall, D., Child sweatshop shame threatens Gap's ethical image, *The Observer*, 28 Oct. 2007, accessed: http://www.guardian.co.uk/world/2007/oct/28/ethicalbusiness.retail

[16] Brown, H., Gap admits possible child labor problem, *ABC News*, 28 Oct. 2007, accessed: http://abcnews.go.com/WN/story?id=3787304

[17] McDougall, D., Gap plans "sweatshop free" labels, *The Observer*, 4 Nov. 2007, accessed: http://www.guardian.co.uk/business/2007/nov/04/3

While this case also demonstrates the lack of control discussed earlier (much like the case of Mattel and their toy recalls), it also shows the shift in how companies react to such situations. A decade ago, this incident would have hit the news, Gap Inc. might have outsourced all responsibility to the Indian subcontractor along with the production, claiming not to know about their business practices and washed their hands of it. Today, however, it's not that easy for large and well-established brands without severely damaging their reputation and business, partly due to the obvious violation of something that has become expected business standards – i.e. CSR – and partly due to the fact that consumers today are well aware that, despite the complex supply chains, it is ultimately down to Gap Inc. to take responsibility for their actions either by imposing sufficient controls or by moving production.

As a result, CSR has been escalated all the way to the top, right into the boardroom, making CSR a strategic matter. Research shows that CSR has risen dramatically in the priorities of CEOs.[18] But still, as Porter and Kramer[19] point out in their award winning article "Strategy and society", many companies have already spent time and resources to improve the social and environmental consequences of their activities, without realising its full potential. This is partly due to the fact that in their approach they pit business against society and partly due to insufficiently integrating CSR with their specific company strategy. As Arena points out in her book: "Many companies expend much time and money 'giving back' to the community, when really they should first focus on eliminating the damage they create through their most

---

[18] "Just good business", a special report on corporate social responsibility, *The Economist*, 19 Jan. 2008.

[19] Porter, M.E. and Kramer, M.R., Strategy and society: the link between competitive advantage and corporate social responsibility, *Harvard Business Review*, 84, 12, 2006: 78–92.

basic business activities."[20] Each company should assess for themselves how CSR fits into their strategic framework, considering all alternatives, the impact, and the skills and competencies present in the same strategic and disciplined way they would with any other strategic programme. One of the core tenets of Porter and Kramer is that CSR can "be much more than a cost, a constraint, or a charitable deed – it can be a source of opportunity, innovation, and competitive advantage" for businesses and thereby contribute substantially to social progress – if it is treated with sufficient strategic discipline and rigour. Porter and Kramer suggest mapping the positive and negative social impact of their entire value chain in order to focus the CSR activities to best effect: "Rather than merely acting on well-intentioned impulses or reacting to outside pressures, the organisation can set an affirmative CSR agenda that produces maximum social benefit as well as gains for the business." What makes their framework so powerful is the fact that they apply corporate strategy to both, leveraging positive social and environmental benefits and mitigating negative social and environmental impacts with the aim to enhance competitive advantage.

One thing is for sure – if companies do not do this kind of mapping themselves, then someone else will. As transparency, a need for accountability and credibility are reaching new heights, projects like Global Demos emerge. One of the founders, Guido Palazzo, Business Ethics Professor at the University of Lausanne, remarks that understanding and evaluating the social and environmental performance of corporations is quickly gaining interest and relevance. The current situation is characterised by a myriad of ratings and rankings offering non-comparable performance metrics and resulting in a highly fragmented landscape littered with millions of CSR micro-experts all over the world: "What we really need at this point," Professor Palazzo points out, "is a universally

---

[20] Arena, C., *High Purpose Companies*, New York: Harper Collins, 2007, p. 13.

accepted standard for measuring the real social and environmental performance of corporations. Transparency can be created by using the same metrics for everyone, and by collecting information that does not solely rely on corporate self-descriptions." This is, however, a daunting task. The current landscape of CSR initiatives and programmes is very diverse and confusing, and to further add to the intransparency of the situation, up-and-coming multinational corporations headquartered from China, India and other emerging markets largely operate in a black box.

Global Demos aims to increase transparency of CSR activities by mapping the social and environmental risks of the entire value chain for both entire industry sectors and individual companies. For instance, the graph in Figure 1.2 shows the value chain of the

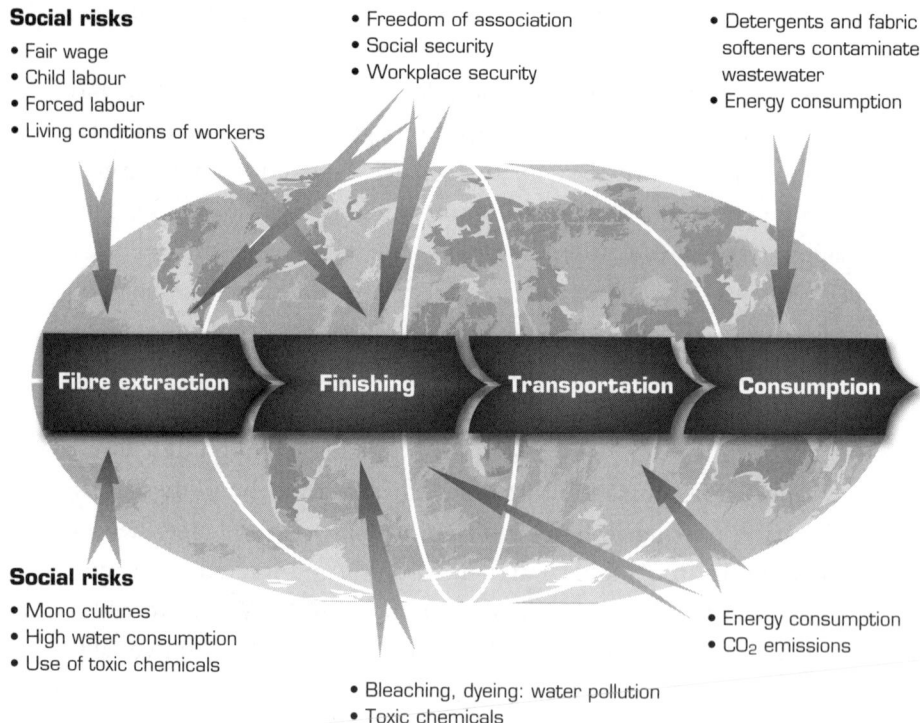

Figure 1.2 Value chain of apparel industry and risks

apparel industry and the social and environmental risks in each step.

The idea is to trace all activities with social and environmental risks. For example, in the phase of "Fiber Extraction", this could refer to anything from work standards, living conditions, and water consumption to the use of toxic chemicals and the impact of monoculture. Palazzo emphasises:

> This project is not about blaming and shaming, it is about introducing transparency into a highly complex network of relationships and interdependencies. At the moment, our main challenge is to feed the system with data. We rely on the cooperation with companies that voluntarily deliver data on their global supply chain and their standards or activities, as well as on NGOs that already have big data bases. In the future, this platform will provide anyone who is interested, for instance consumers, with understandable and comparable information on CSR. And not only for entire industry sectors, but also as it relates to individual products, brands, and corporations. This will create peer pressure. Companies can use the tool as an early warning system, as a benchmark, or for risk analysis. The society as a whole, and local communities in particular, will get access to timely, systematic, comprehensive and reliable data, which can serve as the basis for the development of standards, dialogues, programmes, and educational campaigns.

Why is the issue of CSR significant?

CSR has emerged as a new standard of doing business in the 21st century and therefore needs to be addressed by every brand. However, there is considerable concern that a non-strategic approach to CSR does not sufficiently benefit either the company or society. Equally, there is great danger that companies feel pressured to jump on the bandwagon without proper consideration of brand impact, thereby setting themselves up for creating expectations the brand cannot deliver.

THE INTERNET MEGAPHONE

We discussed earlier how CSR might be seen as a new way to gain transparency into the actions of corporations. But the strong focus on CSR has also resulted in a shift of responsibilities for social and environmental issues from the public domain into the corporate world. This is quite interesting, especially when we consider everything we observe about the breakdown of trust. Would we rather have Apple and Google save our planet than the government? And why? Most companies did not volunteer to take on these issues; on the contrary, they may feel burdened and pressured by it. Is it simply that the mounting issues have reached "emergency state" and corporations are ultimately seen as more skilled, more effective and more efficient in addressing them than an increasingly toothless public policy driven by bureaucracy and sidelined by power struggles? Well, that may be one reason. But we believe the key driver is the increased transparency and the shifting control over information in favour of free content flow which allows the public to hold corporations hostage and exert pressure in a way they could never do with governments. This dynamic represents a new system of checks and balances. Leverage is gained through fear of reputational and financial damage, making it easier and more effective to pressure (global) corporations to address the mounting issues of public responsibilities than a patchwork of national governments. We believe this shift has not occurred because the general public places any more trust and good faith in corporations than it does in the government, but because it has an uncensored, non-intermediated and unmistakably clear way of voting in this arena – with its money.

This shift of control over information has been made possible by the Internet. The Internet has dramatically changed the way information can be accessed, managed and controlled (or rather not controlled). Consumers are talking back to brands, consumers are exchanging their opinions and experiences with each other in unfiltered forums, and single opinions of highly vocal individuals (e.g. bloggers) reach large audiences with unprecedented speed. Web logs (short blogs) have given vocal individuals a means to express their own views and opinions in whichever form they find convenient, and many of the blogs have started to draw significant audiences (so much so, that advertisers are trying to sponsor them now). This mainstream emergence of bloggers occurred over a very short time period, as can be seen by the following quote from Henry Jenkins, the influential MIT professor of media and popular culture, from his 2002 article about the "exotic species" of bloggers (note the "us" versus "them" stance):

> Like cockroaches after nuclear war, online diarists rule an Internet strewn with failed dot coms. [...] Bloggers are turning the hunting and gathering, sampling and critiquing what the rest of us do online, into an extreme sport. We surf the Web; these guys snowboard it. Bloggers are the minutemen of the digital revolution.

Today, of course, Henry Jenkins has his own blog (entitled "Confessions of an Aca-Fan" to be found at www.henryjenkins.org) and blogs have become a mainstream marketing tool used by celebrities, politicians, academics, and, of course, companies; as blogging has become more and more proliferate, it has decreased the power of mainstream media and has lent previously unheard-of powers to uncensored voices. While these voices may or may not be objective or driven by a certain agenda, they are amplified by the instant nature of the Internet, allowing information to spread across the entire globe in virtually no time at all. A famous example concerns the US bike lock producer Kryptonite whose reputation for producing "safes" for bikes was compromised by an amateur video shown in a blog featuring how hilariously easy it was to crack the lock.[21] According to the blog search engine

---

[21] Löwer, C., Digitale Mundpropaganda. *Die Zeit*, 20 July 2006, accessed: http://www.zeit.de/2006/30/Blogs

Technorati more than 1.8 million users were informed in just one week, eventually causing mainstream media to pick up on the story. Kryptonite did not react at first, but eventually had to make a product recall to save face. *Fortune* magazine estimates the damage to be around $10 million.[22] As we can see from this example, blogs can frighteningly quickly "spread the word" and create transparency among interested parties beyond established media. Unfortunately, negative information is often seen as much more newsworthy, therefore potentially creating a situation where brands (and corporate reputations) are at risk of getting severely damaged.

Another technology that facilitates the flow of uncensored information is Web 2.0 or social networking. People are more and more connected through a multitude of online communities and social networking sites, be they for professional purposes or fun, be they very stable or more ephemeral. The emergence of sites like MySpace and YouTube have pushed this idea to new limits, creating an enormous library of written information and videos on almost any topic imaginable. Already the Cluetrain Manifesto (www.cluetrain.com) had pointed out that in the networked economy it will become increasingly difficult to maintain "false" images, and this was a long time before the technology had become so sophisticated. Websites that invite employees to share information, like www.vault.com or www.internalmemos.com, have given employees' voices unprecedented amplification, rendering the term "internal" communication an oxymoron. As a result, it becomes increasingly more difficult to separate audiences, resulting in blurring and dissolving boundaries between stakeholder groups. This in turn creates a situation where messages might not always reach or stay contained within the intended

---

[22] Kirkpatrick, D., Why there's no escaping the Blog, *Fortune* magazine, 10 Jan. 2005, accessed: http://money.cnn.com/magazines/fortune/fortune_archive/2005/01/10/8230982/index.htm

audience. Coupling these developments with the current political and socio-economical context will make it very clear that this ability to get "the inside track", "the real story" or the unadulterated truth addresses a deep rooted need to get information from more than one (trusted) source. While traditionally established media would have been seen as a sufficiently trustworthy authority, the aforementioned breakdown of trust on many fronts, including mainstream media, has made the consumer suspicious. Triangulation of information, a desire to get to the bottom of things, and importance accredited to (assumingly) independent sources are characteristic of the current environment and made possible by the Internet.

Consider, for example, the much discussed controversy Unilever has been embroiled in recently.[23] Unilever, a large consumer goods company, operates what is call a "House of Brands" strategy. They own a large number of product brands which are tailored to the unique needs of the customer segments they are meant to serve. These product brands are the key point of reference in the interaction with the customer, resulting in the fact that "99 out of 100" people are not aware of the entire stable of product brands owned by a single company. Unilever's Dove product brand has been praised for its socially responsible approach to the sensitive topic of marketing female beauty products. Their "campaign for real beauty" exemplifies Dove's social awareness of the impact of beauty marketing on young women and hence has focused on showing women with more "normal body types" in order to boost women's self-confidence. Dove has won several awards and prizes for their courageous stance and to many people stood for an "authentic" brand. However, Unilever incited controversy and became the target of heavy criticism when Dove

---

[23] See, for example, Neff, J., Viral draws heat from critics, *Advertising Age*, 26 Nov. 2007.

launched a viral video campaign entitled "Onslaught", showing a young girl being bombarded by beauty ads and images including plastic surgery and eating disorders and concluding with the line "Talk to your daughter before the beauty industry does". While the video was well received initially, soon bloggers, news reporters and special interest groups discovered and then shared that Dove is owned by Unilever who also owns Axe, a deodorant brand targeted at young men and displaying exactly the type of young, sexy, supermodel-type women in their ads that are being condemned in the Dove video. As a result, Unilever is accused of hypocrisy, the credibility of the Dove campaign is undermined, appearing to many now as just another marketing gimmick. Also, a large portion of consumers now know about the connection between Axe and Dove, making it more difficult for Unilever to operate both brands credibly. To make things worse, one advertising expert was so intrigued with the whole dilemma that he created and then launched on YouTube another viral video that inserted Axe ads into the Onslaught video, ending with the line "Talk to your daughter . . . before Unilever does". This Dove/Axe mashup video received a lot of attention, was shown on CNN news and further amplified the whole controversy and brand damage for Unilever and its product brands.

In summary, the Internet has played and will continue to play a key role in making companies more transparent, simply by bypassing conventional media with all its various forms of control and censorship and by giving employees, customers, and other stakeholders a voice that can easily be heard by a large number of people within a very short period of time. As a result, attempts to cover up incidents, to deny things that actually happened and to "spin" things are less likely to succeed at this point. On the contrary, they will most likely make things much, much worse. For many companies, this "unwanted" transparency is difficult to deal with since it represents a new situation that radically departs from the traditional way of presenting a company.

Why is the emergence of this transparency and instant amplification significant?

As brands struggle to deliver on their promises to their stakeholders, any empty claims, exaggerations, misbehaviours and inconsistencies will most likely be spotted and shared with a large number of people, potentially destroying brand equity very quickly. It also becomes more difficult to contain information and to effectively separate audiences. As more information and more diverse points of view are shared with large audiences very quickly, greater transparency will result, ultimately forcing companies to take the brand promise beyond a communications exercise and to embed it into their every action.

We will now discuss how companies have started to react to these trends in Chapter 2.

CHAPTER 2

EMERGING STRATEGIES TO ADDRESS MARKET FORCES

*I*n this chapter we will discuss how companies have started to address the trends of the current environment.

Companies have started to react to the market forces described in the previous chapter in a number of ways. What all of these emerging strategies have in common is an increased focus on *values*, as opposed to attributes or functional and emotional benefits, in order to build deeper connections with their employees, customers and other key stakeholders. They also increase consistency between brand promise, corporate actions and actual brand experience, all of which work towards re-establishing the trust that is daily being challenged by overstretched supply chains, anti-corporation activists, the scrutiny of bloggers, and half-hearted CSR initiatives.

Some companies have chosen to "bring the corporation into the brand", which means that they are placing more branding emphasis on the corporation behind the products and brands. Other companies subscribe to a new "model of authenticity", whereby all actions emanate from a core set of values. Still other companies find placing greater emphasis on CSR to be an effective approach and yet others are trying to find new ways of engaging

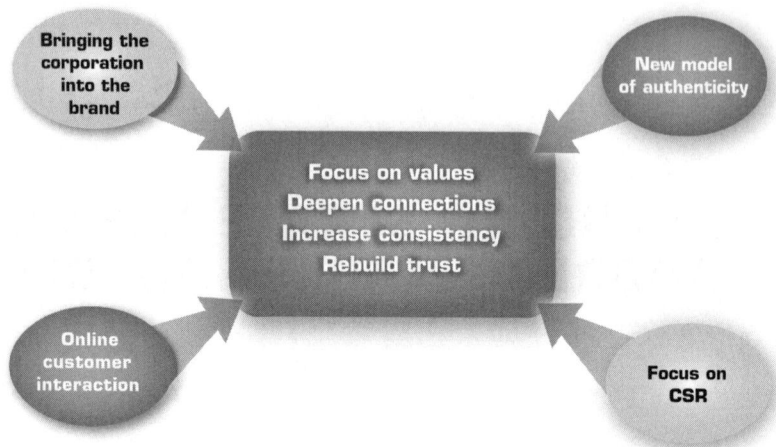

Figure 2.1 Emerging strategies to address market forces

employees, customers and other key stakeholders which are interactive, non-manipulative and non-intrusive. Combinations of these approaches are also used.

We will now discuss each of these strategies in detail and provide an evaluation of what works and what doesn't.

BRINGING THE CORPORATION INTO THE BRAND

One way companies have started to react to the market forces discussed earlier is by shifting their branding emphasis from the product to the corporation behind the product. This shift from product branding towards corporate branding is being documented in marketing literature and has been largely attributed to the impacts of product commoditisation and globalisation.[1] Functional

---

[1] Ind, N., *The Corporate Brand*, New York: New York University Press, 1997.

sources of product differentiation are now so easily and quickly copied (not only by Chinese manufacturers) that they can no longer provide sustainable brand differentiation. Differentiation based on emotional benefits is a route available in some product classes (e.g. high involvement consumer goods, luxury goods, and service-driven categories), but even this approach is becoming more difficult in the current environment in which consumers are more aware of and sensitive to being emotionally manipulated. As companies are forced to find new sources of differentiation, they are starting to develop their corporate brand.

Corporate brands are value based

In contrast to product brands, which have primarily been directed towards the customer, corporations have to speak to multiple and diverse audiences including employees, customers, shareholders, the financial community, the media, NGOs, and so on. In the past, these multiple audiences on the corporate level were addressed by corporate functions such as corporate reputation management, public relations and investor relations. Each of the audiences was typically addressed separately and with different messages. However, due to the convergence of stakeholder groups and the Internet megaphone, this is no longer possible in today's branding environment. Therefore, corporate brands need to find a way to simultaneously appeal to these diverse audiences and this can only be achieved through *value-based* branding. Values have the power to resonate with diverse audiences unlike attributes or functional and emotional benefits. Google's core value of "Don't be evil" is equally appealing to employees, paying and non-paying customers, shareholders, NGOs, partners, the media, and other key stakeholders. In contrast, a key functional benefit such as Google's simple and user-friendly interface may be strongly appealing to search engine users but irrelevant to the Chinese government (whom they had to convince to get entry to China).[2]

Values are also more influential on stakeholder behaviour than attributes, attitudes or any other brand elements[3] and allow the company to build deeper connections and more meaningful relationships with their stakeholders. In an environment of eroding trust, using values as a basis on which to address diverse stakeholder groups can be an effective way to rebuild or fortify this trust. At the same time, corporate branding also satisfies the lively interest in the corporation behind products and product brands displayed by NGOs, customers, and the general public.

Single set of values ("value core")

Strong corporate brands must rest on a single set of values that drives all corporate actions and decisions. These values need to be relevant and appealing to all key stakeholders. This means that all messages, while tailored for each stakeholder group, are rooted in a single consistent "story". The corporate brand thereby unifies rather than fragments stakeholder messages and experiences. Strong corporate brands have the ability to attract and orient all key stakeholders through a single set of recognisable values and symbols that are unique to the organisation.[4/5]

---

[2] Who's afraid of Google? *The Economist*, 1 Sep. 2007, p. 9.
[3] de Chernatony, L., *From Brand Vision to Brand Evaluation – Strategically Building and Sustaining Brands*, Oxford: Butterworth-Heinemann, 2006.
[4] Hatch, M.J. and Schultz, M., Bringing the corporation into corporate branding, *European Journal of Marketing*, 37, 7/8, 2003: 1041–1064.
[5] Balmer, J.M.T. and Gray, E.R., Corporate brands: what are they? What of them?, *European Journal of Marketing*, 37, 7/8, 2003: 972–997.

Role of employees

Corporate value-based branding inevitably places an entirely new emphasis on the role of employees in brand delivery. Product brands connect with their primary audience, the customer, mainly through the product itself, the retail environment, and product-specific communication. This creates somewhat of an arm's length relationship between the customer and the corporation and therefore also the customer and most employees. This is particularly true for packaged goods that are sold exclusively through third parties. If, for example, you buy a Mars bar, you will most likely not come into contact with any Masterfoods or Mars employee, unless you call them up to make a complaint. This has its advantages and disadvantages. On the plus side, it is much easier to create a consistent experience on the product level, in the case of the Mars bar through manufacturing processes that guarantee that each bar has the same look, taste, etc. On the negative side, it is much more difficult for a Mars bar to engage the customer at a deeper, more personal level. This is, among other reasons, why some companies create flagship stores as a point of direct interaction with their customers. Products with higher service components naturally create additional touchpoints between the customer and the corporation, be it the direct sales channel or the customer service department. The more interaction between the customer and employees, the more important it becomes that employees understand the brand and are willing and capable of acting in line with the brand. Corporate brands take this imperative to the extreme – they bring the entire organisation into the brand, putting employees right at the heart of the brand. This highlights the importance of creating a brand that is focused on a set of values that is appealing, motivating, and inspiring not only to the customer and other external stakeholders, but equally so to employees.

Impact on brand architecture

A shift from product branding to corporate branding may require a rethinking of the brand portfolio strategy, in particular in the case of a so-called *House of Brands* strategy. A House of Brands strategy is prevalent with many large (packaged) consumer goods companies like Unilever, Nestlé, Procter & Gamble, or even Henkel and Beiersdorf. It rests on the assumption that a corporation can address the specific needs of a number of market segments with separate product brands that have their own brand positioning and are not visibly connected to the corporation behind the product brand. One of the key success factors of this strategy is the ability to keep audiences separate in order to avoid confusion, contradiction, and brand dilution. However, as we have seen in the Dove and Axe example earlier, the ability to keep audiences separate is deteriorating quickly. This may create unwanted connections between the corporation and the product brand, as well as between product brands, ultimately undermining the effectiveness of this approach.

Shifting the focus from product branding to corporate branding also brings new challenges for companies pursuing a *master brand* strategy. A master brand strategy refers to a structure where one single brand spans the entire offering of a corporation, for example Apple or Virgin Group. Since the corporate master brand is connected with all products and corporate activities, any scandal or crisis related to parts of it has the potential to tarnish the entire product portfolio as well as the corporate reputation.

The key differences between corporate branding and product branding are summarised in Table 2.1.[6]

---

[6] Adapted from Hatch, M.J. and Schultz, M., Bringing the corporation into corporate branding, *European Journal of Marketing*, 37, 7/8, 2003: 1041–1064.

Table 2.1 Product branding versus corporate branding

	Product branding	Corporate branding
Focus	Product	Company/organisation
Target	Customers	Customers, employees, and other stakeholder groups
Creation	Imposed by brand manager	Participative
Primary brand carriers	Product and communication	Product and employees
Delivered by	Marketing	Entire company
Organisational level	Mid-level management	Top management
Time horizon	Short- medium-term (life span of product brand)	Long-term (life span of company)
Importance	Tactical	Strategic

Focus

While conventional product-based thinking typically operates at arm's length with their target audiences, making the product brand the main locus of relationship building and communicative focus, corporate branding brings the entire organisation into the relationship and makes it the key focus point.

Focusing on the organisation instead of the product allows the brand manager to leverage unique aspects of the company culture and vision to differentiate the product offering. However, values are only credible brand drivers if they become embedded in all actions and decisions and are supported by all employees.

Target

Corporate brands address a much wider audience and are not only concerned with the image and associations held by customers, but also employees and other stakeholders, e.g. retailers/distributors, investors, suppliers, partners, media, regulators, special interest groups, local communities, franchisees, activists, analysts, etc. The complexity of addressing such diverse audiences with such different motivations, needs and goals is new territory for many brand managers and marketers.

Take the case of Toyota. Toyota receives many credentials for their environmental responsibility, manifested in their much celebrated hybrid car, the Prius. While this has provided Toyota with phenomenal awareness and positive associations, not to speak of the inflow to Toyota dealerships with customers thinking that all Toyota cars are environmentally friendly, this has also drawn attention to Toyota's corporate actions, demonstrating how the corporation is increasingly pulled into the brand: while Toyota actively communicates their environmental concerns, for example in their latest TV commercial called "Why not?", they have at the same time joined forces with GM and Ford to lobby *against* tougher fuel economy standards in the USA.[7] Loyal Prius owners, special interest groups and NGOs are puzzled with this move by Toyota since it seems not only out of character, but set to undermine both the corporate brand and the Prius product brand.

Creation and Brand Carriers

In the case of product brands, brand elements are often decided by the brand manager alone without much regard for the company

---

[7] Miller, S., Green Toyota ads launch into a hostile environment, *Brand Week*, 5 Nov. 2007, accessed: http://www.brandweek.com/bw/news/recent_display.jsp?vnu_content_id=1003668303

culture. This is understandable particularly in the case of fast moving consumer goods since there are very limited interactions between employees and customers. In the case of corporate branding a more participative approach is required[8] since brand values need to be compatible with the corporate culture and need to be embraced by employees.

Delivery

The communications focus of product brands has often limited the brand delivery to the marketing department. By contrast, corporate brands bring very large parts of the organisation, if not the entire organisation, into brand delivery. While marketing can and should still drive brand strategy and coordinate all inputs and initiatives, marketing alone will very rarely have the remit to align all necessary processes, systems, and structures with the brand.

Organisational level

Ultimately, this means that the corporate brand needs to become a strategic matter worthy of CEO attention. Ideally, the CEO puts the brand on the strategy agenda – not just for a short project, but for good. We have come across some very brave marketing teams who were ready to push the brand agenda up the corporate ladder; but without actually getting to the very top there is little hope for aligning an entire organisation behind the brand. If branding is limited to communications and/or design, it is usually placed at mid-management level.

---

[8] de Chernatony, L., Would a brand smell any sweeter by a corporate name? *Corporate Reputation Review*, 5, 2/3, 2002: 114–135.

Time horizon and importance

In the case of product branding, the time horizon is driven by the product life cycle and therefore is more of a short- to medium-term nature. By contrast, corporate branding is tied to the life span and strategic orientation of the organisation, making the time horizon (in most cases) much longer term. Notable exceptions might be cases where the management are looking for a quick exit strategy (e.g. as might be the case with venture capital or private equity).

CASE STUDY: SUCCESSFUL DIFFERENTIATION THROUGH CORPORATE BRANDING IN INSURANCE

> The link between the needs of employees and those of clients demands creation of a supportive internal environment that encourages employees to treat clients in the expected way, time and time again. A brand that is consistent internally and externally is a good way to achieve this – employees deal with customers in the same way that they themselves are dealt with on the inside.
>
> Carel Nolte, Hollard

Background

Hollard is South Africa's largest private insurance company (in terms of assets), providing short-term (property and casualty) and life insurance policies to over 6 million policyholders across the social spectrum of South Africa and also abroad. The company was created 28 years ago, mostly out of a frustration with traditional insurance practices, and has grown to more than 1300 employees today. In 2003, Hollard developed a new brand strategy with the aim to build a consistent image as an efficient and reliable insurance company that would fuel their ambitious growth plans.[9]

Based on thorough analysis and input from key stakeholders, Hollard defined their new brand values as *entrepreneurship, partnerships* and *innovation*; they also produced a new tag line – "With Hollard it's sorted" – to describe in one short, to-the-point and easy-to-remember phrase the company's personality and the brand promise. The new brand promise was not a radical departure from Hollard's brand heritage of "innovation and cooperative enterprise", but further evolved and leveraged these brand strengths to appeal to a new generation of employees. Since the new brand was seen as a key differentiator and thus driver of the Hollard growth strategy, it was very important that all the right key stakeholders were on board from the beginning. Inclusion of the executive team, the CEO, public relations, marketing and communication, as well as human resources right from the outset, was to ensure that the brand could be embedded in the culture and all business processes.

As a service provider, Hollard was acutely aware of the pivotal role their employees would play in delivering this brand promise and, therefore, they designed and launched a highly effective internal brand building programme before the new tag line was advertised externally.

Challenge

Hollard's key insight was that insurance is all about conversation – between employees, between employees and management,

---

[9] See also Nolte, C., Delivering the brand promise at Hollard Insurance. Transforming brand strategy into satisfied employees and customers, *Strategic Communication Management*, 8, 4, April/May 2004: 18–21.

and, of course, between employees and customers. Carel Nolte, Hollard's communication manager, comments:

> Insurance is what many would call a "grudge purchase". It is indeed a very peculiar product – you buy something that does not come to fruition until that one day where something bad happens to you. Then you are in a state about what happened and need to call your insurance company, and the last thing you need at this point is someone who can't listen. On the other hand, if that voice on the other end of the line can give you a sense of "don't worry, it's sorted", then you will feel better about it.

Of course, dialogue is also very important when selling insurance – in order to determine the right type of policy, the right type of cover, the right type of premium. If through each and every conversation employees are having with their customers and potential customers, this attitude of "it's sorted" were conveyed, and in addition to that employees would also approach each other with this same positive and proactive attitude (for example, in the formal and informal conversations between sales people, underwriters and actuaries), Hollard would truly build a unique and highly differentiating brand in an industry that suffers chronically from a bad reputation. "Anyone can copy products and processes," says Nolte, "but our culture around 'it's sorted' would be very difficult to copy."

Approach

Hollard set out to embed the brand values and "it's sorted" in every aspect of their business, from the new corporate headquarters to their selection of suppliers in the area of executive search to the catering company all the way to their choice of CSR activities. Most importantly, however, employees had to learn which behaviours were expected of them in order to reflect the new brand promise in everything they do.

Preparation phase – creating the right environment

"With Hollard it's sorted" was meant to resonate with both customers and employees, albeit with a slightly different "translation". To employees "it's sorted" was to mean a results-oriented and proactive interaction with clients, while also assuring employees that Hollard cared seriously about them. To customers it was to indicate a very clear service promise for every interaction, be it setting up a policy or handling claims. Therefore, Hollard knew the key to their success was to encourage employees to adopt a "sorted" attitude in their dealings with each other and with their customers. Nolte remarked that:

> The link between the needs of employees and those of clients demands creation of a supportive *internal* environment that encourages employees to treat clients in the expected way, time and time again. A brand that is consistent internally and externally is a good way to achieve this – employees deal with customers in the same way that they themselves are dealt with on the inside.

Since the theme of "conversation" had emerged as a key framework, Hollard started out by facilitating dialogue by creating an environment conducive to interaction. First of all, they had bought an old mansion called Villa Arcadia that was lovingly restored by an architect who was deemed to have a strong cultural fit with Hollard. This villa was mainly used for social occasions and "conversation". Hollard believed that their working environment was an important way to make a statement to their employees who were then working in four different offices across Johannesburg. So they built a state-of-the-art new office block next to the villa, putting employees under one roof and allowing for a continuous flow of interaction between them and management. As Nolte points out, this new office block is a source of employee identification, since it makes employees proud of their environment and to be "Hollardites". The physical environment played a key role in communicating "it's sorted" not only to employees, but to customers as well, through adding more concrete meaning to the intangible aspects of the brand. The newly built office building is structured around a big, double volume, open space – an atrium – which they called Lionel's Eye (referring to Sir Lionel Philips who had a glass eye and built the original Villa Arcadia in the early 1900s) – it is characteristic for the "vibe" and "culture" Hollard wanted to create: open, transparent, inviting conversation. Nolte highlights: "The brand character is intrinsic in the visible openness of the physical building, in other words the building represents the brand promise."

The communications team was heavily involved in the restoration of Villa Arcadia and the creation of the new modern office complex. They created formal and informal meeting spaces including booths and coffee shops, they made the call centre (which is usually tucked away somewhere) a highly visible feature in their working environment and even turned the CEO's office walls into glass in order to signify constant conversation and transparency. In addition, they introduced an open door policy where anyone was allowed to talk to their superiors without pre-agreed meetings.

Introducing brand values and demonstrating desired employee behaviour

For the internal launch of the brand campaign, the communications team decided to bring in an element of humour in order to pique employees' interest and increase identification. So, on the first day, employees arrived at work to find punching bags in their offices. The implied message was that employees should take out any frustrations on those bags and adopt a positive attitude to their work.

Following through on the "conversation" theme, Hollard made sure that employees would be spoken to in the same way they in turn would be expected to speak with their customers.

Integrity, passion, openness and transparency were seen to form the foundation of a "sorted" attitude. Therefore, the organisation did not tell a fairy-tale about a wonderful world where everyone loves each other, but decided to inform all employees about the actual business reality, which was that Hollard had ambitious growth targets and therefore needed to grow and increase profits. Promoting this kind of openness and transparent interaction with employees was meant to become not only a role model for customer dialogue, but also pre-empt any cynical attitude. Nolte mentioned: "We told our employees that we wanted to make money, because it is important to be open and explain your goals otherwise employees become cynical."

To demonstrate the importance of the new brand promise and the "sorted" campaign, all 1300 employees had to go through brand training. The then CEO Paolo Cavalieri set up Paolo's café, where he himself and the marketing communications manager prepared cappuccino for groups of 20 people at a time and then talked them through the new brand promise. During one of these days, the CEO talked to 60 people until he very famously lost his voice. This little story about the CEO losing his voice over sharing his passion for the brand with employees took on the nature of a corporate myth. Cavalieri's engagement brought huge energy and passion to the project, and not only helped employees to understand what "it's sorted" is all about, but also its priority in the company's business strategy.

The communications team was constantly looking for ways to demonstrate what "sorted" could mean in the everyday work of their employees. For instance, neck straps for the security discs were introduced to solve the frequent problem of misplaced or mixed-up discs. As Nolte remarked, such a simple change had a very positive impact on "it's sorted" since it demonstrated expected employee attitude and behaviour towards problem solving with a concrete example.

Once employees were familiar with the brand values and related desired behaviours, the focus shifted to brand enactment. All Hollardites were given the responsibility of inventing and suggesting approaches to problems that they encountered at work on a daily basis. This increased creativity and job appeal, especially among frontline employees. As people who experienced the challenges of brand delivery more than anyone else in the organization, they were able to come up with very innovative ideas that management might have never thought about.

Embedding the brand in business practice
Hollard was committed to make "it's sorted" transpire into an attitude shared by the whole organisation and designed a comprehensive, multifaceted programme to achieve this.

The first step was to adapt recruiting and induction training to reflect the new brand promise. Hollard began to work with recruiting agencies that supported its brand values, thereby cascading the "sorted" attitude down to their suppliers. They chose suppliers that were capable of identifying people with integrity and passion, two key ingredients in a Hollardite. Nolte explains: "Of course skills are very important, but we provide a lot of training on the job, making personality and cultural fit an even more important factor. What sets us apart is our culture: our brand is ultimately made up of people. Therefore, it is very important that we hire the right ones from the start."

Hollard took an usual approach to their induction training by hiring Dennis Beckett, a South African media guru and well-known social commentator, to lead the induction seminars. Beckett's role is to help new employees to understand the thinking around "it's sorted", through motivating them to talk about their reasons for joining Hollard, soliciting their ideas for contributing to the brand promise and sharing management's expectations regarding their performance. In these four-day induction seminars employees will hear about the challenges ahead of them, and they also get to meet the CEO who still pays a personal visit to every induction session. One month after each induction session, new recruits are expected to share their experience of issues they considered to be "sorted" and are asked to pick out things they thought were not "sorted" and suggest ways of improving them. This way the organisation continuously gets the benefit of feedback from "fresh eyes" while bringing on board those who are new to the job.

When Beckett was hired to contribute to the induction phase, he was not briefed about the internal ethos. Rather he was asked to experience it first hand by speaking to people within Hollard randomly. His role was like that of a cultural auditor who, through a critical analysis of the actually experienced internal culture versus what was claimed, was supposed to hold up the mirror to Hollard. Nolte pointed out that "There is always room for improvement, and in order not to become 'arrogant', the critical voice of an outsider can be very helpful."

Launching "it's sorted" inspired Hollard to focus more on the professional training of employees as a way of enabling a "sorted" attitude by helping them to better understand products and the insurance industry as a whole. In addition, the company started investing in enhancing the soft skills of its staff. These skills are vital when conducting dialogue with clients. Furthermore, Hollard became involved in "Proudly Insurance", a programme aimed at teaching insurance employees and the general public about the relevance of the insurance industry to their lives.

Then, Hollard cascaded the brand values all the way down to their suppliers, including the catering company and the gym by selecting these external providers on a number of criteria that also included the "it's sorted" culture and attitude.

Next, Hollard started to revamp business processes to reflect brand values better. For example, they redesigned the claims process to get customers' claims sorted quicker; on the internal side, they introduced an organisational development system to help Hollardites get their career and development path sorted while addressing issues around succession planning and team structure.

Lastly, Hollard decided to reflect its brand values also in the way they look at CSR. For example, each business unit within Hollard has adopted a CSI (Corporate Social Investment) project which they support and manage. The projects are overseen by the Hollard CSI Steering Committee, which liaises with project representatives and helps with logistics.

Ongoing employee involvement

Just like customers need to be reminded of a brand now and then, employees equally need a boost every so often to avoid the brand promise drifting into routine and oblivion. Hollard is trying to surprise and excite their employees and found that humour and metaphors are a good way of renewing energy and enthusiasm provided the key message does not get obscured. For example, Hollard encouraged their employees to report fraud by putting up a poster featuring a toilet that read "Don't flush away your bonus. Be sorted. Report fraud."

Measuring outcomes

After introducing "it's sorted", Hollard measured employee understanding of the core brand values and related desired brand behaviours. It discovered that employee awareness of the brand strategy had risen, while their support for the brand was soaring.

Hollard also measured customer impact of the new brand promise and found that the number of customer complaints dropped significantly, claims-handling times in the life insurance business were improved, sales and business results improved, Hollard was voted best commercial insurer by brokers, and for the first time, Hollard made it into the top 20 unlisted companies in South Africa.

Major challenges ahead

In July 2007, a new CEO replaced Paolo Cavalieri who had introduced the "it's sorted" campaign. Although both CEOs incorporate passion and care for people, they have very different personalities. Yet Hollard needs continual support from the CEO as a role model in further building and nurturing the brand internally.

Another issue concerns how Hollard will be able to keep the "it's sorted" brand promise when the organisation is growing so quickly and internationally, with burgeoning business already in countries like Australia, China, the UK and India.

Furthermore, as Denis Beckett, the external cultural adviser muses on the Hollard web page,[10] there are some signs of brand fatigue. He points out that Hollard needs to re-energise the "sorted" attitude in order to leverage all the strengths within the organisation and stay the truly great place with a highly unique culture that Hollard aspires to be.

Finally, as Denis Beckett also points out, much in line with all we have discussed in earlier chapters about transparency, authenticity, and ethics: "I think the industry is heading for, sooner or later, a wholesale raising of the ethical bar. I'm expecting to see Hollard leading the way, openly, publicly, expressly." That would involve engraining it right in the heart of the brand.

In order to address all these challenges, Hollard is currently analysing the link between their "internal" and "external" brand drivers and brand image. They are constantly looking for new ways to keep the brand fresh and relevant to all key stakeholders, namely shareholders, customers and Hollardites.

---

[10] http://www.hollard.co.za/default.asp

Conclusion

Corporate branding is quite different from product branding and has its own set of challenges and perils to deal with. In particular, it means that all the company's actions – not just advertising and PR – have all of a sudden moved into the area of public interest, thereby making business practices and ethical standards part of branding. To some degree, this will happen whether companies actively manage it or not.

Corporate branding can be very powerful if the values that drive the brand and the corporation are embedded in all the actions and decisions of the company. This will also allow companies to build deeper connections with all internal and external stakeholders, helping to counter the current market forces. As a result, employees and their behaviour relative to the brand will become more pivotal to brand success than ever before. Great emphasis is put on the issues around how to guide and steer employee behaviour in line with the brand. After all, it is the employees that are the foundation of branding by building relationships with all stakeholder groups and by contributing to the meaning of the brand (for example, by representing to others what the company stands for).

FOCUS ON AUTHENTICITY

Authenticity has been hailed as a new branding paradigm and possible source of differentiation in a time of eroding trust. While at first glance it makes intuitive sense to counter distrust with authenticity, this warrants a closer look. First of all, when talking about authenticity, a number of different meanings and definitions are implied. To some, authentic means original; to others it means "true to yourself", etc. Here is what we mean when we talk about authenticity:

> Authenticity is the degree to which one is true to one's own personality, spirit, or character, despite the presence of certain pressures.[11]

It follows that for companies authenticity implies

- a strong ethos or sense of purpose that drives all thinking; we will refer to this as the *value core*
- the communication of the value core to all key stakeholders
- unrelenting compliance to the value core in all actions and decisions

Unfortunately, like the term "organic", authenticity has become confused with other, related issues such as environmental friendliness, social responsibility, and ethical behaviour. In order to better understand what authenticity is in the context of branding, it is worthwhile examining what authenticity is *not*.

Authenticity does not prescribe values

Authenticity as such does not automatically mean ethically or morally sound. Authenticity does not imply that the value core is right or wrong, good or bad. The only thing it does imply is that the value core is proclaimed and then acted upon. For example, a terrorist cell could be highly authentic, but their value core is not appealing for most of us. Authenticity in the branding context will only matter if the value core the organisation subscribes to is compelling and relevant to key stakeholders.

---

[11] http://en.wikipedia.org/wiki/Authenticity_(philosophy)

Authenticity is often also equated with quirky, different, and original (meaning highly distinctive and different from those of competitors). However, authenticity does not necessarily imply either of these attributes.

Authenticity is not the same as CSR

We have already established that authenticity does not prescribe values. By the same token, it is also not necessarily founded on a value core of sustainability or environmental and social responsibility. Yet, authenticity and CSR are often used interchangeably. While CSR cannot excel without authenticity (i.e. the underlying CSR values need to enter the value core), authenticity does not have to involve CSR at all.

Authenticity is not heritage branding

Authenticity is sometimes understood to be heritage branding or a type of "origin" branding where a brand makes allusions to a particular (existing or mystical) culture, its symbols, and associations. While our view of authenticity is not limited to this understanding, we would like to briefly discuss the various forms of heritage branding. The connection can be overt (like in the case of Kerrygold butter where the use of Irish stereotypes is almost comical), subtle (like in the case of Baileys Original Irish cream where the subtle use of colours and Celtic symbols creates the desired effect), genuine (like the Bohemian lifestyle of Italy incorporated in the Vespa scooter brand) or manufactured.

The latter is repeatedly the subject of controversial discussions, since it includes elements of manipulation and is intentionally misleading the consumer. Famous examples that have been exposed as "impostors" include Häagen Dazs ice-cream which is long known not to be of Swedish origin despite the Scandinavian sounding name and maps of Sweden supplied with the original product, or Bombay Sapphire, the premium gin brand which taps into the myths of colonial India through imagery (picture of Queen Victoria, Empress of India), the name and square, brilliantly blue bottle (alluding to the famous jewel), and recipe (allegedly dating back to 1761), despite being only 30 years old.[12] The strategy is one of "fake" authenticity and aimed at leveraging consumers' unquenchable thirst for special places with secret and magical powers. Whether consumers actually care about genuine heritage is difficult to tell. It may well be that the enjoyment factor of the "perfect illusion" outweighs concerns about "fake" authenticity.

Authenticity is not a marketing strategy

Pushing "fake" authenticity a step further is definitely crossing the line. Nevertheless, some marketers suggest that "a perfectly lived lie" could still be seen as authentic, with the added benefit of a more interesting and compelling story that can be told. In our opinion, this is an oxymoron since authenticity rests on the commitment to act on a proclaimed value core. If that value core is only a "marketing gimmick" that is fabricated because the company sees a fantastic marketing opportunity in it and not because they genuinely believe in it, that does not constitute authenticity in our book. The "fakeness" can come from several sources: the story is based on an illusion (e.g. fake heritage branding), the company does not mean what they communicate (for example, "greenwashing" is very common these days), the story is based on a flat out lie (e.g. falsely proclaiming food is organic when it is not).

---

[12] Clegg, A., The myth for authenticity, Brandchannel, 15 Aug. 2005, accessed: http://www.brandchannel.com/features_effect.asp?pf_id=276

We would caution against a strategy based on fakery. It seems difficult to say where stakeholders will draw the line and move from being amused by a perfect illusion to feeling deceived and betrayed by a lie. As some of the "invented" heritage brands prove highly successful, they seem to fall into the former category; however, fake authenticity does not seem suitable as the basis to build strong, resilient brands in the current market environment. Instead of rebuilding trust, it runs the risk of further destroying trust if or when they are being found out.

Greenwashing – the misleading or unfounded use of environmental promises – appears to become increasingly pervasive as companies are trying to exploit the growing concern for the environment. According to a 2007 report by TerraChoice Environmental Marketing,[13] an overwhelming majority of environmental marketing claims made by companies in North America are inaccurate, inappropriate, or unsubstantiated. Using metrics from the Federal Trade Commission (FTC) and the Environmental Protection Agency (EPA), TerraChoice concluded that all but one of the claims, out of more than 1000 products reviewed, raised red flags. Ranging from cleaning and personal care products to televisions and printers, the report concluded that the claims in question are "... either demonstrably false or risk misleading intended audiences". Similarly, a recent report in the UK revealed that an erroneous equation of ethical investing and green investing may harbour some disappointment for socially responsible investors: ethical funds' top 10 holdings were "surprisingly mainstream" with some even investing in oil giants such as BP, Shell and Total.[14]

---

[13] Jedlicka, W., Greenwashing: a dirty job? Brandchannel, 4 Feb. 2008, accessed: http://www.brandchannel.com/start.asp?fa_id=406
[14] Murray, J., Report warns ethical investments may not be so green, Business Green, 13 Feb. 2008, accessed: http://www.businessgreen.com/business-green/news/2209594/report-warns-ethical

A few dimensions of authenticity

Transparency and consistency Authenticity requires the proclamation of a value core which the corporation then sets out to live by. This necessitates a large degree of transparency with regards to the value core and consistency between proclaimed value core and actions.

Accountability Authenticity is also connected to accountability. Having the courage to admit that things might go wrong here and there instead of creating impossible, artificial ideals is a good route towards re-establishing trust. Traditional branding creates impossible ideals on both sides – on the side of the consumer (e.g. women's beauty ideal, what makes a good mother/parent) and on the side of the company (e.g. failing to portray themselves as flawed by human error and incontrollable external factors). This results in a world that is quite far removed from reality. After all, businesses are run by humans and humans are never perfect. Practising authenticity will help companies and brands to shift from an impossible quest for perfection to setting attainable goals, making realistic promises and creating value for all stakeholders involved.

Leadership Our definition of authenticity above suggests that authentic companies have a strong sense of self-directedness, a high degree of independence, resilience and also courage. In other words, authenticity is closely linked to leadership and involves staking out a chosen path and sticking to it with determination and resolve. Followers typically cannot achieve that.

Employee motivation and orientation Since authenticity creates transparency about what an organisation values, this can help to orient and guide employees. Companies with an appealing value core that is embedded in their actions and decisions attract not only customers, but also employees with a strong value affinity (positive self-selection). This in turn creates positive reinforcement of the value core and is highly engaging and motivating to employees.

Discretionary commitment versus true employee engagement One of the problems employees suffer from the most is inconsistency between corporate values proclaimed in corporate memos and *actual* values driving the performance and incentive metrics. For example, if a call centre employee is told that customer centricity is one of the key brand values but their payment is per call completed, there is a fundamental conflict of interest between the brand and the incentive system. In this case it is ultimately up to the individual call centre employee to decide which of the two contradicting systems she chooses to live up to. This is what Irish brand consultancy Genesis calls "discretionary commitment". The discrepancy between what is said and what is done usually results in frustration, disappointment, negativity and finally cynicism – first on the part of the employee, and subsequently on the part of the customer and other stakeholders. By contrast, authentic brands facilitate consistency between proclaimed value core and corporate actions, including performance and incentive metrics.

Gary Joyce, Managing Director of Genesis, explains:

> Every business is on a journey; communicating to employees where the company is going (vision) and how they plan to get there (strategy) will help employees better understand the goals and values of their organisation. Since we know that employees who understand the journey are more engaged than those who don't, this is a good start. But it's not enough. If leaders want to make a real difference to attitude and performance of their employees, they have to invite and encourage them to actively participate in building the journey. So employees don't just understand it, but believe it and own it. Then, and only then, will they take action with the commitment

that will really make a difference – to how customers and all other stakeholders experience the brand. Only if employees feel involved and that they're contributing to the big picture, that they're listened to and valued, will they be prepared to give their best, and turn discretionary commitment into true employee engagement.

Differentiation through authenticity? Authenticity is often hailed as a new-found source of differentiation. By definition, something is differentiating if it is more or less unique. What could make authentic brands so unique? We have already discussed that authenticity does not prescribe values; however, some of the most famous authentic brands are (or were) driven by a value core that was unique at the time of their launch. For example, the Body Shop with its bold rejection of animal testing or Ben & Jerry's with their organic ice-cream. However, while this is true for those examples, authenticity does not necessarily imply quirkiness, originality, or any other differentiating quality of the value core.

The most likely source of differentiation in authentic brands is their power to attract, engage and motivate employees, customers, and all other key stakeholders. Through the unrelenting compliance to the chosen value core they create a culture that permeates the organisation and radiates outwards in a way that creates a unique brand experience for all stakeholders.

The fact that companies actually *live* the values they proclaim should not be differentiating in its own right. Sadly, this is not what consumers and employees have come to expect.

Maintaining authenticity through the company life cycle

Authenticity and growth Which companies come to mind when talking about authenticity? More likely than not, readers will be thinking of smaller companies rather than large corporations when trying to answer this question. Why is that? Can large corporations be authentic or is this the exclusive territory of small (and sometimes quirky) market entrants? It appears that authenticity and company size are highly correlated. Small companies with a strong value core find it easier to stick to their values. They may be founded on a value core that is in direct opposition to the pertinent industry ethos or practice, and as new market entrants they can position themselves as "challenger brands" in order to take market share off the incumbents. This often has appeal with employees, customers, and other key stakeholders, giving the company a big boost in morale and motivation. As companies grow, however, they will typically have to broaden their appeal in order to expand their customer base. By necessity, they will start to compromise their value core and become more and more mainstream – unless they grow entirely through geographical expansion.

One key stage on this development path has often been the first mass media advertising. Loyal customers of an allegedly "undiscovered" authentic brand often get enjoyment from the feeling that the brand is not ubiquitous or a "real find". When seeing the first mainstream advert, this feeling will definitely disappear, and possible alienate the original customer base.

Another key milestone is often a change in distribution strategy. A shift from only being available through a small number of selected outlets that have high affinity with the intended target group to mass marketing through a national retailing chain can provide a decided loss in perceived authenticity. Things can get even trickier if pressure is exerted from investors or shareholders who are focused on a quick exit strategy or short-term financial results and not the long-term development of the brand.

On the employee side, growth will also provide a major challenge for the safekeeping of authenticity. The more employees a company has, the more difficult it is to ensure that they all understand and live the value core that drives authenticity. This is not simply a matter of induction and brand training; it might become more difficult to find the right people as larger numbers of new recruits are needed; it might also become challenging to defend the original culture against newcomers if they outnumber the founding crew and veterans.

Authenticity and ownership structure The current business paradigm around having to grow in order to survive is definitely a challenge to authentic brands. Often, growth also goes hand in hand with ever-increasing financing needs. However, the financing structure can also have significant impact on the development of a brand. Venture capitalists and private equity firms typically have their eyes on exit strategies, either through a sell-out or involving Wall Street through an IPO. This can mean that the underlying ethos and culture are undermined. This is something not all start-ups are sufficiently aware of, but YouBloom,[15] for example, is. The Internet start-up co-founded by Sir Bob Geldof and Phil Harrington aims to create a social networking site for musicians by musicians, with the stated goal to create a level playing field for artists and creatives both in the developed and in the developing world.

The company is built on a strong ethos of social and environmental responsibility, which it considers one of their key assets. "Anyone can build an internet site these days," says Phil Harrington, CEO and key driver behind YouBloom, "but building a unique culture is much more difficult to do and also much more difficult to copy." Thanks to its authentic culture and strong ethos, YouBloom has been very successful in attracting a pool of highly talented people who work together in virtual offices around the globe, from Los Angeles to Suzhou, China. When seeking

---

[15] www.youbloom.com

financing, Phil Harrington had a strong preference for angel money from like-minded investors, in particular in the early days of the company when the culture was more fragile. Very aware of the potential threat venture capital and private equity money could represent to the culture and ethos of YouBloom, which are at the heart of the emerging brand, he tirelessly reached out to people with affinity. "Even if this means that we will be a bit slower in building this company, we will make sure that we can continue to build this culture and value system true to our convictions. This allows us to build something that is unique and has meaning to all people involved, including our investors, and very soon, also to our customers," comments Phil Harrington.

Ownership and financial control usually have a significant impact on perceived authenticity. Take, for example, Google. Based on a simple idea (albeit with a sophisticated algorithm), they set out as a company with a strong ethos around "Don't do evil". With a product that is aimed at helping people and making their lives easier and better, they were quickly able to establish trust and credibility under the ownership and leadership of the two founders. However, as the company has gone public and is facing more external pressure to grow, they are frequently accused of hypocrisy, hidden agendas and ulterior motives; this requires Google to reach out to various stakeholders directly and indirectly affected by the accusations and to proactively fight against the gradual erosion of brand authenticity. They need to protect and continually reinforce their value core – failure to do so could seriously harm the brand.

Authenticity and transferability And finally, is authenticity transferable from one owner to the next? We have mentioned the early Body Shop, Ben & Jerry's and Green & Blacks as "trustworthy" companies. Actually, all of them would exemplify authenticity – if it had not been for their sale to large corporations. Naturally, these corporations ensure those concerned that they will continue to preserve the "authentic" values and identity of those companies even under the new ownership by ring-fencing them within the larger corporate environment. However, it seems that concerns about the "authenticity" are not unfounded. We all understand that these companies are bought so that their latent potential can be "leveraged". Being ring-fenced within the larger corporation sounds good in theory, but in reality many issues emerge. For example, will the Body Shop be able to hold fast on their opposition to vivisection under the wings of new owner L'Oréal who has historically tested cosmetics on animals?[16] And if not, what will it do to the Body Shop brand? Or will Unilever work out their problems with the Ben & Jerry's scoop store franchisees in line with the original Ben & Jerry's corporate philosophy or will the temptation of taking the ice-cream brand mainstream be too great?[17] And will Cadbury Schweppes be able to maintain the positioning of Green & Blacks around organic and green? We have all observed how Snapple fared under various owners.[18] This case really demonstrates that authenticity might indeed be transferable, but only if the new owner understands, respects and nourishes the underlying values that drive an authentic brand. As soon as the larger corporation introduces new rules, new processes, or new structures and tries to cut back the independence of the smaller, authentic brand, it will suffer and stop thriving.

---

[16] The Body Shop and L'Oréal: Why can't big be beautiful? *Ethical Corporation*, accessed: http://www.ethicalcorp.com/content.asp?ContentID=4284

[17] Entine, J., The Contrarian – Ben & Jerry's – socially responsible meltdown? *Ethical Corporation*, accessed: http://www.ethicalcorp.com/content.asp?ContentID=4550

[18] See, for example, Collins, J. and Porras, J.I. *Built to Last: Successful Habits of Visionary Companies*, New York: Harper Collins Business Essentials, 2002.

CASE STUDY: INNOCENT DRINKS IS STAYING AUTHENTIC

Background

One company that has carefully managed the major risks to the authenticity of its brand along its phenomenal growth path is UK-based smoothie maker innocent drinks. This is an extraordinary success story of how a (simple) product of pure fruit (and nothing but pure fruit) turned into one of the best loved brands in the UK over just eight years. Their success is based on two key ingredients – unwavering commitment to keep their smoothies 100% natural and a brand that is natural, engaging, and humorous. Headquartered in London's Shepherd's Bush, they occupy an industrial building lovingly known as Fruit Towers. The floors of the office are covered with Astroturf (synthetic grass) and their car park is littered with a herd of cow vans and grass-covered vans.

Although this is the UK's fastest growing company in the food and drinks sector, innocent so far has successfully avoided turning into a "corporation". All their communications avoid corporate speak; from job titles to job ads to product labels, the language used is always laid back, playful, and deceivingly effortless. In a way, one can't help but create associations with the old Ben & Jerry's "all natural" ice-cream, founded by two self-confessed hippies who built their brand around unique flavours of ice-cream and a socially conscious ethos. Take, for example, the story of how innocent was founded. The founders, three young English guys who were college friends and worked in various consulting and advertising firms, bought £500 worth of fruit in the summer of 1998, turned it into smoothies and then sold them from a stall at a little music festival in London. They put up a big sign saying "Do you think we should give up our jobs to make these smoothies?" and put out a bin saying "YES" and a bin saying "NO". As a means of voting, customers were asked to put the empty bottles in one of the bins. At the end of the weekend the "YES" bin was so full that they went in the next day and resigned from their respective employers. The theme of the little music festival carries through – every year, innocent holds "the village fête" (previously called "Fruitstock"), their own festival, in London's Regents Park. They select lesser known and unsigned bands to play at the main stage (the music needs to be nice to listen to when you are lying in the grass) and also have the innocent Drum Club perform.

This brand is formally designed around the five key values of Be Natural, Be Entrepreneurial, Be Generous, Be Commercial, and Be Responsible. These are the values that drive the company's actions and decisions, from getting suppliers to adhere to their standards to creating new smoothie recipes. Naturally, social and environmental responsibility has been embedded in the innocent brand DNA from the outset. Not only do they purchase the very best fruit, they also try to purchase fruit from farms that look after their workers as well as the environment. They continually work on improving the sustainability of packaging (e.g. in 2007 they became the world's first food and drink company to use 100% recycled plastic bottles), they take responsibility for the social and environmental impact of their business, they try to run a resource-efficient business, and they donate 10% of their profits to good causes (e.g. the innocent Foundation: www.innocentfoundation.org).

How were they able to grow and still keep the appeal of their brand?
For one, despite having grown into a £100 million company, responsible for three-quarters of the smoothie market in the UK, they have managed to stay true to themselves and to their stated goal of "making sure everything we do is good". They have resisted the temptation to change the tone of their communications which is one of the key drivers of their brand's appeal. It

Figure 2.2 innocent logo

is this disarming use of words, the innocent way of looking at the world and doing things differently, the laid-back non-aggressive approach that successfully positions them as the antithesis to the "evil corporate world" that seems so devoid of authenticity. They call their products "little tasty drinks" and tell us on their website that they want to make life a little easier and a little better – "Just think of innocent drinks as your one healthy habit – like going to the gym but without the communal showers afterwards." Even their logo, "the Dude", seems homemade and unpretentious.

On their website they explain why the drinks are called innocent: "We call them innocent because our drinks are always completely pure, fresh and unadulterated. Anything you ever find in an innocent bottle will always be 100% natural and delicious – and if it isn't, get on the banana phone and make us beg for forgiveness." Even their product labels do not contain the usual boring list of ingredients, but light-heartedly inform the customer about the fruit required to make the smoothie (e.g. half a pureed banana, 12 crushed raspberries and 62 cranberries), the fact that they will never put additives of any sort into their smoothie and that you can "tell our mums if you are not absolutely satisfied with the product". In Germany, they also use the product label to recruit people, to tell the story of Mr Boysen and his berry, or to explain their eight-year history of loving fruit and becoming best friends with raspberries.

Most importantly, however, they have stuck to their conviction that their drinks are supposed to be healthy, ensuring

EMERGING STRATEGIES 65

Figure 2.3 innocent product label and bottles

they contain nothing but the finest fruit. Given the absence of chemicals and concentrates, they had to address the logistical challenges of transporting and stocking products with a very short shelf life, putting great emphasis on keeping the product properly chilled and the production line meticulously clean. This is actually one of the reasons it has taken innocent quite a long time to become profitable. Matthew Gardan, the innocent communications manager in France, otherwise also known as Garlic Smoothie, reflects: "If the founders had taken our company public, we would probably no longer exist in this form. Stockholders would have never had the patience for us to grow our business while remaining absolutely true to our brand promise. Time has proven us right, but it took a lot of courage, persistence and determination." innocent knew they had to protect the authenticity of their product if they wanted their company to succeed. This meant that they could under no circumstances jeopardise their very core, their commitment to "100% natural" and they resisted the path of least resistance, i.e. making things easier by "fudging" it. They are very proud that their smoothies have nowhere to hide behind – so it is absolutely pivotal that they buy the finest fruit available. They have a team of six who are constantly travelling the world in search of the best fruit. For instance, they will only buy one kind of mango – the Alphonso mango which grows at the eastern shores of India – for their Mango & Passionfruit smoothies. Although this costs them up to four times the per-ton price of other, lesser quality mangoes, it takes the Alphonso mango to make a smoothie of innocent quality. So far, their customers have been willing to pay for it – a rather pricy £2.70 a 250 ml bottle or £3.99 for 1l.

Another reason they manage to stay authentic is the fact that they see their people as key assets and take recruiting and people development very seriously. They have repeatedly been ranked in the "best place to work" list by *The Guardian*. As Gardan points out: "Like our products, our brand is 100% natural. Our brand is not manufactured, it is lived. From the very beginning, innocent was about producing tasty drinks that are healthy for people, working with nice people and doing good. It really shows, you can feel it if you work here. We have a lovely, unique brand that we are all extremely proud of." Very clearly, all this can only be achieved with the right kind of employees. Innocent is very aware of how pivotal employees are to their success and the delivery of their brand; therefore, they have a very stringent recruitment process, it can take up to six months to get through the entire screening process. But once you are welcomed into the "family" (as they call it), you can benefit from a very positive culture based on praise and support, where people are recognised and managed as a key asset and encouraged to creatively contribute to the firm and the brand. They all participate in weekly Monday meetings where all things important are discussed. There are also quarterly company meetings and away days like Nature Weekend in the Alps. But there are also lots of informal gatherings, from picnics to Film Club movie screenings to Cheese Club meetings. Innocent is, however, starting to feel the fragmentation that comes with growth. Beyond a certain number, it gets more difficult to find activities that are appealing to everyone and can accommodate large numbers. Naturally, people gravitate to affinity groups.

Lastly, it is their intuitive approach to handling big milestones with ease. For example, when they first started to advertise on TV, this could have been potentially tricky for their brand, catapulting it into the echelons of "large" brands in the consumer's mind. However, they found a simple solution to this potential threat to their authenticity – they made the ads themselves. While in the case of almost any other company this would have been perceived as amateurish, in the case of innocent this came across as authentic. And to this day their ads are simple, home-made almost, and they certainly capture this laid-back, understated way of engaging stakeholders.

Upcoming challenges

As companies grow, they need to adapt their distribution strategy. Originally, innocent was distributed through upmarket delicatessen stores and small outlets targeted at health conscious and socially aware customers like yoga studios. As innocent was slowly growing more popular, their distribution became more and more mainstream, including supermarket chains like Waitrose and Sainsbury's. While this certainly took away the feeling of small and undiscovered, it did not negatively impact the brand; however, when they took it a step further and announced a trial of their kids' products with McDonald's in the north of the UK, brand loyalists were upset since McDonald's in their mind stands for the exact opposite in many ways – unhealthy food, no nutritional value, terrible treatment of their workers and the environment, greedy and profit-oriented. Although innocent positioned the opportunity as a way to get healthier drinks in front of underprivileged children, explaining that 90% of UK children do not get an adequate fruit intake on a regular basis in their blog, not everyone could see this angle. They polled their regular drinkers and received more than 73% support for the trial, so they went ahead with it, but one of the co-founders took the trouble to write a lengthy explanation on their blog, assuring everyone that doing business with McDonald's does not mean that they would in any way sway from their principles and their path. This trial certainly seems risky from a brand authenticity point of view, but the fact alone that they are even given the benefit of the doubt that their motivation is not only commercial but also in the interest of children is amazing. At the moment, this trial in McDonald's is still continuing; innocent is one of several juice/smoothie/fresh fruit options in a revised healthy option kid's meal McDonald's are trialling. Ultimately it will be McDonald's decision whether innocent remains a part of their children's menu.

innocent has now expanded into a number of European countries. The challenges of transporting the authenticity of the innocent brand to France, Holland, Austria, Switzerland, Germany, and Scandinavia are obvious. First, there is a language issue. The light-hearted, playful messages that roll off the tongue in English very easily are a bit more difficult to create in other languages. In German, for example, they sound a bit less playful and a bit more translated. Second, these countries may be united in the European Union, but they still have very different cultures with very different protocols and preferences. It can therefore take some time for the brand to grow its own, authentic voice in each market. It is only recently that the French tone, for example, is coming of age. Gardan explains: "To be truly pertinent to consumers, the French tone has evolved into a slightly more edgy tone than its UK parents, reflecting the mild cynicism inherent in the French ethos."

Conclusion innocent case study

As can be seen in the case of innocent, authenticity can be a very successful strategy, but it takes a lot of hard work, determination and skill to pull this off, pretty much across all stages of development to date. Timing certainly worked in favour of innocent – just as its drinks appeal to cash-rich, time-poor workaholics in need of their daily servings of healthy fruit (in enjoyable liquid form), its laid-back and earthy approach to business successfully counters the current environment of distrust and backlash against the dubious ethics of large conglomerates. However, as they keep growing, new challenges will arise – we shall watch with interest. Naturally.

Conclusion

Authentic brands define and proclaim a set of appealing and relevant values which drive all corporate actions and decisions. Following a set of bold values can constitute a unique corporate culture which radiates outwards and helps to create a differentiating experience for employees, customers, and other stakeholders. Authenticity requires transparency and consistency, and is therefore a suitable strategy to rebuild trust. However, authenticity as a strategy seems to be limited in a number of ways: it seems to inevitably come under threat when companies grow, it is difficult to instil in hindsight, and it is difficult to transfer through mergers or acquisitions.

FOCUS ON CSR

CSR has become such a buzz-word and so hyped up, that many companies believe they need to make CSR the centre of every activity, without taking the time to strategically evaluate their options. These companies go beyond taking a strategic approach to CSR and make CSR a key driver of corporate strategy, often unnecessarily. In this section we discuss how some small and some large companies use CSR to respond to the CSR *imperative* discussed earlier and the general erosion of trust in corporations. We will show how CSR can be used to engage employees, customers, and other stakeholders, but will also draw attention to the scrutiny companies need to expect for CSR activities they choose to communicate publicly.

CSR is here to stay

As we discussed earlier, no brand can afford *not* to address CSR as part of their business and brand strategy in the current environment. But this does not imply that every company has to evolve around CSR or become a leader in CSR. What it does mean is that companies should evaluate the social, environmental and compliance issues and risks inherent in their value chains and then strategically address these, ideally in a way that builds competitive advantage and has a positive impact on society. CSR initiatives historically were born of crisis and conflict – defensive strategies designed to safeguard standards and reputations. Therefore, it is not surprising that companies still have difficulties in embracing CSR as a strategic opportunity. Forward thinking companies understand, however, that CSR has the strategic power to energise businesses and brands and will eventually become inherent in the way business is done.

Consumers are looking to brands for guidance

In today's environment with a growing CSR imperative, brands have to be inspirational in a socially responsible way. Rachel Simmons, a brand and CSR expert, comments:

> Consumers are increasingly looking to brands to help define their role within society and for a purchase that counts for something meaningful beyond an acquisition. Companies reaping the benefits are those that proactively and strategically build their Social Brand Capital. Put another way, the stand these companies take on a social issue is not a result of their business but one of the reasons they are in business.[19]

Not every company needs to be a leader in CSR

As the CSR imperative for companies grows, there is much confusion as to how to make sure that CSR is congruent with business and brand strategy while also benefiting society at large. A burgeoning industry of social impact consultants and advisers is testimony to this confusion. Addressing CSR within the framework of business and brand strategy means to develop strategic alternatives, assess them for their impact in terms of risks and benefits, establish criteria for selecting the most suitable ones, and seek ways to measure progress and impact (as with any other investment or strategic programme). For some companies, it will make sense to become leaders in CSR, for others it won't. Key drivers in this decision are the nature of the industry companies operate in (e.g. stigma industries need to think very carefully about their approach), the nature of the product offering (in particular

---

[19] Simmons, R., Social Brand Capital: the loyalty nucleus of CSR, June 2007, Brandchannel Paper, http://www.brandchannel.com/papers_review.asp?sp_id=1309

in relation to key competitors), and the corporate culture and ethos (both existing and desired).

CSR includes a wide range of topics and issues

Companies have to decide (a) which strategic topics of CSR they should best focus on and (b) whether they should adopt a leader strategy or a follower strategy. As a leader, CSR can become an overall strategic driver. This would, for example, be the case with Marks & Spencer, who have made CSR a key focus for everything they do and every decision they take. However, one can also be a leader and focus only on selected aspects of CSR, like Faber Castell, the well-known German brand of pencils and artists' supplies. Faber Castell have been integrating environmental responsibility into their brand and products for a long time. They continuously search for environmentally friendly processes and materials. In addition, they started their own 25 000-acre pine plantation in Brazil some decades ago, providing the raw material required for making 1.8 billion pencils per year.

As indicated in Figure 2.4, CSR is made up of three broad topics.

1. Environmental issues and concerns

These address the impact a company has or can have on the environment. A leader strategy would require that environmental responsibility is deeply integrated into every aspect of the business, from production and packaging to new product development. Rachel Simmons points out:

> Over the last decade, we have seen a lot of companies emerge that have this innate sense of responsibility for the environment and the

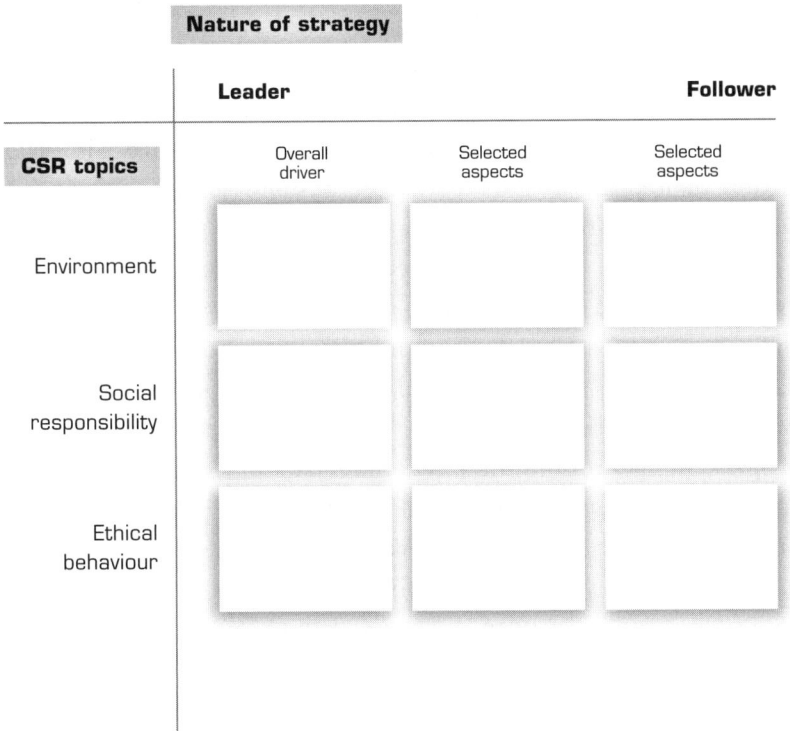

Figure 2.4 CSR strategy framework

individual, where health and a healthy environment are ingrained in their culture and brand from the outset. They start out small or niche but then quickly steal market share from major market incumbents and grow fast – their Social Brand Capital being their major point of distinction. Cliff Bar, innocent drinks and Stonyfield Farm are all good examples. The good news is – these companies are pushing the CSR envelope hard and fast and defining whole new ways of doing business in terms of what they sell and the relationship they build between employees and customers. For example, when Stonyfield Farm was looking to decrease its negative impact on the environment, they thought that transportation and packaging would be obvious places to look for maximum impact. However, as they looked deeper inside their value chain they found that they could make the biggest impact by optimising milk production.

"The good news is," says Simmons, "that many companies have understood the message. They no longer need to be converted; they are ready to act and want to make it happen. Many just don't know how to get the buy-in from their business or how to develop a concrete plan that anchors the very idea of CSR deep within their operational and strategic business reality."

While examining the environmental impact of key processes, companies often discover that reducing negative impacts on the environment usually also results in cost savings. For example, in the case of Faber Castell, the pine plantation not only conserves natural resources but also helps the company cope with the volatility of wood prices and reduce bottlenecks in supply. Common programmes addressing the environmental aspects of CSR include carbon footprint reduction, development of more energy-efficient processes and the use of alternative sources of energy. Many companies are actively investing in this form of CSR, partly in anticipation of tougher standards and regulations, partly because they believe in it, and partly because they can reap financial benefits at the same time. Whatever their motivations and intentions, these will ultimately drive the link between CSR and branding.

As the consuming public is showing a sheer insatiable appetite for "green" products, many companies wonder about the potential contribution *green* can make to their brands. This is strongly linked to the efficacy and authenticity of any green campaigns. For example, many environmentalists might consider Honda the greenest car company with regards to both manufacturing process and product, but it is Toyota that managed to commercialise the idea of green with their hybrid model Prius.[20] If a green campaign lacks authenticity and is seen as greenwashing, it will cause serious damage to the brand.

---

[20] Rusch, R., Best global brands: how valuable is green? Brandchannel, 30 July 2007, accessed: http://www.brandchannel.com/features_effect.asp?pf_id=379#more

CASE STUDY: BP – "BEYOND PETROLEUM"[21]

> One of the pioneers of using "green" as a brand strategy was the UK-based global energy company BP (formerly known as British Petroleum). A recent *Adweek*[22] article was reviewing the green marketing strategy of BP and concluded that it worked with consumers, but not necessarily with media, special interest groups and watchdogs.
>
> For more than seven years now, BP have been focusing their messaging strategy around their alternative energy initiatives, trying to position themselves as environmentally friendly. As one of the world's largest producers of fossil fuels they had associations around negative environmental impact and a lot of cynicism to overcome. Their campaign "beyond petroleum" was launched in 2000, leading to a stir in the energy sector at the time. They were a pioneer in the oil sector with their new green and yellow logo, the Helios, and the green positioning, which was considered a bold move then. Backed by Lord John Browne, the highly visible and much revered CEO at the time, this message managed to capture the attention of the public. Anna Catalano, then Group Vice President, Marketing at BP, recalls:
>
>> In 1999, BP had just begun a series of acquisitions, including Amoco, adding thousands of employees to the BP organisation who shared no common past but a common future. Therefore, we were looking for a platform of values that could create a

---

[21] In their time at BP, Anna Catalano and Charles Perry contributed significantly to driving change in BP towards the "beyond petroleum" promise of a green energy company, together with other passionate colleagues.

[22] Solman, G., BP: Coloring public opinion? *Adweek*, 14 Jan. 2008, accessed: http://www.adweek.com/aw/content_display/news/strategy/e3i9ec32f006d17a91cd72d6192b9f7599a

shared purpose that would equally excite and motivate all employees. In other words, the reason to define a new brand was internally driven.

In order to identify these shared values that would become the new BP brand, the marketing team conducted a large number of focus groups with employees in various parts of the organisation. This work resulted in the definition of the new BP brand around the four values of green, progressive, innovative, and performance. Catalano highlights: "What we really wanted to achieve at this point was that our employees would embrace the new brand. We did not want them to be surprised by the new direction, but to recognise that they had been part of this conversation." For the internal launch of the new brand, the company's 25+ group vice presidents each chose a location to travel to, from China to Philadelphia, so that they could unveil the brand values, new logo and tag line simultaneously in all corners of the world. Each group vice president was equipped with a packet containing a presentation and supporting materials. "As far as the tag line was concerned," Catalano explains, "we had developed a number of variations that were all plays on BP – bright people, big planet, and beyond petroleum. The initial plan was to perhaps use more than one and rotate them. But since we had started with our favourite, beyond petroleum, and it turned out to capture so much attention, we decided to stick with it." A couple of days after the internal launch, the external launch followed suit.

Hailed as visionary and a role model of corporate social responsibility by the consumer business press, BP and its rebranding campaign seem to have been able to convince the public that it is more eco-friendly than its competitors. According to *Adweek*, BP said its brand awareness jumped from 4% to a recent high of 67% over the past seven years; a Landor study showed BP as "more green" in the last five years than any competitor, including Shell; the campaign won the 2007 gold Effie from the American Marketing Association for "Sustained success", recognising that "against a backdrop of scepticism, the world's second-largest energy company wanted to be different. The BP corporate reputation campaign communicates the company's progressive values in a distinctive, non-glossy way", calling the campaign "a landmark platform for a company trying to change the way the world uses, and thinks about, the fuels that are vital to human progress".

However, BP also quickly started to attract critical voices over alleged "greenwashing", with critics persistently pointing to alleged proofs of hypocrisy, including the fact that BP's portfolio is still heavily favouring fossil fuels and more recently BP's stance on exploiting oil sands. Let us take a peek behind the scenes to see if what went on inside BP at the time sheds some light on the continuing controversy.

Charles Perry, former strategic marketing manager at BP who joined the company when he saw the new tag line, remarks:

> I was attracted to BP because of the new tag line and what I expected to find behind that. However, as I found out to my surprise, when the tag line "beyond petroleum" was launched in 2000, it had buy-in only with certain parts of the organisation and unfortunately did not yet signal strategic intent. It is truly mind-blowing in hindsight that it was unveiled under the new BP brand – a very courageous move indeed by a small group of people led by Anna Catalano who wanted to make a difference and drive real change. Its impact certainly took people both inside and outside the company by surprise. And there was, from my perspective, not enough explanation or supporting communication to follow up. Like other oil companies, marketing had never been a big focus at BP and very few professional marketers resided there – the company as a whole did not understand that a tag line presented a brand promise that had to be fulfilled – the entire focus was on upstream, never really downstream.

From a marketing and branding point of view, BP was spot on when they launched "beyond petroleum"; it put BP on a completely different trajectory, but the corporation behind the brand was neither prepared nor sufficiently confident to back the brand promise. The branding team had launched a bold statement into the marketplace, creating attention and also huge expectations. This was the point where the branding team faced their biggest challenge – they had to bring the entire organisation on board with a claim that had already gone public. This created confusion and tension inside the organisation. Perry remembers:

> It was a bit of a civil war in corporate HQ when I got there – there was a massive rift between a small group of visionaries who saw the need for change and a much bigger group that were backward looking and wanted BP to remain an oil company with a focus on upstream like it had always been. Funnily enough, the new logo itself was liked by everyone – the Helios was not the issue, it served to unite a very diverse and much bigger company. The issue was what came underneath the logo.

After the launch, the beyond petroleum tag line was not really used anywhere except in the USA; in Europe BP fell silent, void of any explanation, and leaving stakeholders to interpret the situation for themselves. Mainstream media had a field day, filling the information gap with all sorts of mocking interpretations of "bp". The City (the financial community in London) would take particular issue with the void of information on the part of BP. For example, Goldman Sachs, who were one of the biggest institutional investors at the time, wrote a report about how confused they were about BP's business focus and whether they were trying to get out of oil altogether or not. "As a result," Perry highlights, "they recommended to drop the beyond petroleum tag line – and BP almost did!"

Well, good thing for BP that investment banks are not brand advisers. The marketing team carried the torch and fought the battle tirelessly, conducting workshops and sessions to engage key internal stakeholders, relentlessly communicating the brand promise, until after three-and-a-half years of battling they finally won. Catalano recalls:

Without the continued support of Lord Browne, this would have never happened. In order to change any company, you need to get employees engaged, and the leadership factor in this is huge. There was a critical meeting held in New York, during which Lord Browne decided he needed to re-up his commitment by sending a letter clearly stating his commitment to the brand. Another break-through for us was the elimination of brand fragmentation; so many different departments were talking to their respective key audiences without there being a co-ordinated messaging strategy. It was time that someone took on brand ownership. We identified 12 key audiences, developed a content strategy together with the relevant functions and departments and thus ensured that everyone was pulling in the same strategic direction. This was a real step forward.

In addition, the marketing team also developed 360° communications packages, established a "helios award" which recognised projects that best expressed either one or all of the four brand values and was conferred in an evening event by Lord Browne in London, developed a large scroll of paper where they collected stories about people living the brand, equipped senior managers with communication materials to support them in talking about the brand and moved along the rebranding of retail sites (gas stations) as a visual signal of the ongoing change. Perry points out:

BP nearly made the very worst of this by dropping the tag line; meanwhile, Lord Browne's early speeches about climate change were a hit from the outset. His landmark speech at Stanford in 1997 made people sit up and listen. And still, the internal battle about "beyond petroleum" went on for too long. For years we were not allowed to use beyond petroleum in the UK – not in speeches, press releases, or advertising. Some of us wished that Lord Browne's letter had come sooner, clarifying once and for all that "this is who we are, both now and in the future" as it eventually did.

Perry continues: "As a result of this internal battle, BP lost a lot of time and opportunities. Today, many companies have overtaken BP's position in green leadership, including Marks &

Spencer and GE." Yet, both Catalano and Perry believe that many of the efforts undertaken by the more progressives in the industry were encouraged and inspired by BP's example. "Many are intrigued by how a company in such a stodgy industry can imagine breaking out and setting a bar for others to reach," Catalano explains. "It was a courageous step to take. BP demonstrated that a small and committed group of people can achieve a lot, and that the brand can be a very effective vehicle for change. However, it also shows that promises create expectations and hence the risk of reputational damage if a company fails to live up to these expectations."

To conclude, it seems that the divide in public opinion about BP's true green intentions is somewhat a reflection of the internal struggle that seemingly has continued to this day. Latest announcements by CEO Tony Hayward to focus the business strategy back on petroleum make the green promise increasingly less credible. With crude prices of above $100 per barrel and a primary concern to restore BP's financial standing, BP does not look particularly concerned with the environmental impact of their move into the oil sands of Canada, the growth of their alternative energy portfolio or the need to clean up their carbon footprint. Nevertheless, Hayward claims he is "keen as ever to ensure BP's greener image remains".[23] The question remains – is it just an image?

2. Social responsibility

In a corporate context social responsibility refers to

- how employers treat their employees, e.g. working conditions, health and safety, training, etc.
- health and safety of products

---

[23] Macalister, T., BP goes back to petroleum, *The Guardian*, 21 Feb. 2008.

- social impact of corporate activities on the communities that host them
- fair trading

Social responsibility deals with deeply human issues and, unlike environmental responsibility, is much more difficult to translate into financial benefits to the corporation.

Social responsibility programmes traditionally included the donation of cash to good causes (traditional corporate philanthropy), often directed at local communities impacted by corporate action. This arm's length cash donation approach seems to be losing importance as more active involvement is replacing money donations. For example, many professional services firms like KPGM or IBM encourage their employees to work on pro bono projects or pay them to donate their time to good causes.

CASE STUDY: STARBUCKS

> Starbucks has been a pioneer in corporate social responsibility. Not only do they offer healthcare benefits and stock (called "bean stock") to their employees and part-time workers, but they have also been forging partnerships with coffee growers around the world. These partnerships are designed to give coffee growers a fair price for their beans – often higher than the so-called Fair Trade price – and to promote sound environmental practices.[24] With this approach Starbucks is effectively addressing an issue of contention that is becoming more and more visible in the coffee, tea, and chocolate industries where end customers are being charged a fortune while the farmers are left with hardly enough to survive. While it is

---

[24] Gunther, M., How UPS, Starbucks, Disney Do Good, Fortune: America's Most Admired Companies, 25 Feb. 2006, accessed: http://money.cnn.com/2006/02/23/news/companies/mostadmired_fortune_responsible/index.htm

undisputed that Starbucks treat their employees well, they raise eyebrows in certain places when it comes to their business practices. For example, it has been widely publicised that they propagate a café monoculture by moving in across the street from small independent and highly successful cafés, in some cases even buying out the buildings where competitors operate.[25] This tactic does, of course, not reflect social responsibility and sustainability from a community point of view and breeds a cynical attitude. But a cynical attitude on the part of special interest groups and NGOs will accompany almost all CSR efforts by large corporations. This is partly due to the fact that they are trying to push the envelope by trying to pressure companies into taking a more active role in CSR, and partly because of the fundamental assumption that all corporations have ulterior motives and hidden agendas. For example, when Starbucks took over Ethos Water from the initial founder Peter Thum, who wanted to change the world by providing clean water to poor, dying children, they almost immediately attracted heavy criticism, being accused of disguising a profit-making enterprise as humanitarian relief and exploiting the plight of poor countries to sell more bottled water in the USA;[26] other key points of contention are the disproportionately small amount of donation (5 cents per bottle) versus the product price ($1.80 per bottle), with some people suggesting that donating directly to a reputable charity dedicated to water projects in Africa would be a better way to address the issue if serious about it. There are some simple things Starbucks could do to bring those interested into the conversation and to mollify criticism, for example they could create a donation option on the Ethos

---

[25] Prendergast, M., *Uncommon Grounds: The History of Coffee and How It Transformed Our World*, New York: Basic Books, 1999.
[26] See, for example, the campaign against Ethos, www.thetruthaboutethos.com

Water website. Of course, the Ethos "project" also suffers from inopportune timing, when bottled water has become highly controversial from an environmental point of view (e.g. major bottled water companies like Pepsi, Coke and Nestlé are working hard at the moment to battle the bad reputation of bottled water in terms of energy consumption, pollution concerns, and issues of social responsibility around water access rights and water control). Starbucks has now teamed up with Pepsi for a new campaign of print ads, fronted by actor Matt Damon and launched in April 2008 in a number of magazines including *Time, GQ,* and *Vanity Fair*. The ads read:

> Over 1 billion people around the world lack clean water. . . . Every time you buy a bottle of Ethos, money goes to help provide children with the access to clean water they need. So if you choose to drink bottled water, please choose to make a difference.[27]

All the criticism is entering the stream of associations the Starbucks brand stands for. If you have ever paid attention to their store decoration, you will have seen the pictures of smiling and proud coffee farmers which are meant to warm the customer's heart while she sits there and enjoys her coffee. However, it might just also remind the customer of these accusations of hypocrisy and tarnish the intended experience along with the brand.

3. Ethical behaviour

All companies with strong brands have a basic code of conduct or ethical standard defined. However, these codes of conduct are rarely linked to the brand and typically are not actively communicated or managed. This tends to change when a company's reputation is

---

[27] http://www.sustainablelifemedia.com/content/story/brands/pepsi_starbucks_tout_eco_charity_in_ethos_ad_campaign, 11 March 2008.

threatened or when a scandal is engulfing the corporation. These situations usually create enormous pressure to demonstrate to the outside world that the root cause of the misbehaviour or non-compliance is eliminated, putting a lot of focus on compliance-related processes and standards, including the code of conduct. Naturally, this leads to a power shift in the organisation. Those in charge of "cleaning up" get the mandate and the authority to interfere with business practice and business processes, often leading to increased bureaucracy and organisational inefficiencies.

The temptation for these compliance efforts to overpower everything an organisation does is sometimes so big that the brand is in danger of being hijacked. However, we would caution any company in this situation to consider that it might be dangerous if a code of conduct, born out of a crisis or at least a somewhat extraordinary situation, starts to drive the brand. The code of conduct is focused on rectifying a situation, and so will be limited in its motivational, strategic, and aspirational qualities which are required to engage all key stakeholders (not just misbehaved employees). Moreover, it is typically designed by a corporate department that operates in a different communication paradigm – namely, signing statements and ticking boxes – than the marketing or branding team. Making employees sign an updated code of conduct will most likely be seen as window dressing and not have the desired effect of actually changing behaviour. Therefore, companies in this situation should try to find a way to satisfy both external pressures for demonstrating action is taken to rectify the situation and internal needs to boost morale, increase confidence and rebuild trust.

Sometimes, a scandal is brought on the company by unethical behaviour of an influential senior manager, for example the founder or CEO. This can be particularly risky for a brand if it is founded on ethical principles, like the US retailer Whole Foods for example, famous for its green and ethical standards; the behaviour of a senior manager would then become infinitely more relevant to the credibility of the brand. John Mackey, co-founder and CEO of Whole Foods, had been an active contributor to the Yahoo!

Finance stock forums for more than eight years. He wrote under the pseudonym Rahodeb (a play on his wife's name "Deborah"), and used his online alter-ego to write online attacks against Whole Foods' primary rival called Wild Oats. Mackey trashed Wild Oats' management, questioned their corporate structure, and constantly undermined the value of the company's stock, predicting that the company would fall into bankruptcy and then be sold after its stock fell below $5 per share.[28] On the flip side, he praised Whole Foods, commented on the efficacy of his own financial models and predicted stock increases. In February 2007, Whole Foods announced it would buy Wild Oats for about $565 million, or $18.50 per share. While Mackey's anonymous contributions do not constitute an anti-trust violation (the whole incident was exposed by the FTC in an anti-trust investigation seeking to block the buy-out), they were certainly unethical and in sharp contrast to the ethos on which Whole Foods was founded.

This case is also interesting because Mackey is not only the CEO, but also the founder of Whole Foods. Founders of companies that grow around a strong ethos (e.g. in the case of Whole Foods organic, environmentally concerned, humane treatment of animals, caps to executive pay) typically carry particular weight in terms of making the claim credible and a scandal involving the founder personally could undermine the efforts of the entire company. However, if the brand values have been so deeply embedded in everything the company does, and adequately anchored within the broader company culture, then the brand becomes more resilient to threats like this. In the case of Whole Foods, the backlash appears to be surprisingly short-lived, demonstrating that the brand has taken on a meaning beyond the founder and hence is robust enough to absorb the impact of the scandal.

---

[28] Kesmodel, D. and Wilke, J., Whole Foods is hot, Wild Oats a Dud – so said Rahodeb, *Wall Street Journal*, 12 July 2007, accessed: http://online.wsj.com/article/SB118418782959963745.html?mod= googlenews_wsj

Strategic approach to CSR

As more and more companies are searching for ways to integrate CSR into their corporate strategy, CSR is being transformed in many ways: its standing and attention within companies is growing and management of CSR is demanding more strategic skills. CSR activities are being shifted out of the PR or compliance team into separate CSR functions. Most large companies now have a CSR officer, vice president of CSR or director of CSR. Rachel Simmons remarks: "With the introduction of marketing and branding to CSR everything changed for the better. Finally, we have moved from CSR being a defensive strategy or a retention strategy to now actually being seen as a strategic opportunity. This is when real change will happen. Companies will start to look much deeper for ways to incorporate CSR."

Companies that address CSR strategically Companies that address CSR strategically manage to leverage CSR to benefit both the company and society. They can be grouped into four categories:

- CSR entrepreneurs
- CSR leaders
- Vocal (*or proud*) CSR converts
- Quietly conscientious

CSR entrepreneurs CSR entrepreneurs are companies who have been founded with CSR in mind and who embrace CSR as part of who they are and what they do. These companies tend to be smaller and are often just starting out. They generally have the advantage that they do not (yet) have to offset the baggage of being large and global, and can work from a clean slate. Take, for example, EDUN, the Irish clothing label providing socially conscious fashion, launched in spring 2005 by Ali Hewson and her husband Bono (of U2). The company's mission is to create beautiful clothing that supports sustainable employment in developing areas of the world, particularly in Africa.[29] EDUN is founded on the principles of "trade, not aid", aimed at building sustainable communities by improving the skill sets of factory workers. EDUN also promotes Africa within the fashion community, encouraging others to do business there and help bring the continent out of extreme poverty.

Bridget Russo, Global Marketing Director at EDUN, explains:

> Our brand vision is to become synonymous with beautiful clothes made in Africa. We really want to prove to the world that Africa is a modern place and that it can be done. We take pride in the beauty and quality of our clothes and do not want them to be a pity-purchase. However, it will be a lot of work before "Made in Africa" will take on this meaning and it can be quite challenging at times.

While the fashion and garment industry overall has started to focus more on social responsibility and sustainability, certain pressure points remain the same. Russo explains:

> One of our key challenges is on the functional level. The industry works to certain turn-around times, putting a lot of stress on lead-times. Our customers run on tight retail calendars, so delivering outside the expected window can hurt both our business and theirs. L.A. brands with factories in their back yards therefore have a natural competitive advantage. Also China has made a lot of progress in terms of speed and product quality. Hence, we need to spend a lot of time and effort in building capacity and quality control to improve our competitiveness.

As fashion brands with a sustainability focus have become more and more popular, this has also attracted pretenders who "fake it" and hope that nobody will check their claims of "organic", "natural", or even "sweat-shop free". Russo highlights:

---

[29] They also have knitware from Peru and silk products from India.

Having a strict code of ethics is very important to us and adhering to it means that you constantly have to check and monitor what is going on locally. We have made significant progress, but at the same time we also know we are not perfect. When we find that our standards are not met, we help the factories get back on track. There are also some no-tolerance issues like child labour and physical violence. We hope that brands recently jumping on the sustainability trend are also sincere and in it for the long haul.

The EDUN label has been received with great anticipation and enthusiasm in the marketplace, partly aided by the celebrity status of their owners, but also by the bold combination of for-profit principles and sustainability principles. "The worst thing that could happen to us now is that consumers will start to show signs of green-fatigue," Russo continues. "We really hope that EDUN has helped to shine a light on something that is important and will inspire others to follow. The consumer has enormous power to make things happen and if the big brands turn sustainability simply into the way of doing business this would be a real achievement." The ethos of brands like EDUN is often shaped by the passion, vision and personality of their founders and a small group of people around them. "We are a tight-knit family here at EDUN. All our people have strong credentials and strong convictions; we are dedicated to the EDUN vision and we are all prepared to give our best to make it come true", says Russo.

At the moment, EDUN is sold in a small number of selected departments and specialty stores around the world; however, in 2009 EDUN will also introduce the first freestanding EDUN shop. Clearly, the retail environment is one of the key interaction points between the EDUN brand and its customers. Russo confirms: "We feel that having our own store will enable us to fully express the brand and to better communicate both our aesthetic and company ethos."

The Economist predicts that the future will see a flurry of CSR entrepreneurs who benefit from being nimble and savvy, creating an ethos of entrepreneurs with a conscience, a strong network of business relationships and deep expertise.[30]

CSR leaders CSR entrepreneurs may one day grow up to be CSR leaders. CSR leaders are established brands with a core of environmental and social responsibility values. One of their key characteristics is that they have the scale and the ambition to transform their industries. Take, for example, beauty and wellness brand Aveda, founded in 1978 "with the goal of providing beauty industry professionals with high performance, botanically based products that would be better for service providers and their guests, as well as for the planet".[31] Aveda has since grown into a global company and is viewed by many as a leader in sustainability. Aveda's sense of environmental responsibility stems from its founder, Horst Rechelbacher, who launched the plant-and-flower-based beauty line.[32] They focus on organic ingredients, strive to set industry benchmarks for environmental packaging, manufacture with 100% certified wind power, raise money for social and environmental causes, and continually work to reduce the impact of their production techniques. But they do not only strive to continually improve their own sustainability, they also want to create awareness in the beauty industry and foster change. Dominique Conseil, who left L'Oréal to become president of Aveda, mentioned in an interview with *Green@Work* magazine:[33] "I discovered that Aveda really has pure and good intentions – there is a little light in the darkness of the beauty world. My duty is to take care of it and make sure it

---

[30] Just good business, Special CSR Report, *The Economist*, 19 Jan. 2008.
[31] http://aveda.aveda.com/aboutaveda/index.asp
[32] Sacks, D., It's easy being green, *Fast Company*, 19 Dec. 2007, accessed: http://fastcompany.com/magazine/85/aveda.html?page=0%2C1
[33] Bonda P. and Sosnowchik K., Aveda finds sustainability from within, *Green@Work* magazine, March/April 2004, accessed http://www.greenbiz.com/news/reviews_third.cfm?NewsID=26806

doesn't go out. So, that's what I'm doing. The beauty business, when it's well done, is not a superficial thing." And so Conseil believes that sustainability, like beauty, must come from within. This is also expressed in their mission "Beauty is as beauty does". This conviction seems to be shared by many of Aveda's employees and helped the company through some rather tumultuous times, caused by the departure of founder Rechelbacher as president and the purchase by Estée Lauder in 1997, a huge influx of capital from a new parent company that resulted in rapidly increasing sales and a workforce that tripled during a six-year period; and, finally, a period of remote management before Conseil took residency in 2000 as president, headquartered in the company's Blaine, MN, facility. It has survived these changes, Conseil notes, because its dedication to the environment is part of its culture and not a marketing position. It is their mission to do that "Soil to Bottle". The objective is to set up sustainable business partnerships with the producers of all ingredients so that not only do they benefit the consumer, but most especially the farmers and harvesters who work in the fields.

Aveda also has started a new campaign around "Beauty is as beauty does" which will focus on a new "green issue" every six to eight weeks. The first series focuses upon wind energy and how Aveda use wind turbines to power one of their US factories. In mid-February 2008 they started to promote their efforts to use 100% recycled materials for their product packaging.

"Aveda has many years of evolution of people working together and it's very precious and it's very, very powerful," Conseil comments. "And it can change the industry – it is changing the industry."

Vocal CSR converts Vocal CSR converts are large global brands which have fairly recently started to embrace CSR as part of their brand in reaction to the growing CSR imperative. Unlike CSR leaders, they have yet to convince the public that their CSR efforts are genuine and long-term. The list of these companies is growing as more global brands are finding a way to bring CSR into their business and brand strategy. However, convincing the public is no easy task for them. Whether they have to overcome legacy issues or severe cynicism, many large corporations come under attack when they shift their messaging and communications to embrace CSR issues. This is particularly true if it is a major campaign like GE's Ecomagination. In a recent interview with CNET, GE's Vice President of Ecomagination Lorraine Bolsinger explained how anticipation of tougher environmental standards in the future, scarcity of resources and growth have driven the company to develop a strategy that takes a fresh and detailed look at sustainability. According to Bolsinger, GE quickly realised that the company would hugely benefit from such a strategy while also doing a lot of good for the environment, and so GE was one of the first US-based companies to take a bet on making money in cleaner technologies. GE then launched the Ecomagination campaign and started to incorporate the key underlying values into all energy-related businesses. Bolsinger explains: "Ecomagination was never based on 'we're doing this for philanthropy' or 'we're doing this to make the world safe'. We're glad to be doing that as a result of making money. It's a different lens that informs your decisions about where to spend money and what resources you're going to invest. [. . .] Ecomagination is for us, above everything else, a growth strategy."[34] GE uses a third party to certify products as Ecomagination that have both measurably better operating performance and environmental performance in order to make sure that the "green" products are also competitive. While Ecomagination has given the GE brand a big awareness boost, it has also attracted criticism, mostly claiming that targets have not been set

---

[34] LaMonica, M., Newsmaker: stirring GE's ecomagination, 26 Oct. 2007, CNET News Interview, accessed: http://www.news.com/stirring-ge-s-ecomagination/2008-11392_3-6215496.html

ambitiously enough, questioning the accounting of which products are Ecomagination or not, given that it is not a separate division, etc. Despite Bolsinger's pragmatic approach of doing what is good for the business and the environment, a certain legacy reputation may be hard to overcome.

UK-based Marks & Spencer also falls into this category with their "Plan A", a 100-point five-year strategy which was launched in 2006. "Plan A: because there is no Plan B"[35] is based on five pillars – by 2012 Marks & Spencer aims to become carbon neutral, send no waste to landfill, extend sustainable sourcing, help improve the lives of people in the supply chain and help customers and employees live a healthier lifestyle – and seems to be less controversial. The programme won the 2008 World Economic Center gold medal for International Achievement in Sustainable Development, for linking sustainability extensively with its supply chain, operations, and customers. Stuart Rose, Chief Executive, Marks & Spencer, said:

> We are delighted to receive this prestigious award. Our customers, shareholders and employees have also embraced our Plan A ambitions, and it's now how we do business. While we still have a long way to go and face many more challenges ahead, we are making good progress and this recognition will provide even more motivation for our teams as we continue to deliver our plan.[36]

Not all vocal CSR converts make sustainability a key focal point of their business and brand strategy; some have identified causes to support that are relevant for certain strategic aspects of their business, like Coca-Cola with its initiatives to conserve fresh water in collaboration with Greenpeace, or the global delivery

---

[35] http://plana.marksandspencer.com/?mnSBrand=core
[36] Andrews, K., Marks & Spencer to receive 2008 World Environment Center Gold Medal, 21 Dec. 2007, accessed: http://primeconcern. wordpress.com/2007/12/21/marks-spencer-to-receive-2008-world-environment-center-gold-medal/WEC

company TNT for its programme to address hunger through improved logistics.

Quietly conscientious While some companies choose to publicise their CSR activities, hoping that it will benefit their corporate reputation and brand, others fear that such publicity may invite criticism instead of praise. Therefore, they work quietly in the background to reduce carbon emissions, to find alternative suppliers or change the way their current suppliers work, to revamp production processes and to review their ethical and social standards. Understanding the potential negative impact on their brand, none of these companies would make sustainability part of the brand, while still trying to contribute their share for the benefit of society and the planet. For example, DHL, the Germany-based global express and logistics company, has just revamped their brand after a series of acquisitions. Outwardly, their brand is all about the customer – communicating their dedication to customer satisfaction as well as their capabilities. But they also introduced a "GoGreen" option in 2007 that allows customers to offset the CO_2 emissions caused by the transportation with carbon dioxide reduction projects ranging from alternative vehicle technologies to renewable fuels, solar panels and reforestation projects against a 3% "green" premium which will go towards certified carbon management programmes. The programme is verified on an annual basis by an external certifying body.[37]

Conclusion

Corporate social responsibility or sustainability needs to be addressed in a strategic way. However, a focus on CSR is no

---

[37] http://www.dpwn.de/dpwn?skin=hi&check=yes&lang=de_EN&xmlFile=2002182

panacea for branding woes. Committing to a strong CSR stance will invite heightened scrutiny, so chances are that while the brand might get a boost with certain target audiences, it may also get criticised for not doing enough with others. CSR can only be an effective strategy to counter distrust and provide a source of stakeholder engagement if it is genuinely embedded within the corporate and brand strategy and benefits both the corporation and society. Seeking differentiation is the wrong motive for committing to CSR; equally "greenwashing" or putting on a façade of good corporate citizenship is unlikely to prove successful in this environment.

This means, naturally, that companies who have spotted this a long time ago and made the switch quietly and in time, as well as companies who were founded on these principles, have a significant advantage over those who just woke up to the new world of green. Jumping on the CSR band wagon is possible, but will take a lot of determination and commitment. Any company deciding to make CSR a key strategic driver needs to be sure that they understand what they are signing up for: (1) high expectations on the part of all key stakeholders, from employees to customers to NGOs and partners; (2) high risk of being attacked with accusations of hypocrisy and greenwashing by activists and other small but vocal groups; and (3) very hard work and determination. CSR needs to be approached with strategic rigour and synchronised with the culture, the brand and business strategy in order to benefit the company (and not "just" the planet).

As CSR becomes a way of doing business, it will lose its differentiating qualities and no longer provide this energising factor to a brand or a story that is worth telling. Unless, of course, it is so deeply ingrained in the corporation that it shapes everything they do, but then there is no need to communicate since it will speak for itself.

ONLINE CUSTOMER INTERACTION

Brands can and must learn to use the power of the Internet to their advantage by embracing it as a brand-staging medium. The perceived integrity of brands is challenged by the pervasiveness, speed and broadcast power of the Internet, giving customers not only a voice, but also a platform to be heard. The Internet is facilitating the distribution of information but also the connection between people. While initially user-generated content was all the hype, now the focus has expanded to include online conversations and relationship building, supported by Web 2.0 technologies – including wikis, blogs, news alerts and social networking sites such as Facebook, YouTube and MySpace. But there is no reason why brands could not also use the Internet as a connection device, and even more, as a constant stream of feedback. We will now discuss how companies have started to do that.

Overall, it is fair to say that enterprise social networking is still in its exploratory stages. Some companies simply take their offline advertising efforts into the online world without regard for the different dynamics and rules prevalent there. This typically is not experienced as engaging by online customers and mostly disregarded, sometimes even creating alienation or backlash. For example, embarrassing situations tend to occur when employees randomly chime into online discussions about the virtues and drawbacks of various products offered by their company, sounding like clumsy sales people and almost always eventually being exposed. Equally blunt are some pop-up ads that do little more than mimic the classical TV advertising, which is based on a one-way and intrusive communication paradigm. Their use is controversial at best as they are seen as annoying by many and hence less suitable for building strong brands.

The myriad of possibilities for users and companies to engage with each other online are still intimidating to many brand managers who as a result have not yet fully embraced the medium.

96 CONNECTIVE BRANDING

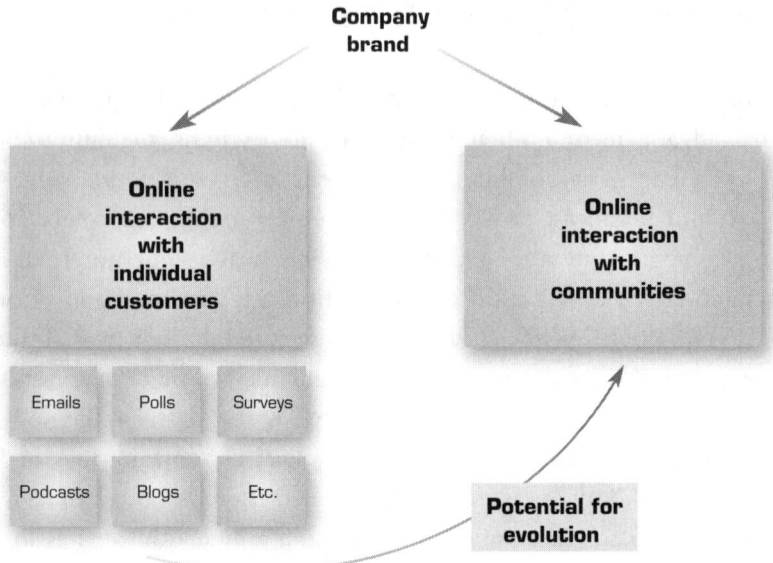

Figure 2.5 Categories of online activities

At the same time, courageous and creative companies experiment regularly with online interaction, making interesting forays into unknown territory.

On a very basic level, online activities can be separated into two categories – activities directed at individual customers and activities directed at communities (see Figure 2.5).

It is important to note that interactions directed at individual customers such as blogs or online forums can sometimes pick up sufficient momentum to evolve into an online community.

Online interaction with individual customers

Let us first take a look at how companies can interact with individual customers through the Internet. The tools range from simple emails to more complex devices as companies try to increase the intensity of interaction levels.

While the spectrum from merely providing information to actively involving the customer is nothing new (see Figure 2.6), it is astonishing to see that even online transactions can still be challenging to some companies.

Inform

The most basic form of online contact between company and customer is the one-way provision of company and product information, and this has become a prerequisite for any brand. Easy navigation, clearly organised information, tone and style in line with the brand have all become must-have features and are simply expected.

Interact

The next level of online interaction allows for a bare minimum of a basic dialogue. Customers can contact the company via email or online forms, ask for call-back, search for information of particular interest to them, sign up for a newsletter, watch podcasts, etc. Click-through ads fall into this category since they allow interested customers to follow a context-specific lead for more information.

Transact

Transacting online is still not possible for every product category due to a number of impediments, including logistics (e.g. perishable goods), restricted distribution strategy (e.g. luxury goods), ticket size (e.g. too small or too large), intangible nature (e.g. services), low penetration of credit cards (e.g. Germany), low

98 CONNECTIVE BRANDING

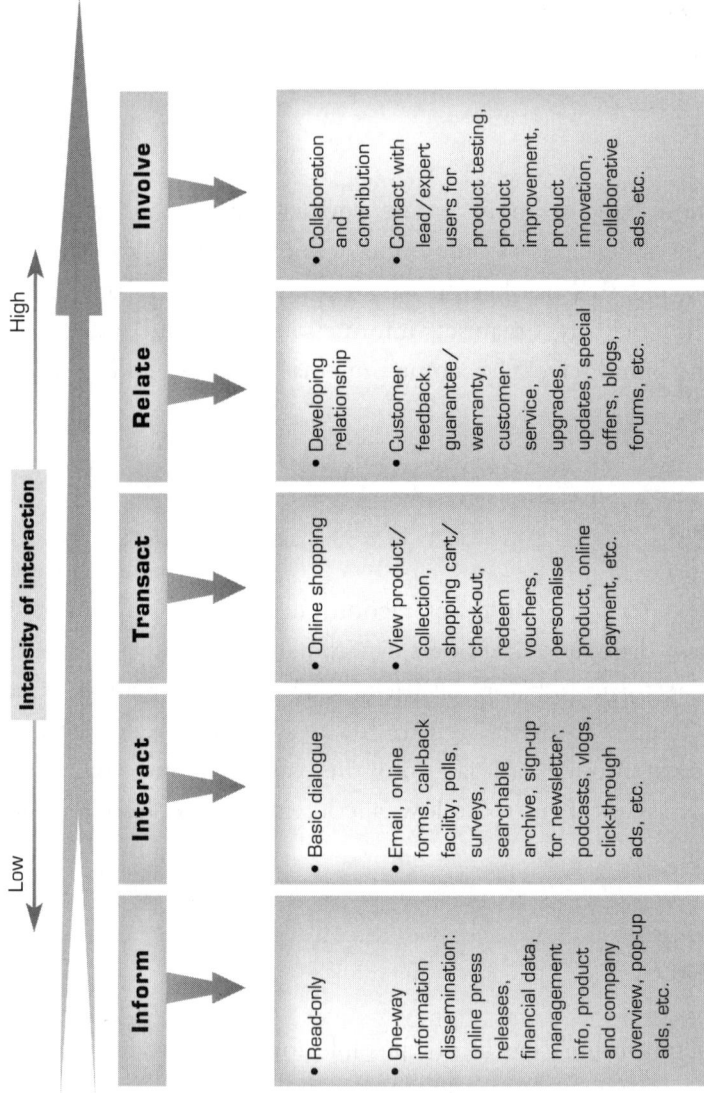

Figure 2.6 Online customer interaction spectrum – reaching out to individuals

penetration of PCs (e.g. China), and low penetration of fast Internet connections like broadband (e.g. Ireland). An interesting point here is that for fast moving consumer goods, for example confectionary or chewing gum, it is still not feasible to sell these products online directly from their corporate or product home page. Take, for example, Wrigley's, the famous confectionary and chewing gum company based in Chicago. Their website, Wrigley.com, hosts a wealth of information about their product portfolio, oral hygiene and healthcare, ingredient and nutritional information, the company and its history, the famous Wrigley Building in Chicago, etc. However, the transactional online relationship will be controlled by third parties, like online retailers or supermarkets with an online shopping service, making it more difficult for the brand to establish an online relationship.

Of course, a large number of companies have mastered online transactions, with companies like Nike or LEGO Group already offering personalisation features online (e.g. customers can design their own pair of sneakers or custom-build their LEGO model before ordering the necessary blocks online).

Relate

In order to develop a relationship and serve as a platform for building loyalty, online interaction needs to be more sophisticated. Simply transferring offline techniques into the online world without adaptation will not work. For example, company blogs can be an interesting way to bring customers back to the corporate website on a regular basis. However, this requires original and relevant content as well as a feedback facility where readers can also post comments. Moderated and unmoderated forums where customers can meet and discuss various topics are another popular form of relationship building both between customers and between the customer and the brand; however, for this to turn into a thriving community a great deal of work and skill is required. Empty forums with no posts or members do not impact positively on the brand.

Involve

For companies who are ready to fully embrace online interaction, collaboration can be a great way to bring lead users, early adopters, expert users and opinion leaders into the brand dialogue. For example, lingerie brand Passionata (owned by French company Chantelle) is moving away from the traditional life-size outdoor billboard ad as the main means of communications and instead is focusing almost entirely on reaching out online to a younger and Internet savvy female target group. For the launch of their new logo (a purple heart with an inscribed P) and their new collection, they not only launched a new ad on their website[38] (shot by famous director David La Chapelle in the Crazy Horse establishment in Paris), but they also invited 60 popular fashion bloggers from across the globe to come to Paris. These bloggers were identified as opinion leaders and "multipliers", telling their respective audiences about the presentation of the new Passionata collection and the new ad, creating buzz and traffic for the website, the product and the brand.[39]

Online interaction with communities

A plethora of online communities has emerged over the relatively short life span of the Internet. They vary widely in terms of topics,

---

[38] http://show.passionata.com/en/
[39] Schaefer, U., Dessous Party im Crazy Horse, *W&V*, 12, 20 March 2008: 24–25.

EMERGING STRATEGIES

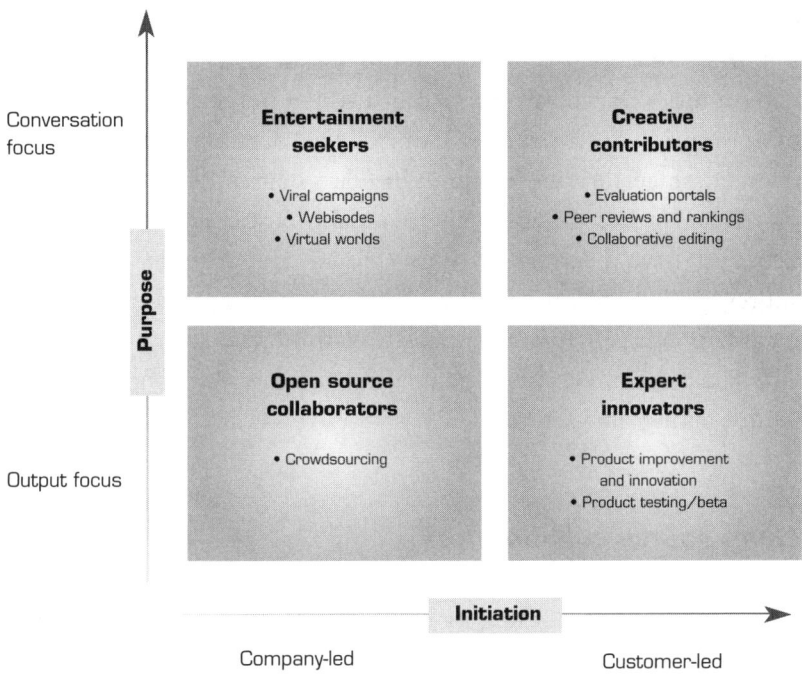

Figure 2.7 Online interaction with communities

purpose of gathering, frequency and nature of interaction, membership size and reach, rules and dynamics, etc. In order to bring some structure to this daunting variety, we present a framework that categorises online communities by purpose and initiation[40] (see Figure 2.7).

The *purpose* dimension describes the focus of community activities – they can be directed towards a specific output/result or they can be focused on the conversation itself. The *initiation* dimension describes who leads the community at the outset – it

---

[40] This framework was inspired by the work of Kozinets, R., Hemetsberger, A. and Schau, H., The wisdom of consumer crowds: collective innovation in the age of online community, forthcoming *Journal of Macromarketing*, 2008.

can be led either by a company or by customers themselves. It is important to note that leadership can also be dynamic, for example communities that start out as company-led might be "taken over" by customers or vice versa. Control is a fleeting concept in this context, since thriving communities are constantly evolving.

As a word of caution – there are also customer-led communities that have been known to "move" (= relocate to a new address) when feeling disturbed by the commercial pressure of intruding companies.[41] Therefore, it is important for companies to familiarise themselves with general community rules and dynamics before taking any actions.

Open source collaborators

Communities in this category gather for the purpose of planning, managing, and/or completing well-defined projects launched by companies. A new business model based on this category is emerging – it is called *crowdsourcing*.[42] Crowdsourcing is a new form of outsourcing whereby companies take a function previously performed by employees into an undefined (and generally large) network of people in the form of an open call (an interview or audition without specific appointment); this can take the form of collaborative peer production (where several people work together – offline or online) or can be undertaken by individuals. Internet and crowdsourcing specialist Jeff Howe explains: "The crucial prerequisite is the use of the open call format and the large network

---

[41] Fisher-Buttinger, C., New media branding with online communities, Unpublished honours dissertation, University of Innsbruck (Austria), 2002.
[42] Kozinets, R., Hemetsberger, A. and Schau, H., The wisdom of consumer crowds: collective innovation in the age of network marketing, *Journal of Macromarketing*, **28**(4) 2008.

of potential laborers. [. . .] Basically, this is everyday people using their spare cycles [*meaning free time* and *capacity*] to create content, solve problems, and even do corporate R & D."[43]

Crowdsourcing is becoming increasingly popular as a way of online customer interaction in a number of industries, ranging from financial services (e.g. stock trading companies collecting top stock tips from their most successful customers) to the entertainment industry (e.g. the Beastie Boys providing 50 enthusiastic fans with hand-held digital cameras to produce a concert film in Madison Square Garden).[44] It seems to be particularly popular in the apparel and garment industry, where users can design, produce and sell their own artwork and models. For example, Zazzle.com is an on-demand retail platform allowing users to instantly design and sell everything from T-shirts to tote bags, giving them a cut if others like and buy their products. Zazzle.com features over 3.4 billion user-designed products, benefiting greatly from users' quick response to breaking news and events (e.g. according to chief strategist Jack Heckman, eight of the top 10 best selling products in March 2008 were related to the fall of New York Governor Eliot Spitzer due to links with prostitution).[45]

Companies who use crowdsourcing leverage the intelligence and efforts of crowds who gather around a particular point of interest. This can allow companies to focus more on what they consider a core activity or competence, but must be weighed carefully against considerations of inherent risks, like potentially (but not necessarily) compromising quality standards. Andrea Hemetsberger, University of Innsbruck, explains: "Companies who want to

---

[43] Howe, J., The rise of crowdsourcing, *Wired Magazine*, 14 June 2006, accessed: http://www.wired.com/wired/archive/14.06/crowds.html
[44] Manly, L., This is not Spinal Tap, *The New York Times*, 19 Jan. 2006, accessed: http://www.nytimes.com/2006/01/19/movies/19awes.html
[45] Gunnison, L., Scandal: your ad here, Condé Nast Portfolio, 13 March 2008, accessed: http://www.portfolio.com/news-markets/top-5/2008/03/13/Spitzer-Cottage-Industry

collaborate with communities in order to harness their collective creativity and intelligence, must be prepared to give something back. This is all about fair exchange and principles of reciprocity, best illustrated by the case of Linux and open-source code."

Expert innovators

This category describes online communities that gather around a shared goal, for example testing, improving, or creating a particular product or object of interest. Typically, these communities are initiated by like-minded customers who enjoy the output-driven exchange with other enthusiasts. They tend to have a sufficient number of highly knowledgeable and well-informed leaders who devote their time to improving product design, product quality, or product performance, or even to add new product features. Newcomers ("newbies") are often lovingly educated once proven worthy, and hierarchy levels within the community (typically based on expertise and contribution) are often sacred. For example, alt.coffee is a place where coffee enthusiasts meet to create the perfect cup of espresso. They spend a great deal of time tinkering with their favourite "trio" of coffee roaster, grinder, and espresso machine.[46] While they are customer led and independent of a company or brand, companies will find it useful to "lurk" (= listen to their conversations) to learn about the standing of their own as well as competitive brands.

Many companies wish to seek out interaction with this type of community, not only because of their innovation ideas, but also because they tend to be trendsetters, early adopters, and often even opinion leaders. However, interacting with these expert innovators

---

[46] Fisher-Buttinger, C., New media branding with online communities, Unpublished honours dissertation, University of Innsbruck (Austria), December 2002.

is no easy task. They can be quite fickle and most companies lack the resources, the patience or the skills to do it in a mutually agreeable fashion. But help is on the way: an entire industry of online and social media consultants has emerged. They act as intermediaries between company and community, first identifying appropriate communities, then learning the social protocol before identifying the most suitable contacts, and carefully entering into a dialogue with them. Depending on the consultants' experience and skill levels, they will be able to identify communities for product testing, co-invention, or simply brainstorming and sound-boarding. Increasingly, interaction with these communities also augments or even replaces traditional market research formats like focus groups and in-depth interviews.

Creative contributors

This category consists of a wide variety of communities. It includes those that gather around individuals who rightly or wrongly think of themselves as experts in a certain field and who are quite vocal about their opinions, for example bloggers and Wikipedia editors. The blogosphere has firmly established itself as part of the online culture, with a majority of Internet users reading or contributing to blogs[47] and blogs attracting increasingly significant sums of advertising money.

Creative contributors can also take the form of "evaluation portals" where users share their experience with products and services in the form of product reviews and rankings. These portals can be specialised in one subject, for example travel portal tripadvisor.com, they can be part of an online provider, for example retailer Amazon.com, or they can take the form of an opinion

---

[47] Rainie, L., The state of blogging, Pew Internet, Jan. 2005, accessed: http://www.pewinternet.org/PPF/r/144/report_display.asp

exchange covering many different topics from appliances to MP3 players, for example ciao.com. Evaluation portals have become very popular and there is virtually no subject that is not being evaluated by users; however, portals vary considerably in quality and depth, with number of reviews posted, currency of information, and sophistication of quality control systems being critical factors. Portals with high standards in terms of eliminating overly critical reviews, suspicious entries and obviously manipulative texts have gained more critical mass than those that simply take feedback at face value. With the proliferation of evaluation portals customers have quickly learned that online reviews are a more informative and reliable source of information than company-created self-descriptions. For example, evaluation portals like tripadvisor.com or holidaycheck.de have transformed the travel and tourism industry – travel agencies and hotels can no longer ignore the criticism and rants on popular evaluation sites as user reviews have proven to be a much stronger influence on purchasing decisions and brand image than marketing messages.

"The central principle behind the success of the giants born in the Web 1.0 era who have survived to lead the Web 2.0 era appears to be this, that they have embraced the power of the web to harness collective intelligence."[48] Most famously, Amazon and eBay rely heavily on the collective intelligence of users for their market platforms; a system that reduces the (perceived) risk of doing business with unknown third parties and hence transaction anxiety. Yet this is a particular kind of collective intelligence: the collective intelligence of relatively large groups, with everyone providing relatively small contributions, unaware for the most part that their online activities are, en masse, contributing value to the capital ventures of corporations.

---

[48] O'Reilly, T., What is web 2.0: design patterns and business models for the next generation of software, 30 Sep. 2005, accessed: http://oreillynet.com/pub/a/oreilly/tim/news/2005/09/30/what-is-web-20.html/

Creative contributors also encompass the many, often small individual contributions that occur as a part of a more playful interaction with a particular topic. Through social networking sites these contributors have suddenly found an audience for their musings and creative activities. Sometimes, these can involve a brand – whether to the brand's advantage or disadvantage. On the positive side, in 2006 the candy brand Mentos received $100 million worth of publicity[49] as a result of an amateur video of an oddball experiment: people dropping Mentos candies into bottles of Diet Coke. The video, which was put into a weblog and viewed nearly a million times in one week, was made by two people who spent their own money to buy 100 litres of Diet Coke and dozens of packs of Mentos. They made a Fantasia-esque musical fountain with cascading streams of beautiful goop. Considering that Mentos' annual ad budget is nowhere near $100 million, Mentos marketing people were understandably delighted, wanting to feature the video in advertising and hire its creators to tour on Mentos' behalf.[50] While this consumer-generated ad turned out to be a great success for the company, the video discussed earlier showing how easy it is to crack a Kryptonite lock impacted very negatively on the Kryptonite brand. Similarly, the discussion about the Dove and Axe brand ownership outlined earlier as well as the mash-up video also negatively impacted on Dove, Axe and Unilever.

Companies trying to interact with creative contributors have not always been successful to date, in particular if their interaction attempts are seen as trying to manipulate reviews and evaluations. There seems to be quite some temptation for using in-house staff

---

[49] Vranica, S. and Terhune, C., Mixing Diet Coke and Mentos makes a gusher of publicity, *Wall Street Journal*, 12 June 2006, accessed: http://online.wsj.com/public/article_print/SB115007602216777497-1mzdx_pOFlMBwo9UAiqbsgY6MZ0_20060619.html

[50] See the video: http://consumerengagement.blogspot.com/2006_10_01_archive.html

or hiring an agency to post fake comments or recommendations, getting buzzers to hype up a product or service or even asking fans to disguise their involvement in a campaign. Any number of well-established brands have been "caught" in the process. But, as these tactics are all bound to surface ultimately and damage the brand in the process, a more successful strategy is to be honest about identity and affiliation, and to take any criticism to heart by trying to improve the offering accordingly.[51]

Entertainment seekers

This category includes communities who gather with the purpose of being entertained. A number of methods and techniques catering to entertainment seekers is currently emerging, including viral campaigns, webisodes, and virtual worlds, among others.

Viral campaigns

Companies increasingly try to engage customers in viral campaigns where the customer spreads the word to other customers. For example, Nestlé produced a short viral video where French comedian Jamel Debbouze interviews "Zimzim Zidane" (bearing a slight resemblance to legendary French soccer star Zinedine Zidane), about his on-field exploits and his other great passion: Nescafé Dolce Gusto, a capsule-based espresso and cappuccino maker aimed at younger customers. The video has been seeded on an advertising-focused social networking site called Blogbang owned by Publicis Groupe and spread to other video sites and

---

[51] Sernovitz, A., The truth will out, 25 April 2008, MarketingProfs, accessed: http://www.marketingprofs.com/news/marketing-inspiration/index.asp?nlid=348&cd=dmo121&adref=NmiF448

blogs from there. According to Publicis Groupe, the videos have been viewed more than 1 million times.[52]

Online soap operas – webisodes

Procter & Gamble, the original producer and inventor of soap operas on radio and television, is taking this strategy of combining entertainment and advertising online. They have created an online series called "Crescent Heights" to engage customers in their detergent brand Tide. The story centres on a new college graduate who moves from Wisconsin to Los Angeles to start a career in public relations in the big city. As her story unfolds, viewers learn about her emerging circle of friends and her romantic pursuits as well as the benefits of Tide.[53] Procter & Gamble is by no means alone in creating online entertainment around a featured product brand. Other companies like Unilever, Anheuser-Busch and now even retailers like American Eagle Outfitters are producing webisodes.

L'Oréal went a step further with their viral campaign that spoofs the concept of embedding brands in entertainment programmes. The humorous campaign is comprised of a website, video clips and a blog and introduces a line of hair care products called Garnier Fructis Style Bold, aimed at men aged 18 to 34.[54] The campaign is presented to consumers as if Garnier executives had entered into

---

[52] Pfanner, E., Letting the consumer do the work, *International Herald Tribune*, 27 Jan. 2008, accessed: http://www.iht.com/articles/2008/01/27/technology/ad28.php

[53] Tedeschi, B., P&G the pioneer of mixing soap and drama, adds a Web instalment, *International Herald Tribune*, 15 Oct. 2007, accessed: http://www.nytimes.com/2007/10/15/business/media/15ecom.html

[54] Elliott, S., L'Oréal spoofs product placement in US ads, *International Herald Tribune*, 18 Dec. 2007, accessed: http://www.iht.com/articles/2007/12/18/technology/adco.php

an agreement to include the new product in a new sitcom called "The Harry Situation" (theharrysituation.com). However, the heavy handed product plugs in the first episodes have so enraged the creator of the show that he has hijacked the site and wants to expose the commercial exploitation. His angry blog entries are supported by video clips which supposedly are excerpts from the offending first episodes, and there are also mock memos from Garnier, fictitious reports of focus group interviews and imaginary reactions of test audiences to the series. As L'Oréal is trying to engage customers in this mock situation of hijacking and conflict, they are walking a fine line. It is not clear to everyone that this is a spoof and the joke might not be appreciated by everyone. On the other hand, this ambiguity might precisely be what creates the buzz, engaging consumers and encouraging them to pass it along.

Virtual worlds

Another approach to engage customers online is to build virtual worlds. Coca-Cola, for example, created a virtual "island" on there.com which is shaped like a Coke bottle and called CC Metro. Visitors at the island can set up a virtual alter ego (an "avatar") which can then shop, dance, visit a movie theatre to watch short films, etc.; furthermore, they can "buy" clothing and accessories for their avatars by exchanging the codes from Coke bottle caps for reward points. Virtual worlds are a difficult endeavour, however. First of all, they attract much less traffic than social networking sites do, and second, they will repulse visitors if they feel too much like an advert.

Engaging with customer-led communities

For most companies, it is much more intuitive to initiate interaction with individual customers or to create a company-sponsored community than to reach out and interact with existing customer-led communities. Therefore, we will now describe which basic steps need to be taken.

Stage 1 – Listen and learn

Companies have started to use the Internet like a "wiretap" – they trawl through user-generated online forums and communities in order to identify opportunities for customer interaction. Some companies have dedicated resources for this task, others rely on dedicated employees to spot any noteworthy entries as part of their routine Google search (this also highlights the importance of search engine optimisation).

While it is wise to develop the necessary skills and experience in-house before reaching out, ignoring this channel can also be dangerous. For example, a former *FT* journalist repeatedly reports in his blog about a bad experience with Wells Fargo, the financial services company, and how over the past year despite a continually growing collection of posts with bad customer experiences and other bloggers picking up the story[55] the company did not make an effort to reach out to him and his readers.[56]

Stage 2 – Comment and connect

Once the groundwork is laid, companies can start to comment and connect. However, only few companies have managed to

---

[55] See, for example, Brand Autopsy, Would you miss Wells Fargo, 22 March 2007, accessed: http://brandautopsy.typepad.com/brandautopsy/2007/03/would_you_miss__4.html

[56] Foremski, T., Case Study in Online Brand Management: Wells Fargo continues to ignore the conversation, 26 March 2008, accessed: http://www.siliconvalleywatcher.com/mt/archives/2008/03/case_study_in_o.php

successfully connect with user-led online communities. For example, Starwood hotels was one of the first to do it well. They employ one person named William (who identifies himself as the "Starwood Lurker" and is quite well-known by now) specifically to trawl through travel forums and to check for postings about his employer, Starwood Hotels & Resorts. He works through any comments relating to brands operating under the Starwood umbrella (including Westin, W, Sheraton and St Regis) to provide helpful responses and clear up misunderstandings. What is noteworthy here are two things: (1) William does not operate covertly, but very openly communicates his affiliation to Starwood; (2) this one person has been able to create a lot of positive reactions and goodwill for the Starwood brand. Overall, this programme is an amazing success story for Starwood, in fact they just received a Freddie Award for Industry Impact.[57]

Stage 3 – Engage

Once companies feel comfortable interacting with online communities in general, they can set out to identify suitable communities for more involved interaction. For example, Mercedes-Benz decided to engage with a small community of trendsetters called "A small World" comprised of highly influential people with large personal networks. Instead of simply advertising on the community website, Mercedes decided to lure the members with VIP tickets for Fashion Week in Berlin or invitations to the Laureus World Sport Awards in St Petersburg. Olaf Goettgens, Vice President Brand Communications Mercedes-Benz, explains: "It is very important that we adhere to the community rules. No disruptive ads, but relevant benefits."[58]

---

[57] http://www.freddieawards.com/events/?event_key=6
[58] Bell, M., Marketer unterschaetzen Communities, *W&V*, 13, 27 March 2008: 10–13.

Figure 2.8 LEGO bricks

CASE STUDY – BRINGING THE ONLINE WORLD INTO THE LEGO CUSTOMER EXPERIENCE

In the case of LEGO Group, the online world presented a serious challenge through the emergence of a whole new world of online and interactive games, almost making the legendary building blocks a toy of the past. But they managed to turn a corner when they figured out how to bring "online" into their brand.

The Danish LEGO Group, founded in 1932 by Ole Kirk Christiansen, has come a long way over the past 76 years – from a small carpenter's workshop to a modern, global enterprise that is now, in terms of sales, the world's fifth largest manufacturer of toys.

The founder hit upon the LEGO name by putting together the first two letters of the Danish words LEG GODT, meaning "play well" – allegedly unaware that it also means "I put together" in Latin. Today the LEGO name is both the name *and* the idea behind the company: the LEGO philosophy poses that "good play" enriches a child's life – and subsequent adulthood. The LEGO Group has developed a wide range of products founded on this philosophy and the principles of "learning and developing through play".

In the late 1990s, the LEGO Group faced challenging times partly due to the emergence of a new type of competition: high-tech computer games. At the same time, the LEGO Group had diversified into theme parks and merchandise, including clothing, books, watches and multimedia games, resulting in a higher cost structure and ultimately millions of dollars in losses in the years leading up to 2004. This nearly brought the company down. Some experts like the toy researcher Torben Hangaard Rasmussen were quick to dismiss LEGO toys as a relic of the past: "LEGO bricks belong to the industrial era when children liked to build things, playing wannabe engineers. Nowadays, the most popular toys are inspired by the virtual world."[59]

But the LEGO Group was not going to give up that easily. At the height of its crisis, owner and CEO Kjeld Kirk Kristiansen injected more than 800 million kroner ($178 million) of his personal fortune into the business and developed a plan to bring the company back to financial stability. The seven-year strategy, internally known as *Shared Vision*, was launched in 2004 and is designed to refocus the business on its core strengths while revitalising the LEGO brand.

Jacob Kragh, Senior Director at the LEGO Group, explains:

> We started out by defining industry basics like providing lasting play value, and a good price/value relationship. These criteria are entry level requirements; they need to be met but don't make you special. We think what makes us special is our heritage, the brand values rooted in our culture and spirit, and our ability to make these relevant to the needs of children who live in the modern, partly virtual play world.

The brand mission of the LEGO brand is to establish the brand as a synonym for *fun of building*, and *meaningful play* for children, teens and adults. This is a challenging task in an environment where virtual games are dominating children's play time

---

[59] ABC News, At 50, Lego still going strong, 29 Jan. 2008, accessed: http://abcscience.net.au/news/stories/2008/01/29/2148368.htm

and where quick engagement and portability are key characteristics of toys. "Every toy is compared [by children] to video games and DVD/TV entertainment. We have to accept this reality," highlights Kragh.

The company believes that offline play offers many benefits, including interaction with other children or adults, fostering creativity, nurturing intellectual curiosity and the natural desire to explore with all senses. Kragh explains:

> The LEGO brand offers a unique play experience to children of all ages. However, in today's world this has to be actively communicated. Before the arrival of video games, this may have seemed more intuitive. But the fact is, children will always be children, and they love the magic of traditional toys that play into their innate creativity and never become boring, even in today's digital world. Our brand is grounded in three brand values: *fun – creativity – quality*. These values are found in the unique LEGO play experience.

Kragh continues:

> The interlocking principle with its tubes makes LEGO toys unique – it makes it an intuitive game while at the same guaranteeing high quality. LEGO toys are very flexible, able to respond to any child's needs and capabilities – it is the child who drives pace and complexity. There are different building blocks for different ages and motorical skills, and there is no limit to building possibilities, nurturing the creativity of children. You can really see the pride in children's eyes when they have built a new model. We are proud that LEGO toys are playful learning and that we have the privilege to play such a positive role in children's lives and development.

This pride is also shared by employees; they understand that they make toys that help children to develop skills, pride, and self-esteem.

In order to ensure that the LEGO brand remains relevant in today's digital world, the company has extended its reach into the virtual and interactive world. CEO Jørgen Vig

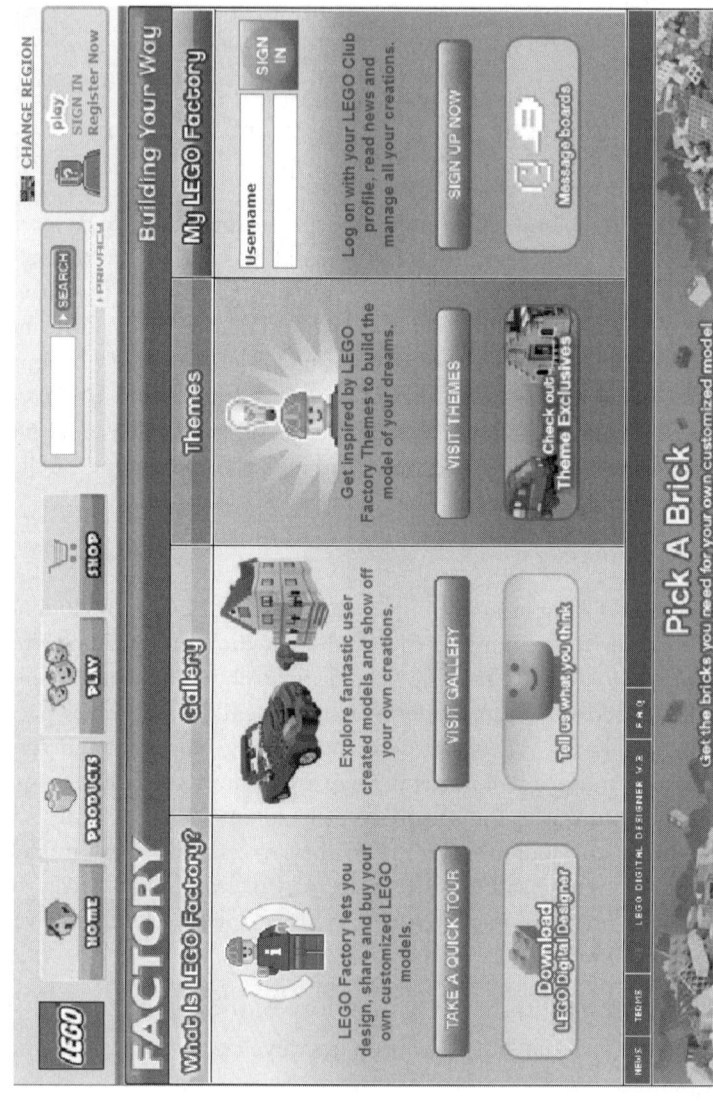

Figure 2.9 LEGO Group website

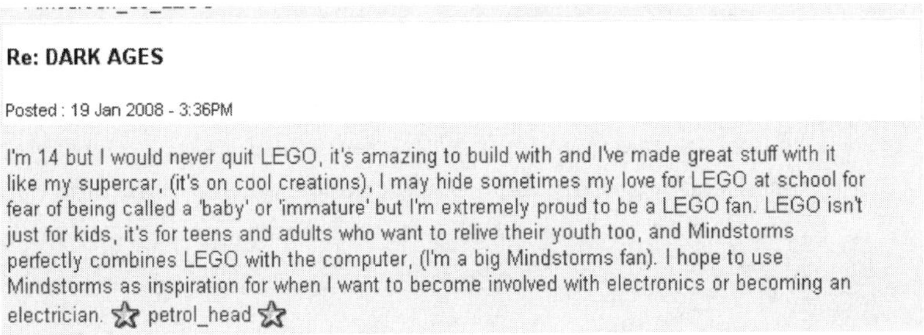

> **Re: DARK AGES**
>
> Posted : 19 Jan 2008 - 3:36PM
>
> I'm 14 but I would never quit LEGO, it's amazing to build with and I've made great stuff with it like my supercar, (it's on cool creations), I may hide sometimes my love for LEGO at school for fear of being called a 'baby' or 'immature' but I'm extremely proud to be a LEGO fan. LEGO isn't just for kids, it's for teens and adults who want to relive their youth too, and Mindstorms perfectly combines LEGO with the computer, (I'm a big Mindstorms fan). I hope to use Mindstorms as inspiration for when I want to become involved with electronics or becoming an electrician. ☆ petrol_head ☆

Figure 2.10 Messageboards.LEGO

Knudstorp explains: "I don't see us leaving plastic and bricks behind but digital technology will take us into a new world over the next 10 years," he says.[60] For instance, in 2004 the LEGO Group launched LEGOfactory.com where customers can build, share and order their own models; in 2009 they will launch LEGO Universe where children interact online, bound together by their shared interest of building LEGO models. Social networking sites like YouTube and Flickr are awash with lovingly created LEGO models, further facilitating for like-minded enthusiasts to connect and share their creations, ranging from robots to knitting machines.

While children certainly are the main consumer group, LEGO enthusiasts can be found in any age group. For example, a 14-year-old posted the contribution show in Figure 2.10 on the official LEGO website.[61]

Kragh explains:

> There is a growing number of AFOLs [adult fans of LEGO]. We define the aspirational LEGO associations for this group as follows:

---

[60] Sibun, J., Lego renaissance builds on key strengths, telegraph.co.uk, 28 Jan. 2008, accessed: http://www.telegraph.co.uk/money/main.jhtml?xml=/money/2008/01/27/cnLEGO127.xml

[61] http://messageboards.LEGO.com/ShowPost.aspx?PageIndex=15&PostID=321252

> I loved LEGO when I was a child, it made me so proud of what I can do and I enjoyed sharing the LEGO experience with my friends. I still find it exhilarating to play with LEGO, it takes my mind off things and is fun. I am glad that I can share my LEGO experience with a community of people who feel the same way and with whom I can easily identify.
>
> As it is with children, for AFOLs we deliver the fun of playing and the challenge of creating new things. However, we can also provide them with a unique additional benefit, namely access to a large and thriving community of like-minded people.

Over time, the LEGO Group has actively developed relations with many AFOL groups, who have their own websites, organise public events, and take part in LEGO development projects. In one of the best known independent online communities, Lugnet (which describes itself as a community of LEGO enthusiasts), participants discuss the endless possibilities inherent in the LEGO construction. While this community is not sponsored by or connected with the LEGO Group, it still promotes the brand through its endorsement and enthusiasm and becomes a classical demonstration of brand co-creation.

Brand success that is rooted in heritage

On 28th January 2008 the LEGO brick celebrated its 50th birthday. In addition to official activities, LEGO fans all over the world contributed to make this a special occasion. For example, the British newspaper *The Independent* sent buckets of LEGO bricks to some of Britain's most creative minds and then ran an article reporting about their reactions.[62] This is, for

---

[62] Chung, A., I love Lego: Celebrating 50 years of the tiny building blocks, 25 Jan. 2008, accessed: http://www.independent.co.uk/arts-entertainment/art-and-architecture/features/i-love-LEGO-celebrating-50-years-of-the-tiny-building-blocks-773703.html

example, what Right Said Fred, a famous band with hits like "I'm Too Sexy", "Don't Talk Just Kiss", and "Deeply Dippy", came back with:

> My brother and I knew straight away that we wanted to make a guitar out of our LEGO, but it was trickier than we thought because there are no curved pieces – LEGO is geared more towards houses or structures. [. . .] Fifty years is quite amazing but when the idea behind something is so clean and simple then it's not affected by the technological advances that sweep by. Children have endless options of things to play with now but they seem to enjoy the physical, hands-on aspects of LEGO. So many things these days are virtual but you can actually hold LEGO and create something with it. LEGO gives them the tools so they can make it up as they go along.

The rich heritage of the LEGO brand is the key driver for their future brand success. Kragh comments: "We must never ever forget this . . . Our programme *Shared Vision* takes the company back to its heritage, acknowledging the fact that the LEGO brand is the BRICK and vice versa. All we have to do is make sure that the LEGO brick is not marginalised, but stays relevant to the current and future generations of LEGO fans of all ages."

Conclusion

There is a plethora of new ways to interact with customers online. As companies are starting to find their feet in the online world, they are experimenting with new ways of interacting with both individual customers and online communities. The challenge will be to identify programmes that can help build meaningful relationships with customers.

When selecting appropriate means of online interaction, companies should steer clear of outdated formats like pop-up ads, as well as unethical approaches like fake blogs, undercover members, etc. Also, interacting with online communities is not meant as a replacement for company resources or a means of cheap labour; exploitation is to be avoided at all costs. After all, there is a fine line between voluntary involvement and industrial exploitation. Online communities thrive because they respect a certain set of values and rules called "netiquette"; companies are strongly advised to familiarise themselves with these before taking the plunge.

In order to make online interaction a meaningful way of reaching out to customers and other stakeholders, companies need to develop the necessary skills, devote appropriate resources to the task and keep it relevant and interesting at all times.

PART II

A FRAMEWORK FOR COPING

Chapter 3 Brand framework for building connective brands

We put forward a framework for building and maintaining connective brands. The model is built on two major brand equity drivers – engagement and alignment, which are discussed in detail.

CHAPTER 3

BRAND FRAMEWORK FOR BUILDING CONNECTIVE BRANDS

*I*n this chapter we will discuss the key brand levers a company can work with to create strong brands: brand strategy, brand management, brand building through engagement, and brand building through alignment.

In Chapter 1, we discussed the four market forces that shape the current branding environment: lack of control, Internet megaphone, CSR imperative, climate of distrust. In Chapter 2 we outlined how companies have started to react: by bringing the corporation into the brand, focusing more on authenticity, taking a more strategic approach to CSR, and finding ways to engage stakeholders online to (re)build trust and strengthen the brand.

Our review of these strategies in the context of concrete case studies provided a number of insights into critical success factors as well as key challenges. Each of the four strategies discussed in Chapter 2 can be effective in building brand equity:

- As the corporation is brought more into the brand, alignment between corporate actions and brand promise builds trust and credibility; at the same time, a greater focus on long-term relationships and more deeply anchored brand principles such as values helps to build more emotional connections.
- A greater focus on authenticity results in better alignment of intended and actual brand experience, potentially delivering a highly differentiated experience.
- A strategic approach to CSR requires better alignment of competitive strategy, CSR initiatives and underlying business processes along the entire supply chain, resulting in a credible, appealing promise that benefits both the company and society at large. CSR can also be a meaningful way to engage employees, customers and other key stakeholders.
- Engaging employees, customers and other stakeholders in a dialogue instead of one-way information dissemination (and manipulation) improves the relationships with all key stakeholders. In addition, continuously engaging employees in a way that motivates them to deliver on the brand promise not only helps build emotional connections with them, but also facilitates alignment between what is promised to external stakeholders and what they actually experience.

The two key drivers of building brand equity for each of the four strategies are building emotional connections with key stakeholders and aligning the brand promise with actual brand experience.

We will now use these two key drivers to build a branding framework called *connective branding* that can help companies to systematically create and maintain successful, strong brands which can cope with the challenging branding environment of today.

The two key drivers of brand equity – (i) alignment of brand promise and actual brand experience and (ii) strength of encour-

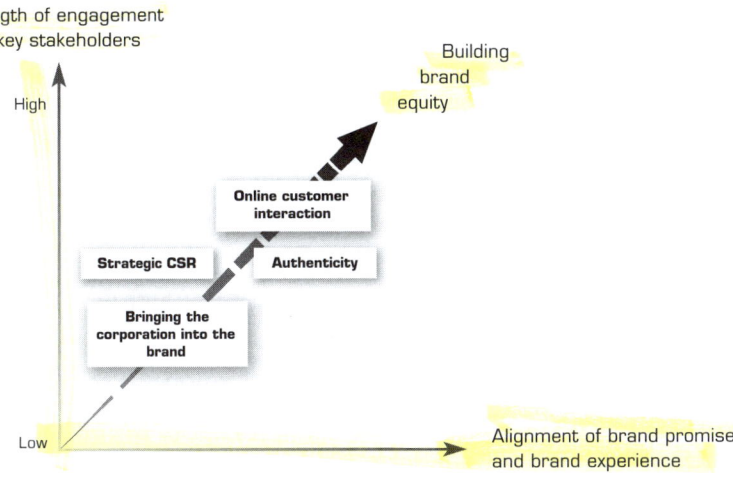

Figure 3.1 Building brand equity in the connective branding framework

agement with all key stakeholders – are at the heart of connective branding (see Figure 3.1):

(i) By identifying and eliminating misalignment between elements that *define* the brand (e.g. brand principles, brand vision, brand architecture) and elements that deliver the brand (e.g. brand metrics, enabling processes, actual employee behaviour), the brand becomes more trustworthy, more authentic and more credible.
(ii) By continuously finding meaningful ways to engage employees, customers, and other stakeholders in a welcome, appealing dialogue, a brand can effectively counter scepticism and build emotional connections with all key stakeholders, and at the same time satisfy stakeholders' heightened need for information and create transparency.

The connective branding framework is designed to build these principles of alignment and engagement systematically into the brand and is organised around four brand levers – brand strategy, brand building and management, stakeholder engagement and enabling processes and structures (see Figure 3.2):

- *Brand strategy.* Connective brands have a clearly defined role that is consistent with the brand's mandate and power to act, they are built around a welcome and engaging brand promise (or purpose), they have a clear brand vision that outlines the future strategic direction, and they are aligned with business priorities and company culture.
- *Brand management.* Connective brands are owned by the CEO, represented by a C-level executive and managed by a branding team that understands the new paradigms of stakeholder engagement and networked collaboration. The branding team is empowered to work with all relevant functions and departments to facilitate alignment of brand promise and corporate actions. A system of actionable metrics provides regular feedback on where to improve and where things are going well.
- *Brand building through engagement.* Connective brands continuously find ways to engage employees in order to create commitment and motivation to act in line with the brand promise; they also seek to engage customers and other key stakeholders such that deep connections and meaningful relationships are created. They also manage the complexities of converging stakeholder groups.
- *Brand building through alignment.* Connective brands are able to deliver on the brand promise to their stakeholders in every touchpoint by continuously improving alignment of enabling processes and structures with the brand promise and brand vision.

BRAND FRAMEWORK 127

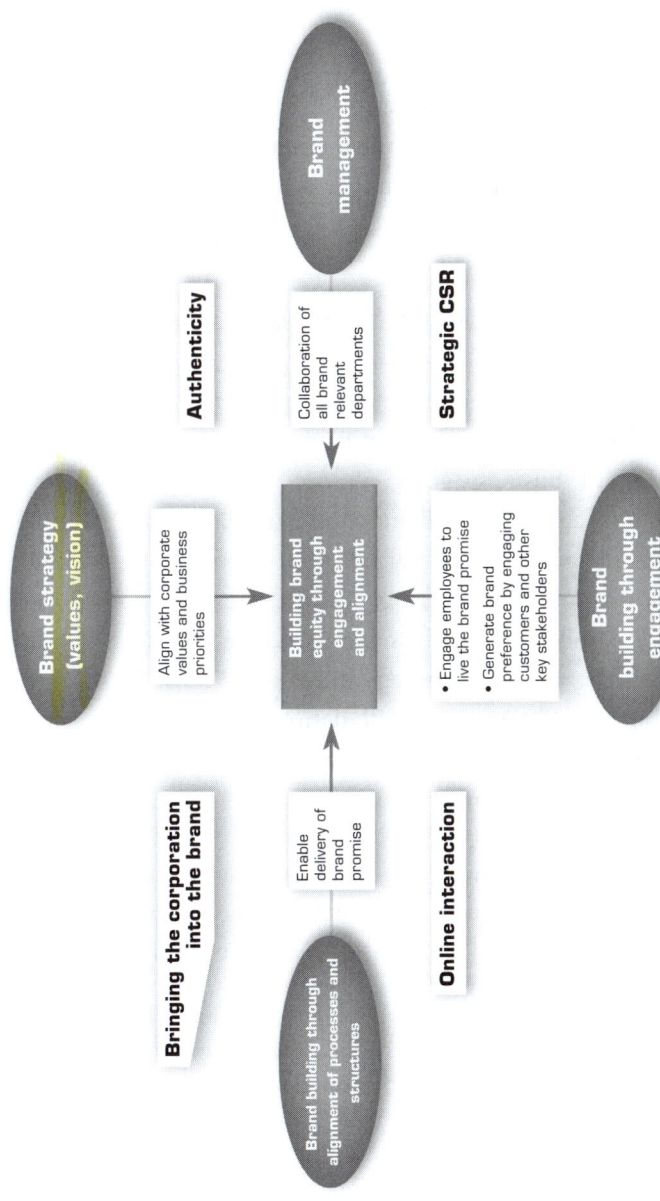

Figure 3.2 Key brand levers of the connective branding framework

BRAND STRATEGY – THE FACE OF BUSINESS STRATEGY

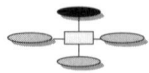

Brand strategy is what defines the DNA of the brand – its role in the organisation and vis-à-vis business strategy, its content in terms of brand principles and brand promise, its future strategic direction in terms of brand vision, and its portfolio structure.

Role of the brand vis-à-vis business strategy

Successful businesses are built on solid business models and driven by a clear business strategy. Brands are designed to facilitate the achievement of business goals set out in the business strategy. While brands are an excellent tool for engaging stakeholders, developing meaningful and sustainable relationships, amplifying differentiation and even driving change, they are not an end in themselves. Although often it is the brand strategy that helps crystallise what the business strategy means for various stakeholder groups, the business strategy will define the strategic parameters within which the brand strategy operates. For example, the business strategy for an airline could be:

> Our vision is to become the number one preferred passenger airline for long-haul flights between mainland Europe and the USA or Asia. We operate a hub and spokes system with major hubs on each continent. Our business model evolves around high service and premium prices, primarily targeting business travellers. We aim to create differentiation through faultless operations and customer centricity. Our tickets are primarily sold through partnering travel agents, we use the same catering partner on a global basis and we will become members of one of the top three alliance programmes. We will place great emphasis on hiring and maintaining excellent people including pilots, flight attendants, and on-the-ground operations.

The brand strategy for this airline would then define how the brand can best facilitate the achievement of the business goals.

If this airline is a new entrant, the brand will have to create awareness in order to let customers know they now have a new option. At the same time, the brand will have to establish basic credibility in terms of safety and financial stability in order to enter the consideration set. Furthermore, the brand will facilitate differentiation in order to create preference over key competitors operating similar routes. Most importantly, the brand needs to appeal to the key target customers by offering relevant functional benefits such as consistently being on time, no lost baggage, no delays at luggage claim. In addition, emotional benefits will help to provide a deeper connection, such as feeling taken care of, feeling valued as a customer, enjoying the plane ride. The brand also needs to appeal to employees, both in terms of attracting talent and in terms of motivating them to act in line with the brand promise.

Strategic role of the brand in the organisation

Connective brands have a clear role that is reflected by the brand's mandate *and* power to act. In some companies, the brand is a key strategic driver, as is the case, for example, with innocent drinks. While innocent drinks offer a great product (healthy pure fruit juices), their differentiation, customer loyalty, employee motivation, and other key stakeholder relationships all rely heavily on the brand. This is only possible if the brand receives sufficient CEO attention. The branding team needs a mandate from the very top to ensure the brand is embedded in the entire business *and* sufficient power and resources to fulfil this mandate. In some companies the branding team will have to convince the CEO and senior management team first that there is strategic value in branding. For example, branding in financial services was only discovered in the mid-1990s when financial services companies started to focus on organic growth instead of acquisitions and mergers. This saw the development of branding teams, branding strategies, and brand building programmes within most banks, insurance companies, brokers, etc. At this point, branding teams were given the mandate to bring on-board other key *internal* stakeholders and furnished with the necessary power to act. Today, most large financial services companies have elevated brand matters to board level.

> **Key questions to be answered**
>
> - What is the role of the brand in the organisation? Is it a strategic driver? Is it only emerging as a strategic driver?
> - Is the role of the brand clear to senior management? Is the CEO capable of and willing to own the brand?
> - How is the brand expected to facilitate achievement of business goals?
> - Does the branding team receive sufficient top-level support? Are mandate and power to act adequate?
> - Is there a clear link between the business strategy and the brand strategy?

Brand content

A brand can be described in many ways, but any brand model must comprise the following three ingredients:

- A small number of brand principles that define the general personality and characteristics of the brand (*value core*)

- A promise to key stakeholders
- A vision outlining the future strategic direction of the brand

It is not the main concern of this book to advise on brand content, but rather to facilitate *delivery* of the brand as well as provide thought provoking new angles and new connections.

Nevertheless, we will briefly run through the key steps in developing brand content.

Brand principles

We have defined a brand as *the sum total of relationships among stakeholders, or the medium through which stakeholders interact and exchange with each other.*[1] Therefore, a brand needs to set out the principles for engaging its employees, customers, and other key stakeholders in meaningful relationships. At the same time, these "brand principles" need to facilitate the interaction and exchange between stakeholders *without* necessarily involving the branding team.

A small number of brand principles (value core)

For a brand to be effective, it needs to be defined by a small number of brand principles that can intuitively create the intended relationships with all key stakeholders. Internally, the brand principles need to act as a behavioural guide and motivational force. Therefore, the brand principles need to be very clear and express a small number of powerful ideas employees can easily relate to. To get through to customers, brand principles need to

---

[1] Myers, D., Whose brand is it anyway? in Ind, N. (ed.), *Beyond Branding*, Philadelphia: Kogan Page, 2003: 21–35.

communicate what a brand stands for in a compact, powerful, and to-the-point way. Brands cannot rely on customers investing time and effort to get to know a complex brand construct. The same is true for other external stakeholders who deal with a multitude of different brands and partners.

Since the brand needs to facilitate the achievement of business goals, all brand principles need to fit with the business strategy. Together, the brand principles need to address the needs of employees, customers, and all other key stakeholders. For example, it is possible that some brand principles are more relevant to employees and some more to customers; as long as they appeal to all key stakeholders and can play together to create an engaging idea, that is no problem at all.

Hierarchy of brand principles

Brand principles can take the form of attributes, functional benefits, intended emotional benefits or values (see Figure 3.3). Attributes are physical features and characteristics of the product or service offered, like the leg-room in an airplane, or the check-in facility at the airport. Functional benefits describe the added value that results from specific attributes. For example, extra leg-room in an airplane might reduce the risk of attracting thrombosis during a flight. Intended emotional benefits describe the emotional reaction a company wants the customers to experience every time they interact with their product and services or the company itself. For example, the airline may want their customers to experience pleasure when travelling with them. The extra leg-room and the reduced risk of suffering thrombosis thus would become examples for how to create an intended emotional experience of *pleasure* for the customer, but also a physical experience. The emotions experienced by customers through interaction with the product, the service or the company itself tend to be short-lived and contained

Brand principles

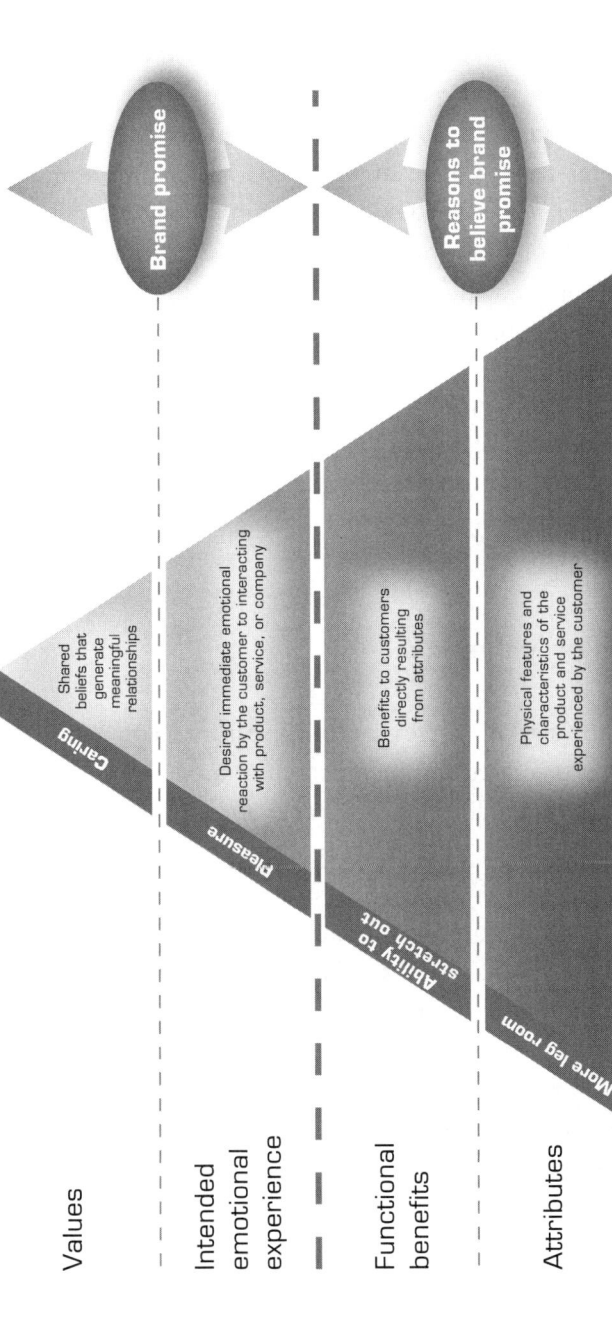

Figure 3.3 Hierarchy of brand principles – example customer. (Based on laddering theory by Gutman[2/3] and adapted from Aaker[4] or de Chernatony and McDonald[5] among others)

---

[2] Gutman, J., A means-end chain model based on consumer categorization processes, *Journal of Marketing*, 46, 2, 1982: 60–72.

[3] Reynolds, T.J. and Gutman, J., Laddering theory, method, analysis, and interpretation, *Journal of Advertising Research*, 28, 1988: 11–31.

[4] Aaker, D., *Building Strong Brands*, New York: The Free Press, 1996.

[5] de Chernatony, L. and McDonald, M., *Creating Powerful Brands*, Oxford: Butterworth Heinemann, 2003 (3rd edition).

in the moment of experience. However, through experience of many such emotions over time a meaningful relationship can be generated. This predicates that the emotions experienced are relatively consistent over time. For example, if the airline operates a number of different planes only some of which have the extra leg room, this could result in a mix of negative and positive emotional experiences depending on which plane serves each flight. As the relationship is reinforced through consistent emotional experience, the customer may slowly come to regard the airline as *caring*. Caring expresses a shared belief among employees, customers, and other stakeholders. This shared belief is a way to transform short-lived emotions into a more stable connection. This shared belief is then called a *value*.

Brand principles on value level

Responding to the market forces outlined earlier, connective brands include a mix of values and intended emotional experiences in their brand definition. Values are not only more deeply rooted than attributes and functional benefits, but they also unite audiences as demonstrated with the Google example earlier. This is particularly important for corporate brands that need to address multiple stakeholders. As discussed in Chapter 2 product brands are typically less credible as carriers of values as they have an arm's-length relationship with customers.

Values are known to be more influential on stakeholder behaviour than attributes or any other brand construct because they relate directly to emotional experiences.[6] This is further

---

[6] Nelissen, R.M.A., Dijker, A.J.M. and Vries, N.K., Emotions and goals: assessing relations between values and emotions, *Cognition and Emotion*, 21, 4, 2007: 902–911.

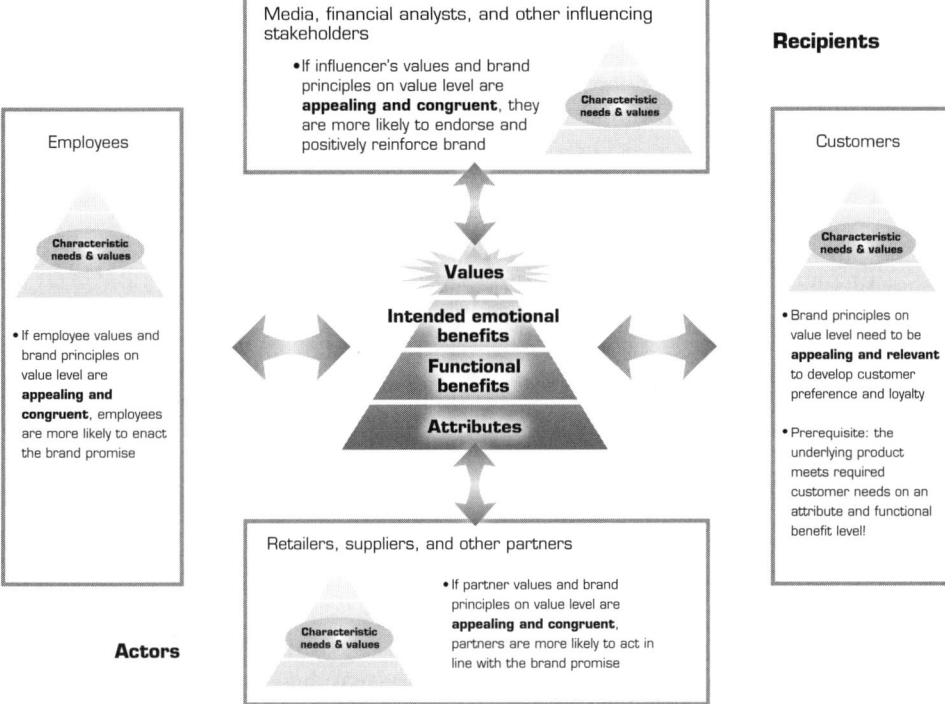

Figure 3.4 Congruency of values

amplified if there is congruency between brand principles on value level and the stakeholder's own values: in the case of employees who need to enact the brand, congruency of values will lead to greater willingness to do that. For example, if the airline employee is a caring person, she will be more willing to enact the brand value of *caring*. In order to consistently deliver on the brand value of caring, the airline will also need partners to enact this value. For example, the catering company should provide meals that care for the health and well-being of the airline passengers. Again, the more congruency between the partner's values and the company's brand values the more likely they are to enact the brand values. For customers, brand values need to be *relevant and appealing* in order to generate brand preference and loyalty (always provided the underlying product or service meets the customer's needs). If the airline customer is receptive to being cared for, he will appreciate the brand value of *caring*, i.e. it is relevant and appealing to him. Stakeholders such as media or financial analysts are also more likely to reinforce the brand values if they are appealing and relevant to them.

Differentiation

When defining brand principles, differentiation is a key consideration. As companies are shifting their branding emphasis from the product to the corporation in search for new sources of differentiation, values and intended emotional experiences gain in importance. While attributes and functional benefits are increasingly less able to provide differentiation, intended emotional experiences and values can provide differentiation through deeper connections. This is much more difficult for competitors to copy, but also much more difficult for brands to deliver. It is not necessary and also in most cases not possible that all brand principles are differentiating in their own right, for example in industries where "innovation" is a key source of product differentiation, most companies in this industry will include "innovation" as a brand principle. This makes "innovation" more of a table stake (i.e. a prerequisite) than a differentiator.

At least some brand principles need to be differentiating or have the power to enable differentiation (e.g. through execution or interpretation). For example, Philips' interpretation of *innovation* (which in itself is not differentiating) as "sense and simplicity" might be seen as differentiating.

Heritage versus aspirational

A brand needs to be an inspirational and motivational force for employees, customers, and other stakeholders. Therefore, some of the brand principles need to be aspirational, pointing towards the future or helping achieve change. This needs to be balanced against brand principles that leverage current brand strengths. Drawing on current brand strengths ensures that the brand heritage is acknowledged, providing a source of *stability and continuity*, while including aspirational elements ensures that the brand is *dynamic and motivational*. Lack of aspirational elements will result in a flat brand; lack of heritage elements will create a brand without roots and authenticity.

Brand promise

Once the brand principles are defined, the brand promise is developed. It serves as a summary of the brand principles and should be both motivating to employees and appealing to other stakeholders. It should also be differentiating in the current competitive context. For example, "Unlocking potential" could be the brand promise of a global service provider. This brand promise motivates employees to unlock their own potential as well as that of their customers. At the same time, to business customers it means that their own chances of success are improved. To shareholders it implies that the financial returns will be stellar, to NGOs it means that CSR potential will be identified, etc. Some companies prefer to work with the definition of a "purpose" rather than a brand promise. A purpose can be equally motivating and appealing – what matters in the end is that it is clear to all key stakeholders what the brand stands for and that employees are passionate about it and willing and able to serve that purpose or deliver on that promise. Only then will the brand spring to life and appeal to other stakeholders, including customers.

Connective brands show a clear link between business strategy and the brand promise. It needs to be intuitive how the brand promise facilitates the achievement of business goals and objectives. Moreover, connective brands are at least to some degree a reflection of the current company culture. Company culture is driven by a number of shared values and beliefs which are reflected in employee behaviour. If there is no congruency between current company culture and brand values, the brand will not be enacted. For example, a German telecommunications company founded a separate company for employees that had been laid off. The new company provided call centre services and was branded as a perky, cutting edge, customer centric organisation. However, the brand values were very much at odds with the corporate culture – in terms of both heritage from the mother company and legacy issues around having been laid off.

Brand vision

The *brand vision* indicates the brand's future direction and aspirations, answering the question "What do we want to be/become/be known for one day?" Coming back to a previous example, the brand promise of "Unlocking potential" could evolve into the brand vision of "Being the adviser of choice to Fortune 500 companies". The brand vision is not something that is typically shared with external stakeholders and therefore is primarily directed at employees. It is therefore very important that the brand vision is motivating for employees. The clearer the picture it paints of what the company and brand want to become and stand for, the higher employee commitment and identification will be.

Connective brands express their brand vision in line with their business priorities, clearly stating how the brand will transform as the business does.

> **Key questions to be answered**
>
> - Are brand principles supportive of business strategy, sufficiently differentiating, sufficiently anchored on a value level, and sufficiently aspiratonal?
> - Are current brand strengths sufficiently leveraged?
> - Do the brand principles together address the needs of all stakeholders?
> - Is the brand promise motivating to employees and appealing to customers and all other key stakeholders?
> - Is the brand vision aspirational and engaging enough for employees?

Brand architecture

Connective brands create a clear link between business strategy, brand content and brand architecture. Brand architecture defines the structure of the brand portfolio (e.g. one master brand versus many brands) and also the role of each brand in this portfolio. Brand architecture is an important but often neglected strategic consideration which can contribute significantly to building brand equity.

In the context of connective branding the key brand architecture issues are:

- *What should be branded?* A company can brand the organisation (e.g. Apple), a product category (e.g. Macintosh for computers), a single product (e.g. MacBook Air for the new superlight Macintosh laptop), an ingredient (e.g. with Intel Core 2 Duo processor), a particular feature (e.g. with iSight camera), or a platform (e.g. Leopard for the new operating system).

140 CONNECTIVE BRANDING

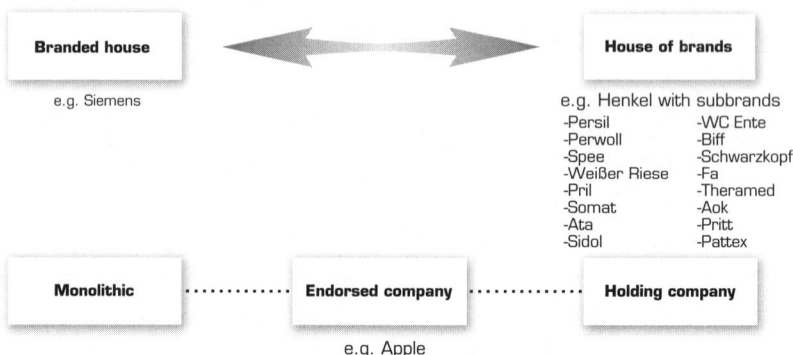

Figure 3.5 Alternative brand architecture strategies

Connective brands place the branding focus in line with the strategic focus of the business portfolio, the communication strategy and customer navigation needs. A combination of different strategies is also possible.

- *How many brands are required to address the portfolio of offerings?* Looking at what David Aaker aptly calls the "Brand Relationship Spectrum",[7] companies can choose a suitable brand portfolio strategy on the spectrum that ranges from the default strategy, namely a "Branded House" strategy where one master brand spans the entire offering, to the other end of the spectrum, the "House of Brands" strategy (see Figure 3.5).

House of brands strategy

On the right side of the spectrum is the House of Brands strategy, whereby companies maintain a whole stable of individual brands

---

[7] Aaker, D., *Brand Portfolio Strategy*, New York: The Free Press, 2004.

geared towards the unique needs of well-defined target audiences. This will give a company the flexibility to address markets with different, inconsistent or non-compatible needs with separate product brands. Their joint owner, the corporation, is not a key point of reference in the interaction with the customer.

It is generally very expensive to operate many individual brands. Therefore, this strategy is usually only employed if there are compelling business reasons to do so, e.g. avoiding cannibalisation, building retail power (the "wall" strategy), addressing channel conflicts (e.g. retailers versus direct), and avoiding non-compatible associations (e.g. appealing to young and old audiences with one and the same product).

A House of Brands strategy is generally accepted as a legitimate brand portfolio strategy. It certainly has proven successful to large consumer goods companies like Unilever and Procter & Gamble in the USA, or Nestlé and Henkel in Europe. But the House of Brands strategy requires some rethinking in the current environment. The House of Brands strategy is more prevalent in the consumer goods markets and often places individual brands at the product level, like the Dove and Axe brands owned by Unilever. At the core of this strategy is the assumption that one and the same company can address the market with a series of different positionings simply by creating several "faces" that in the mind of the customer are not connected to their joint owner. In the past, this has given companies more flexibility, since they did not have to watch out for alignment between the brand promises of individual brands. This allowed individual brands to appeal to smaller segments with more pronounced profiles, making the brands more interesting. However, there are potential problems on the horizon for House of Brands – first, as demonstrated in the Unilever example in the previous chapter, it is increasingly difficult to leave the corporate brand out of the limelight and second, it becomes increasingly difficult to ensure that the various brand messages reach (only) their intended audience (otherwise causing confusion and brand dilution through "spill"). These problems are amplified by the increased desire of customers and other stakeholders to know which corporation is behind a brand (transparency).

Branded house strategy

The Branded House strategy at the other end of the spectrum makes the master brand the key point of reference for the entire product portfolio of a company. This strategy is the default brand architecture strategy for most industry sectors, primarily since it facilitates clarity, synergies, and also leverage. In the case of Virgin Group, the Virgin master brand is defined around elements like innovation (e.g. revolutionising an industry), irreverence, customer service, and fun. Every time Virgin Group enters a new market, they try to bring these elements to bear. Although their product categories are very diverse, ranging from mobile phones to bikes, airlines to financial services, their activities each build equity for the master brand. The equity of the master brand provides positive associations to both existing and new offerings across the entire Virgin portfolio. By the same token, negative associations might also tarnish the entire portfolio. For example, a product recall in one product category might undermine the perceived quality in all other categories served. That is why many companies create stand-alone brands for high-risk ventures.

In the business-to-business (B2B) markets a master brand is often also a corporate brand, meaning that it is the organisation behind the products or solutions that is being branded. Clearly, this places even greater emphasis on corporate actions and decisions. Siemens, for example, subscribes to a corporate master brand strategy for their diverse portfolio organised around the three strategic pillars of healthcare, energy, and industry. All business groups have one thing in common – a shared belief in their three core brand values of *innovation*, *excellence*, and *reliability*. The master brand bundles the efforts of the entire organisation, enhancing visibility and awareness and attempting to build consistent associations around the core brand values. This allows each of the business units (and products, in fact) to benefit from these associations and provides new products and solutions with instant credibility, which is particularly important in a business where innovation, project risk, financial stability and experience are key. However, each of the business units and products in turn also need to continuously nourish and build the master brand to keep up its strength. Managing the intricate reciprocal brand relationships that constitute a corporate master brand can be a challenging task, as Alfred Marquart, Head of Brand Architecture at Siemens AG, highlights:

> Our corporate master brand brings together our diverse businesses, thousands of products and solutions, and more than 398 000 employees around the globe. Managing a corporate master brand for such a large corporation requires a clear vision of what is and is not "on brand", a well-defined set of standards and guidelines that ensure that each business and product contributes to the strength of our master brand and finally, the consideration of brand impact every time strategic business decisions are taken. We need to build brand strength through consistency on many levels – consistent use of the master brand, consistent focus on businesses where we are market leaders or have leadership potential, consistent use of descriptive product names that give the master brand space and do not compete with it, and consistent ways of working with partner and licensee brands. We try to avoid fragmentation and dilution of the master brand; every brand architecture decision we take is evaluated carefully, with one primary goal in mind – to strengthen the brand equity of our master brand while facilitating business success.

One area that is particularly challenging for companies who subscribe to a master brand strategy is growth through acquisition. Siemens has gone through a series of substantial acquisitions in the recent past, creating the need to absorb a number of newly acquired brands into their brand portfolio. Acquired brands typically carry significant brand equity. This brand equity needs to be managed with care and in the interest of both the overarching brand and business strategy. Every time a new brand is acquired, a decision has to be taken with regards to its future role in the brand portfolio. While immediate retirement of the acquired brand would lead to significant value destruction in many cases, retaining all acquired brands would call the master brand strategy into question. Therefore, Siemens has developed a dynamic solution. Alfred Marquart explains:

> We are committed to the Siemens master brand and have found a way to integrate acquired brands into our brand architecture that allows for adequate brand equity transfer while at the same time affirming our master brand strategy: we design a migration pathway for each newly acquired brand right at the outset. This migration pathway can follow a number of options, like a temporary dual brand or continuation of the acquired brand on a product brand level for a transitional period; however, the strategic aim is to eventually migrate all acquired brands towards the Siemens master brand. While these transitional strategies and migration pathways create the impression of a "blended" master brand strategy, the focus very clearly rests on the Siemens master brand alone.

As Siemens is shifting towards a more organic growth model, the importance of the master brand as a key business driver will further increase.

- *What is the role of individual brands and how is the relationship between them defined?* For example, Apple endorses all of their product brands. This makes Apple a master brand with the task to provide instant credibility to all of its products as well as positive associations. The associations inherent in the Apple master brand are great design, innovation and user-friendliness. Every time Apple launches a new product, the new product can draw on these brand equities. By the same token, the master brand needs to be nourished by the equities of the products in the portfolio. When Apple launched the iPod it became an instant success, reinforcing the equities of the Apple master brand. In addition, the positive impact of the iPod was so strong that it provided a halo to the other Apple products. Therefore, the iPod assumed the role of key strategic driver in the Apple portfolio. iTunes was able to further support and strengthen the iPod in its quest for leadership of the music download market.

> **Key questions to be answered**
>
> - How is the portfolio structured? Does it adequately reflect the key drivers of business strategy? Does it clearly present underlying skills and competences? Is it easy to understand for customers? Does it leverage brand equities?
> - Is there only one brand? If so, is it the only brand by default? Is it the only brand by design? Can the one brand accommodate planned extensions and growth? Are all risks under control?
> - If there are several brands, is there a clear reason for having several brands? Are the roles of each brand clearly defined? Are their interrelationships clearly defined? Is the corporation behind the brand prepared to receive more attention from key stakeholders?

BRAND MANAGEMENT

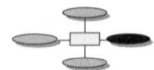

Brand management addresses the question of brand ownership, structure and responsibility of the branding team, interfaces with other functions and departments, and adequate measuring and monitoring systems.

Brand ownership

Connective brands are owned by the CEO and represented by a C-level executive. As brand owner, the CEO needs to make the brand her personal concern and decide what is and is not "on brand". The CEO will bring together business strategy and brand strategy at the very top, ultimately allowing for the brand strategy to come to full fruition within the context of business strategy. Many of our interviewees confirmed the importance of CEO ownership. As the head of marketing of a large US-based financial services company put it:

> Everyone should feel responsible for the brand, but the CEO should be the keeper of the flame. While some younger great brands draw a lot of energy from their owners, like Apple from Steve Jobs, Starbucks (again) from Howard Schultz, SouthWest from Gary Kelly, others have been around for so long that it is no longer possible to do that; however, having a CEO who truly takes the brand under his wings and is willing to fight for that is just as inspiring. If that is not the case, the brand will quickly dissipate energy, resulting in a situation where brand becomes negotiable.

Being the brand owner does not necessarily mean that the CEO has to become the "face" of the brand as is, for example, the case with Sir Richard Branson and Virgin. Not all CEOs are comfortable with such a highly visible role. But the CEO needs to step up to the plate if needed, for example when addressing the public in a time of crisis. A CEO addressing his employees needs to demonstrate that he knows and cares about the brand if he expects the employees to enact the brand. The CEO's appearance, words, and tone of voice will all be clues that reveal genuine brand affinity or betray the lack of it.

The same is true for customers and any other key stakeholder groups. For example, an investor relations manager at a large global insurance company told us: "As Investor Relations, we were always concerned to be taken seriously as an internal stakeholder by the CEO. We knew that his speeches would attract a lot of attention in the financial analyst and journalist circles and we were always trying to raise his awareness of how his statements would impact the assessment of our company."

Structure of the branding team

If the brand is seen as a key strategic driver of the organisation, it is vital that the branding team is not an isolated department, but a well-connected, heavily networked strategy contributor represented on the board. Therefore, on a more operational level, the brand should be represented by a C-level executive, ideally by a CMO (chief marketing officer) or a CXO (chief experience officer).

Core team

Underneath the CMO there will be a branding team that understands the new paradigms of stakeholder engagement and networked collaboration. Many of our interviewees were engaged in "internal" brand building programmes as we spoke to them, confirming that employee engagement is both a pressing and a timely issue. However, most of them were just finding their feet and had started to create stronger links between the branding team and other communications functions.

Connective branding will be organised in a way that facilitates collaboration with all functions and departments that engage employees, customers, and all other key stakeholders.

Customer engagement brings together all brand building activities directed at the customer, including sponsorship, advertising, trade fares and exhibitions, marketing collateral, events and hospitality, the homepage and online activities. Customer engagement needs to reflect how media is consumed today, in particular customers' ability to cut out ads (e.g. through Tivo) and the increasing importance of online interaction and mobile phones. Customer engagement needs to get comfortable with a situation where the interaction between brand and customer can be initiated by the customer himself or by the company. The next section on brand building will address this in detail.

Employee engagement brings together all brand building activities directed at employees including induction for new hires, information, education, measuring, and relationship building. Identification, recruiting and management of brand role models is another key task of employee engagement. They subscribe to an interactive model of communication and encourage employees to take the initiative by getting involved in brand building themselves.

Connective branding requires that corporate reputation, public relations, and investor relations will become members of the branding team (if they are not already). Corporate reputation is defined as "the good will created by the sum of all past actions of an organisation".[8] Although corporate reputation literature insists that a reputation can be managed or at least influenced, it is a much more passive construct that is not really used in the way a brand strategy is used to drive growth and business performance. By making the

---

[8] Rindova, V.P., The image cascade and the formation of corporate reputation, *Corporate Reputation Review*, 1, 2, 1997: 189–194.

BRAND FRAMEWORK 149

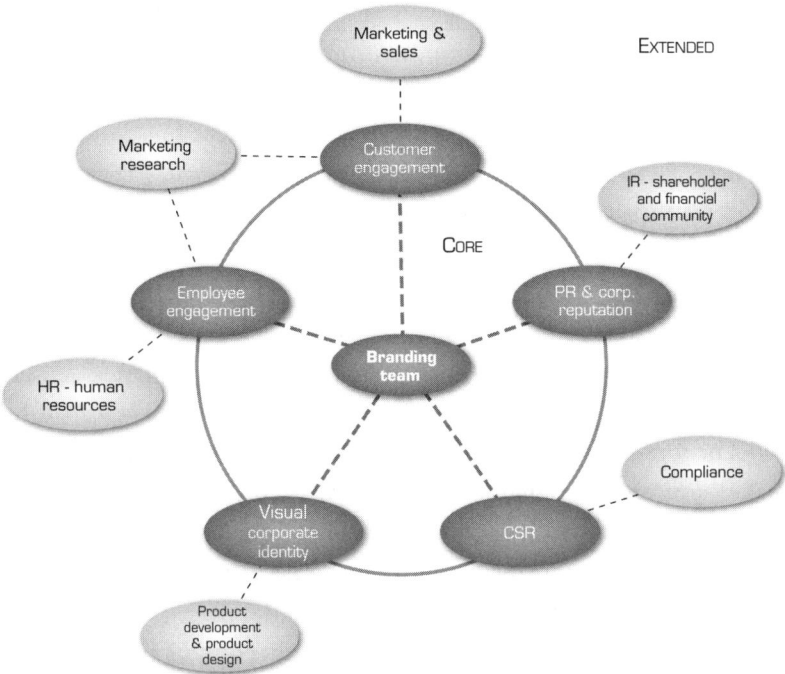

Figure 3.6 Core and extended branding team

corporate reputation department part of the branding team, it becomes easier for the brand to talk to all key stakeholders with one voice.

Similarly, visual corporate identity should be another core member of the branding team looking after all visual elements of the brand including logo, colour scheme, fonts, layout, imagery, etc. and their applications.

Extended team

Connective brands need to build a strong network of collaboration with all other functions and departments that impact the brand directly. These include marketing and sales, investor relations, compliance, product development and product design, human resources, and market research. Depending on the particular driving forces with a company, it may make more sense to include some of these functions in the branding team. For example, if a brand is primarily expressed through product design like the snowboard maker Burton, then product design should be a core member of the branding team. Equally, it may be necessary to expand the extended team depending on the particular powers present. For example, if a company is very finance driven, finance should become part of the extended team.

The branding team will work with product development to make sure the products are in line with the brand in terms of packaging, product design, functionality, quality, etc.; they will work out the distribution strategy with sales; the right price points reflecting the desired positioning in the marketplace vis-à-vis competitors with finance; and co-operate with compliance to ensure that the delivery on regulations like Sarbanes-Oxley does not negatively impact on stakeholder experience.

Interaction with all other functions and departments

Furthermore, connective brands are empowered to work with all relevant functions and departments to facilitate alignment between brand promise and corporate actions. They achieve this by translating the brand content into the everyday jobs of all employees.

Responsibilities of the core branding team

The core branding team has the primary responsibility for designing (and updating) the brand strategy with key inputs from all key stakeholders and gatekeepers. Also, the core branding team needs to make sure the brand becomes sufficiently anchored and embedded in the entire organisation. They will work closely with the extended branding team as well as with brand role models to do this. We will discuss this in more detail under "Brand building through alignment of processes and structures", below.

The complex network of collaborations described earlier makes it clear that the brand is no longer solely owned by the branding team, but actually jointly owned by the entire organisation. The branding team, however, is in charge of making sure that the brand is and remains part of the agenda of all key functions and departments, helping them to interpret the brand within the context of their particular responsibilities and tasks. It is part of the branding team's responsibility to understand the formal and informal powers that shape and steer the organisation. The branding team needs to make sure these forces work in favour of the brand and don't represent obstacles.

Finally, the branding team is responsible for measuring and monitoring brand performance. An actionable metrics and monitoring system will provide the basis for continuous brand improvement.

Metrics and monitoring

As we have mentioned above, connective branding is designed to increase brand equity by improving alignment of brand promise and brand experience and building deeper engagements with all key stakeholders. Brand equity is comprised of all the assets (or liabilities) linked to a brand that add to (or subtract from) the underlying product or service; these assets can be clustered into awareness, perceived quality, brand associations and brand loyalty.[9]

Our research indicates that metrics and monitoring is still an issue for most branding-related areas. In particular, companies feel that many things are measured but not the right things, and that market research is conducted in various parts of the organisation, trying to answer specific questions, without contributing to a big-picture, strategic perspective.

What should be measured?

Connective brands are supported by an actionable measuring and monitoring system that provides regular feedback on where to improve the brand experience for employees, customers, and all other stakeholders.

Many interviewees have shared their particular approach to measuring and monitoring with us and it is fair to say that no two approaches are the same. Some companies focus on hard financial performance indicators. For example, SAP AG measures the success of their brand in terms of their price–earnings ratio. Dr Heitmann, Global Communications SAP AG, explains: "The price–earnings ratio ultimately is a result of the credibility of management, the quality of communications, and the reliability of our products; but the problem is, there are so many influencing factors that it becomes impossible to isolate their relative impact."

---

[9] Aaker, D. and Joachimsthaler, E., *Brand Leadership*, New York: The Free Press, 2000. However, quite in contrast to traditional branding models, we suggest not to limit brand equity to customer associations, but to include all stakeholders' associations. Also, embracing the new communications paradigm, it may not be as straightforward to determine desired associations and then to create programmes that link the associations to the brand.

Many companies have started to measure their brand equity in terms of awareness, product or service quality and brand associations (both prompted and unprompted). This is augmented with conversion ratios along various forms of the purchasing funnel (awareness – consideration – purchase – loyalty). In some cases this results in a single financial "brand value"; however, this is generally not found to be an actionable result.

Another metric that is gaining in popularity is the "net promoter" score. This is particularly prevalent with service providers who are naturally concerned with service quality; for example, a well-known financial services brand is all about "providing world-class service and personal recognition"; the net promoter score measures for each customer whether they would recommend the company to their friends and peers or not; on a monthly basis this is tallied up per customer service representative and integrated into their incentive scheme.

Focusing on the two key drivers of connective branding, namely improving alignment and building deeper engagements, the metrics shown in Figure 3.7 should be measured on a regular basis.

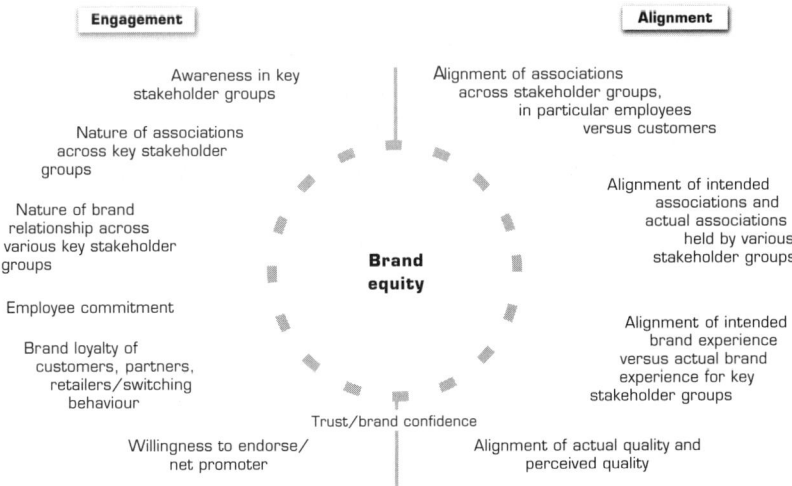

Figure 3.7 Measuring and monitoring

Alignment of intended brand experience versus actual brand experience for customers, employees, and other key stakeholder groups is of particular importance and *will be explained in more detail later*. One way to measure brand experience is through SOPI (Sequence-Oriented Problem Identification),[10] which systematically identifies all interaction points between brand and stakeholder and then captures all critical (positive and negative) incidents[11] at each point of interaction. In order to create the desired brand experience, the internal processes are then optimised to eliminate or at least reduce negative incidents and build on positive ones. For example, for a retail bank, opening an account would constitute one key point of interaction. At this point, many positive and negative incidents could happen – there could be a long queue at the customer service desk and nowhere for the new customer to sit down; there could be a plethora of forms to be filled in, or there could be an unpleasant feeling of scrutiny in terms of several pieces of identification required (e.g. following the new requirements of know your customer which is a result of more stringent anti-money-laundering rules). But there could also be a very helpful and friendly customer service representative, there might be a water fountain with cool spring water to quench the thirst and a television with news to shorten the wait. This technique can help to get information about many things that can be changed very easily to make the brand experience a more positive and engaging one. Clearly, the success of this approach is very dependent on identifying all relevant stakeholder interaction points. The final result of a SOPI study will be a guide of how to prioritise interaction points and, therefore, how to allocate resources to brand building and alignment programmes in the most effective

---

[10] Shostack, G.L., Designing services that deliver, *Harvard Business Review*, Jan/Feb 1984: 133–139.
[11] Flanagan, J.C., The critical incident technique, *Psychological Bulletin*, 51, 2000: 327–358.

way (i.e. maximising brand equity). We will talk more about this under "Brand building through alignment of processes and structures", below.

Key issues

- *Measuring the right things.* Creating a link between brand performance and metrics. Some companies admitted that they measure primarily operational performance metrics (e.g. for an airline this could be the number of flights on time versus delayed, number of bags lost or damaged) while their brands may actually be focused on friendliness. In this case, there is no link between metrics and brand performance, making the measuring exercise rather pointless from the branding perspective. An effective metrics and monitoring system provides actionable information to the branding team. It will tell the branding team where the brand is doing well and where it could be improved, also giving clues as to what the underlying problems might be.
- *Frequency.* Measuring and monitoring should become a regular activity. It is important that insights and results are fed back to the decision makers on a regular basis and in a way that facilitates a reaction. Reams of data tend to disappear in drawers without inspiring action or change.
- *How to measure.* While large companies have an in-house market research department that is well used to working with external research agencies, smaller and medium-sized companies often think that they can do the job themselves. However, there is something to be said for an objective outside evaluation; no matter how unbiased employees think they are, they will still filter all answers and information through their particular view of the brand and the organisation. As Otto Riedl, Head of PR of the Austrian chocolate maker Manner,

commented: "Market research is often used to solve political issues in an organisation. If the management team can't decide, they let market research do it for them."

It is very important to make sure that the study delivers the required information; this typically requires both thorough preparation in terms of objectives and stamina in terms of getting what you want versus what the research agency wants to (or can) sell.

> **Key questions to be answered**
>
> - How can the CEO become the brand owner?
> - Who should be part of the core branding team? Who should be part of the extended branding team?
> - Which departments or functions need to institutionalise collaboration with the branding team? How to create a formalised branding network that pulls into one strategic direction?
> - What is the role of informal branding structures?
> - How should brand performance be measured?
> - How can emotional engagement with employees, customers, and other key stakeholders be measured?
> - How can alignment of brand promise and brand experience be measured?

BRAND BUILDING THROUGH ENGAGEMENT

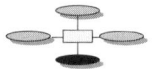

Brand building through engagement helps the brand to spring to life. This requires several things to happen:

- Employees need to understand the brand, embrace the brand and start living the brand.
- Customers need to know about the brand, consider buying the brand, make purchases and finally turn into loyal brand enthusiasts.
- Retailers, suppliers, and other partners need to value the brand enough to adapt their own business practice such that they can enact the brand promise and help deliver the desired brand experience.
- All other key stakeholders, including influencers, need to notice the brand, embrace the brand and positively reinforce brand preference.

This is no easy task. Connective brands achieve this by continuously engaging with employees, customers, partners, and other stakeholders in an *interactive, non-intrusive,* and *non-manipulative* way.

Each of the audiences requires a tailored approach that caters to their particular needs, their ways of consuming media and information, their ability and willingness to engage, and their particular relationship with the brand.

Brand building is primarily concerned with employees and customers since they need to form the most important relationships with the brand. If shareholders play a very active and important role in strategic decision making, they may have to be included in this inner core. Retailers, suppliers and other partners also need to be brought into the brand in a systematic, strategic way in order to enact the brand promise. Depending on the particular set-up

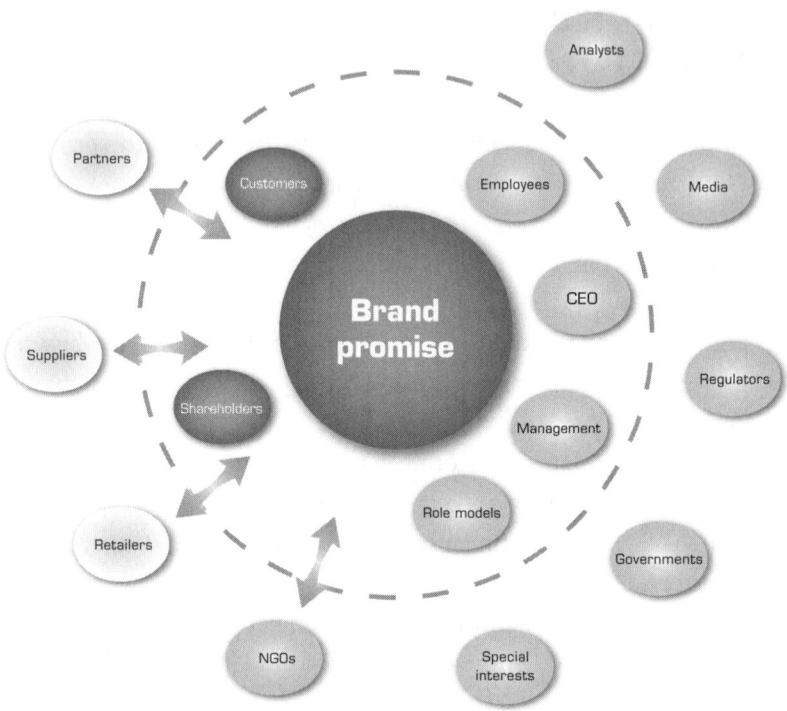

Figure 3.8 Brand building through engaging employees, customers, and other key stakeholders

of a company's relationships and business processes, a number of other stakeholder groups could also become part of this inner core either permanently or for particular initiatives, for example NGOs. All the other stakeholders should also be engaged in a systematic way; however, the interaction may be less intense and less frequent.

We will now discuss how to approach engagement with each of these audiences.

Employee engagement

Employee engagement drives the satisfaction and brand experience[12] of external stakeholders. Whether intended or unintended, verbal or non-verbal, employees permanently communicate the brand through their behaviours. Therefore, connective brands need to increase the willingness of employees to act in line with the brand. This can be achieved through employee engagement.[13] We understand employee engagement to be the extent to which employees identify with, are motivated by and are willing to make an extra effort to the brand. Connective brands are enacted by a large majority of employees.[14]

Companies increasingly become aware of the importance of engaging employees beyond the traditional internal communication activities and are seeking new ways to motivate and inspire employees. Instead of disseminating information one way from the company to the employee, companies are starting to create opportunities for the employee to learn more about the brand and expected behaviours by engaging in a dialogue.

Key issues

Engaging employees means addressing a number of key issues. Over time, employees have been exposed to many company initiatives, not all of which have actually been successful and resulted

---

[12] Homburg, C. and Stock, R., The link between sales people's job satisfaction and customer satisfaction in a business-to-business context: a dyadic analysis, *Journal of the Academy of Marketing Science*, 32, 2, 2004: 144–158.
[13] de Chernatony, L., From Brand *Vision to Brand Evaluation – Strategically Building and Sustaining Brands*, Oxford: Butterworth-Heinemann, 2006.
[14] Rutledge, T., *Getting Engaged: The New Workplace Loyalty*, Canada: Mattanie Press, 2006.

in change. Therefore, employees are often cynical or sceptical when a new programme is launched. They search for signals and clues as to whether this is "just another programme" in a series of many which they can safely disregard, or whether this is something worthy of their attention and interest.

In addition, they are busy with their everyday jobs and the brand will be competing for attention with any number of other programmes and special activities. In some companies, employees are inundated with emails, memos, special reports, surveys, meetings, and announcements of all sorts. This makes it difficult for the brand to automatically connect on a deeper level.

Employees are often treated with a one-size-fits-all approach, thereby neglecting that they are as diverse with regards to needs, skills, languages, cultural backgrounds and ways to consume and perceive information as, for example, customers are. Disregarding this diversity drastically reduces the impact of brand engagement activities.

Failure to translate a brand promise into expected employee behaviour will make the brand less relevant to employees. Companies strategise at the highest levels – the management team develops a business strategy, the branding team crafts brand promises and claims – yet they often forget to inform – and more importantly motivate – their employees. But without truly understanding what a brand means in the context of their tasks and responsibilities they are neither equipped nor willing to deliver.

Approach to employee engagement for connective brands

Connective brands account for the diversity of employees when seeking to engage with them, thus maximising relevancy. By segmenting employees beyond the common dimensions of customer facing/non-customer facing and positive/negative attitudes, it becomes possible to engage at a much deeper level. This results in more meaningful brand relationships and has a positive impact on brand enactment.

Connective brands make employee engagement a priority of brand building and offer their employees a multitude of opportunities to engage with the brand. They make sure that their motivation and commitment remain high over time. They understand that employee engagement is not a one-off activity, but an ongoing programme that informs, trains, supports, motivates and excites employees.

In order to keep employee interest, connective brands continuously find new ways to engage employees but also invite employees to take the initiative themselves.

The employee engagement programme needs to embody the brand promise

Brands aim to create differentiation and deeper emotional connections with all stakeholders. This desire should also drive the design of an employee engagement programme. Connective brands find a way to communicate their brand principles and expected employee behaviours that is unique, memorable, and already a reflection of the brand itself. For example, if a brand stands for "Unlocking potential", then the employee engagement programme should not only *talk about* the value of unlocking potential, but should be designed to actually unlock potential in every employee. For example, by letting employees learn something simple they never thought possible like juggling three balls, they will experience first hand what the brand promise means – to them, to their customers, and to all other stakeholders.

Connective brands engage all levels of the organisational hierarchy

Every company is comprised of a number of different employee types. They can be organised around a number of different criteria, including hierarchy, functional affinity, geography, tenure, intensity of customer interaction, etc. Of these, the organisational structure is typically most helpful for segmenting employees. It allows to create buy-in from the very top and cascade down information by taking advantage of a multiplier system, whereby various levels of management are trained to train their teams.

As discussed earlier, the CEO needs to "carry the brand flame" and assume brand ownership. Therefore, the CEO should be involved in the brand development if at all possible. As a result, the CEO is already on board the new or revised brand strategy, and can help get the buy-in from the most influential top managers. When designing the layered programme, it is important to define the levels in a way that gets to all top and middle management in three or four steps.

This approach can work for both a brand launch (more like a one-off event) and the ongoing employee engagement.

Connective brands engage employees with the help of brand role models

Brand role models are people on all levels of the organisation who have a strong affinity with the brand and like to share their brand excitement with others. They are typically outgoing and very good at motivating others. Brand role models have fully embraced the brand and integrated the brand principles into their work and behaviour. Typically, congruency between their personal values and brand principles on value level is high. Brand role models generate an informal network of influencers that grows over time. They can be managers, subordinates, or peers and are not limited to top or senior management.

The core branding team needs to identify suitable brand role model candidates on all levels of the organisational hierarchy. These candidates are then approached and officially brought on

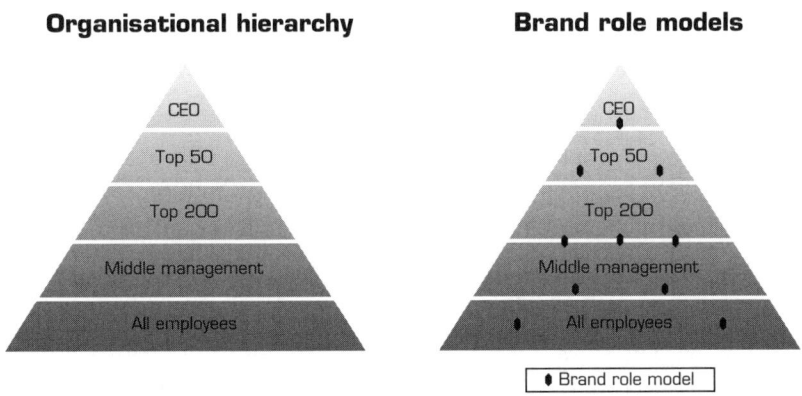

Figure 3.9 Placing brand role models on all levels

board. Training for brand role models can either be conducted in one-on-one sessions or in group sessions, or both. Generally, brand role models benefit greatly from the exchange with other brand role models. It is important that brand role models work closely with the core brand team and provide regular feedback on issues and successes. As brand role models identify additional suitable candidates, they need to bring these into the role model team as well. This will allow constant feeding of the informal branding network in order to ensure it stays alive and grows continually (see Figure 3.9).

Connective brands engage employees by employee type

A somewhat different approach is to cluster employees by the meaning work has in their lives. This is particularly helpful for connective branding since it indicates the level of commitment the employee brings to work. This in turn shapes the commitment towards the brand. In addition, a segmentation by meaning of work provides some clues as to which engagement mechanisms and vehicles are particularly appealing and effective for each segment.

For example, there might be a group for whom work is all about personal growth and excitement. These employees can be found on all levels of the hierarchy, with a slight bias towards younger employees. They can be engaged by appealing to their intellectual curiosity, be it through exchanging ideas with exciting people (e.g. a brand expert), contributing to white papers, or learning something new by attending conferences.

See the table in Figure 3.10 displaying a number of different employee types and ways to appeal to them.

Connective brands engage employees across all phases of brand building

Brand creation

It is one of the key tasks of the core branding team to develop the brand strategy. However, it pays off if enthusiastic, knowledgeable and influential employees are consulted or included in the process from the outset. Not only will they contribute valuable insights to the development of brand strategy, but their participation will also create a sense of co-ownership and commitment.

Brand launch

For competitive reasons it is often not possible to inform employees until the new brand is signed off by top management. However, a cascading approach as discussed earlier works well in most cases,

Employee type	Excitement and curiosity	Social and ambitious	Leaving an impression
The role of work	Work is one way to experience growth and excitement	Work is about being a valuable part of a winning team	Work is about creating something with lasting value
What appeals and engages	**Appeals to: intellectual curiosity** • Learning something new, personal growth • Exchanging ideas with exciting people • Figuring something out • Write white papers	**Appeals to: feeling of belonging** • Assign role in exteded brand team • Dialogue, conversations • Competitions, team events • Teaching and sharing with others	**Appeals to: ability to shape something** • Contribution to brand development • Train as a brand trainer • Moderate a brand forum (online)

Employee type	Recognised but non-committal	Reliable but uninspired	Steady and predictable progress
The role of work	Work is primarily a way to make good money	Work is a necessary evil and not a priority	Work is about moving up the ladder along a predictable path
What appeals and engages	**Appeals to: ego** • Become part of a team to create more commitment • Give access to network • Brand stories and gossip	**Appeals to: sense of responsibility** • Social or peer pressure	**Appeals to: desire to achieve something** • Rules for brand behaviour • Clear criteria for brand performance evaluation

Figure 3.10 Illustrative employee segmentation by role of work[15]

[15] Adapted from Erickson, T. and Gratton, L., What it means to work here, *Harvard Business Review*, 1 March 2007: 104–112.

allowing top management to get a preview before everybody else.

In parallel, internal media can be used to pique interest of employees by placing brand-related information in employee magazines, intranet articles, etc. without revealing specifics or too much detail. For example, TUI AG, the German-based global travel and holiday company, followed this approach in the pre-launch phase of their new master brand at the time. They started to discuss in theory the advantages and disadvantages of House of Brands and Branded House brand architectures without providing any details with regards to a planned master brand. They also published a number of interviews with brand and marketing people who worked on the master brand project, aimed at sensitising employees about the importance of branding and preparing them for the strategic move. For example, they would also discuss the strength of international brands like Coca-Cola and Nivea.

Timing of internal launch

It is very important to launch the brand internally well before an external announcement is made. Employees need to feel that they are special and privileged enough to hear first about the new brand. After all, they are expected to live by this new brand promise almost immediately. The more time a company can allow between launching the brand internally and making an external announcement the greater the chances that the new brand promise can actually be delivered. Connective brands work with trigger points that measure understanding of and engagement with the new brand before an external announcement is made. This makes sure that expectations are not only created, but also met.

Many companies prepare booklets, books, or other means of visualising and describing the brand as part of the launch campaign. For example, TD Ameritrade created the *Power Book*, a small, lime-green booklet in an unusual format that summarises their brand values, and translates them into expected brand behaviours and actions. The *Power Book* simply showed up on everybody's desk one day. Chris Armstrong, EVP of Sales and Marketing at TD Ameritrade, explains: "It is important to pick the right time for doing something like this; ideally there is a context that automatically reinforces one or several of the brand principles. In our case, launching the new brand in the wake of a merger was a perfect opportunity."

The launch campaign in many ways does not only have an information purpose, but also takes on a symbolic character. Employees will be looking for clues as to how important and how serious the intended changes are. Therefore, the launch campaign should connect with elements that symbolise importance and significance within the organisation.

In some companies, this is the involvement of the CEO. In others, it might be a speech by a long retired founder or someone the company would recognise as a celebrity and who is capable of reinforcing the brand message (e.g. for a motorcycle company it might be a famous racer, for a professional services company it could be a highly successful business leader). Whatever it is, the core branding team needs to incorporate these elements into the launch campaign.

It is very important that the launch campaign embodies the brand promise. For example, if a new brand is launched that evolves around "excitement", the launch campaign itself needs to be exciting or the brand building programme will be discounted and discredited immediately. For example, when TUI launched their new brand vision of becoming synonymous with "the most beautiful time of the year" to their top 200 managers, they took great care to select an appropriate venue and programme. The event was held in the German pavilion of the Expo-area in Hannover. The evening saw a multi-media staging of the new "World of TUI" master brand, introduced by an energetic speech by the CEO and supported by a whole range of activities. To reinforce the enjoyment factor incorporated in the new brand, managers were invited to discover the new "World of TUI" logo by solving a puzzle.

Combining the launch with a small but symbolic first change increases interest in the new brand and credibility of the initiative. For example, when Hollard Insurance introduced "It's sorted", they also introduced the new neck straps for employees' security discs thereby "sorting" a small but annoying problem.

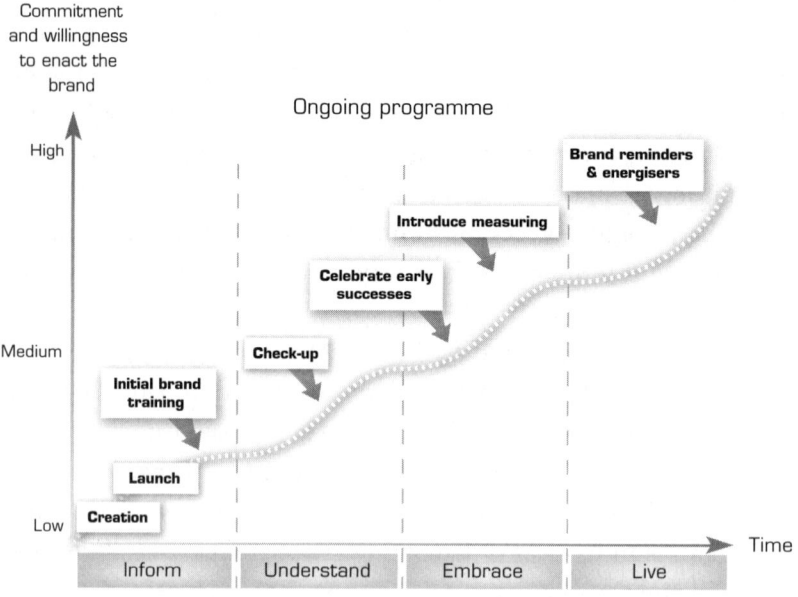

Figure 3.11 Employee engagement programme across phases

Initial brand training

An announcement or a launch generally raises many questions and also creates anxiety. Dovetailing an announcement with as much additional information and training as possible will help to turn anxiety into excitement. Working with middle management as multipliers who pass the information to their teams works well in most organisations. This requires that they are not just adequately briefed and equipped with additional material to take back to their teams (e.g. posters, badges, decoration for their mousepad or laptop), but to be taught how to teach their teams. Supporting elements like online video clips, podcasts, and texts that can be viewed at any employee's leisure are very helpful, since often these trainings are conducted in English and the language proficiency might not be such that everyone can understand the message at first pass. Q&A sessions, roadshows, and workshops are all helpful at a level, but are often very boring and lack practical relevance. Small groups, for example moderated by brand role models, combined with highly interactive content, challenging tasks, and rewards, improve engagement. Viral campaigns can also work internally.

As employees go back and get on with their day-to-day job, they should notice and be reminded of the difference the new brand makes. Maybe their physical environment has changed – a different seating arrangement, a new lick of paint on the walls, a new reception area, new meeting areas, a new canteen, the possibilities are endless. Maybe some processes are starting to change – a different way to send information, a new way to answer the phone, a new way to conduct meetings, a new way to meet or greet the customer. Whatever it is, the first changes are very important. People need affirmation and role models they can copy. It helps tremendously if they see that the CEO and other senior executives live the new brand. Their manager is also a great source of affirmation and motivation. Some companies provide hot lines to answer employee questions, downloads for their iPods and cover answers to frequently asked questions in the employee magazine.

Check-up

A few months after initial contact there needs to be a follow-up. The branding team will want to hear about progress made and issues or challenges encountered. Again, working with middle management as intermediaries might provide just the right level of information aggregation. An online quiz or competition might spark some interest, or an invitation to join a check-up session for randomly selected employees. Ideally, the check-up concludes the information phase and leaves employees comfortable with the new brand. If the core brand team, however, discovers that there are still large information gaps, they need to address them before they move into the next phase of the programme.

Celebrate early successes

After the check-up, there will be enough material to start communicating early successes. This will help employees to start embracing the brand. Stories about how customers react to the new brand promise, how employees are enjoying themselves better, how the media reacted, etc. will be very helpful. These stories should be communicated in a creative, unconventional way in order to engage employees properly. No emails, no publications on the blackboard. Personal, engaging interaction is required.

Embracing the brand

Continuous involvement of the CEO signals that the brand is and remains a top priority. For example, if the CEO has his own blog, he might make the brand a topic of this blog once a quarter. However, this only works if the blog is authentic and not written by a ghost-writer. Many CEOs might find this difficult because they are used to operating in a corporate culture where they need to channel information carefully. Few companies like to be publicly controversial or admit that they make mistakes, living in fear of unwittingly disclosing information that might be considered important to shareholders.

Some CEOs lecture about the role model function of the CEO and then get embroiled in a scandal as was the case with the CEO of Deutsche Post, Klaus Zumwinkel, who had to resign over accusations of tax evasion. Ironically, Mr Zumwinkel had written an article for the employee newspaper *Premium Post* about leaders as role models which was issued just one day before the scandal broke. "Leaders need to live values, their leadership quality is particularly recognised in times of crisis," remarked Mr Zumwinkel.[16] This can set back employee engagement efforts severely and create employee scepticism.

For innocent drinks, a combination of story-telling and the use of a particular vernacular works well to engage employees. We have already mentioned the story about how innocent drinks was founded (you may remember the two voting bins). This story is told in the same unpretentious, fun, innocent way that is also characteristic of all other communications. Their play with words, the insertion of unexpected information about some unrelated

---

[16] Post-Mitarbeiter-Postille: Zumwinkels Märchenstunde, *Spiegel*, 18 Feb. 2008, accessed: http://www.spiegel.de/wirtschaft/0,1518,536152,00.html

everyday affair, makes their communication very engaging, for example: "We also have some Tiny Grass Vans here at Fruit Towers. Although they are smaller . . . they don't feel inferior and are very useful for making emergency deliveries around town, and for giving Katie a lift to the bank when it's raining." It also indicates to employees that the company is human. This is further demonstrated by their use of titles; for example, Matthew Gardan is not called the "French Communications Manager", his title is "Garlic Smoothie".

Arthritis Ireland, a national charity dedicated to improving the lives of people with arthritis, identified several simple, but effective ways to engage their employees and volunteers (= people with arthritis who carry out a lot of volunteer work on behalf of Arthritis Ireland) in their new brand. The idea of "empowerment" is at the heart of the new brand, to inspire patients and those who care for them to keep a positive attitude towards life with this painful condition that currently has no cure. In a first step, CEO John Church called in an occupational therapist and turned the headquarters in Dublin into a disability-friendly facility, opening up the organisation to interaction and empowering volunteers to visit if they were in the vicinity. Then he replaced the dowdy newsletter directed at volunteers and employees with an engaging, glossy magazine that is all about how to live a full life even with arthritis. Next, he bought a self-help programme from Stanford University that allows volunteers to get licensed as a trainer and then deliver the programme to arthritis patients, empowering them to help themselves and to help others. And finally, he was also empowering volunteers in the countryside by eliminating the heavy Dublin bias for all activities. "We really started to be seen as a D4 [Dublin postal code] organisation. Dublin had to get out of its comfort zone," John Church explains. "We are now driving around Ireland all the time, which really is a way of indicating respect to our volunteers in the local branches while also engaging with them."

CASE STUDY: AWARD-WINNING EMPLOYEE ENGAGEMENT PROGRAMME AT GM

The power of word of mouth is rising in consumer decision making, in particular in the case of high-involvement products. Word-of-mouth marketing starts with customer satisfaction: a happy customer is a potential advocate and influencer but unfortunately, an unhappy customer is even more powerful. Employees who are committed to the product and the company contribute substantially in making the brand experience a pleasurable one for customers.

General Motors UK operates out of 10 different locations, with over 5000 employees. Jos Sharp, Internal Communications Manager, explains how their award-winning employee ambassadors programme leverages the potential to turn employees into brand enthusiasts, to promote the company and to sell their products with pride: "In 2006, we won three categories of motivation awards with our program. Basically, there are four key elements to our strategy," Sharp explains: creating pride, engaging employees, adequate incentives and creating opportunities to promote the product.

Creating pride in the company

To create pride, GM aims to make knowledgeable and informed company spokespeople of all employees. Sharp adds: "Even though our recruitment activity is limited, we aim to make GM an employer of choice in the marketplace so that employees feel proud to work there."

The two key internal communication events are the quarterly town hall presentation where all employees are included and the executive conference for the top 300 leaders. "For both of these we ensure we cover subjects of interest to attendees and topical information that they can share with friends and family. One such topical subject is the impact of our cars on the environment. For example, last year we featured Sir Richard Branson receiving his Saab Bio Power," explains Sharp. As well as only covering interesting and relevant content, it is essential that the presenters – coming from within the company and occasionally externally – are motivated and enthusiastic about their subjects and are never just going through the motions.

Becoming an employer of choice in an industry that is struggling to make adequate profits is tough, as obviously there are always trade-offs to be made. "There are always things that can be done at minimal cost," says Sharp, and these include:

- Making sure that whenever legally possible, benefits such as health schemes, flu vaccinations and well person clinics are open to all
- Running a discount programme with genuine special deals on a wide range of products and services
- Giving employees an opportunity to speak directly with the most senior leaders

Engaging employees in the brands

The second element of the brand ambassador programme is engaging employees in the brands – both in GM and in its consumer brands. "Car brands are some of the most exciting and best loved brands in the world – so it is comparatively easy to excite employees about brands like the Astra VXR or the Saab 93 Convertible. We therefore run a lot of product-based engagement programmes. But for our corporate GM brand we need a programme that can unite people behind the many consumer brands," explains Sharp, and continues:

The product-based programmes are self-explanatory – things like advertising previews, new product reveals and "ride-and-drive" events. The key here though is to get buy-in from all areas of the organisation, so that employees are considered first in the planning and launch processes – when the additional costs are minimal, rather than trying to include them once the Internal Comms team become aware of the plans.

As part of the initiatives on a corporate brand level, we launched a behaviours-based programme called EXCITE, which stands for:

- *Enjoy* the challenge of bringing a positive, winning attitude to all we do.
- *X-factor.* Everyone can make a creative contribution – whatever their role.
- *Customer driven.* To give the best service to our colleagues, retailers and customers we have to understand them.
- *In it to win.* We believe in winning, not just taking part.
- *Tell it how it is.* We're direct and engaging with customers and colleagues.
- *Energetic.* We need to act quickly, decisively and always deliver on our promises.

These are the behaviours expected, encouraged and rewarded throughout the organisation. A key initiative is WhateverNext? which gives employees a platform for suggestions, complaints and comments – particularly around the company's working environment and employee engagement. It also covers business etiquettes for voicemail, email and meetings, for example, and it is used to communicate behaviours-based messages and engagement activities. "Another initiative is the 5-a-side, twice-yearly football competition – where all teams are equal – although there may be such a thing as a career limiting tackle, when up against the directors team!" Sharp quips and gets serious again: "We measure the EXCITE programme regularly and have achieved 100% awareness for the last two years – it was developed internally and responds continually to feedback, creating strong buy-in and alignment."

Incentivising employees to promote the brands

The third element of GM's brand ambassador programme is incentivising employees to promote the brands. For instance, the "Mates Rates" programme is designed to enhance the employees' feeling of ownership for the success of the company. This programme rewards employees for making a recommendation to their friends to buy a particular car, and gives their friend a discount off the new car, which they wouldn't have received without the recommendation. Another way to enthuse employees is by providing them with the chance to buy or win bespoke merchandise linked to the various GM campaigns. This again enhances employee buy-in and enables them to promote the brands outside the company.

Giving employees the opportunity to sell the brands

Selling a product requires the ultimate identification and is one of the most important customer interaction points. Therefore, GM invites employees – including plant employees – to apply to work on their Motor Show stands.

Applicants had to go through a screening process and those selected were then trained in product and customer service. The response was great as shown by some employee comments:

"I wanted to show how much enthusiasm I have for the future of the company and its products."
"I mostly spend time working at a computer on a system that monitors the vehicles that are being built in the plant – normally quite boring. But I felt as though I was playing a major role on the stand of the Motor Show."
"A good opportunity to speak to some real customers; not something I normally get to do in my job."

BRAND FRAMEWORK 177

Figure 3.12 GM – giving you a chance to shine!

"A lot of visitors to the stand were impressed with the fact that we were one of the only manufacturers to have 'REAL' employees on the stand, and not just agency staff. This gave them confidence in the information that we give them."

Another new initiative that GM launched allows employees to take a new car home for testing and demonstration purposes; they can test the car on any chosen route – including narrow, winding roads instead of being restricted to pre-selected standard routes; they give their family a ride in it instead of sharing it with another employee; show it off to friends and distribute sales brochures and reminders of special offers. Here are some employee comments:

"I would never usually look at the Corsa as it is too small for me, but the New Corsa has more to it and the interior is much more attractive to look at."

"Friends, relatives and neighbours were commenting on it. 'Nice vehicle, can't believe it is a Corsa!! Spacious, trendy looking'."

"Gives a good impression of the company, I had a wedding that weekend and I felt so special!! Felt proud to be working for Vauxhall."

"Neighbours and family impressed as they are not given opportunity to have a good look at a vehicle, and prod and poke around at the retailers, feeling comfortable."

Sharp adds:

> We also use the following communications methods to promote all of our activities internally including:
>
> - Full size 48 sheet posters in the employee car park
> - A "Hero Wall" celebrating business success or community activity by employees
> - Large impact banners down the employee walkway
> - Changes in the tone of our communications to be less corporate, less dictatorial and more motivating and personal, by using people and teams in the creative department
> - Running feedback focus groups with employees which help to highlight the successes as well as providing a basis for improvement.

Sharp concludes: "Our experience shows that with hard work, customer-facing brand values can be translated across the workforce and are a key brand differentiator in an increasingly com-

> petitive sector." Studies suggest that companies whose employees rate it as a great place to work have grown in share price – and companies with an engaged and committed workforce can double shareholder returns.[17]

Including brand in incentive metrics

Once employees have started to embrace the brand, it is time to introduce brand-driven metrics into the incentive system. This will further boost the importance of branding. Letting employees know that their behaviours are measured will be effective in terms of changing their behaviour, but might also cause some resistance at first.

Measuring customer impact is very important, as are measuring employee understanding of the new brand, willingness to change behaviour and overall commitment and motivation to act in line with the brand. All these metrics provide important information to the core branding team with regards to how to improve the engagement of employees, customers, and other stakeholders. Making the brand promise part of the incentive system also allows the company to reward those who act in line with the brand.

Brand reminders and energisers (regular and spontaneous)

By now, everyone should have heard of and understand the new brand. Now it is time to make sure everyone can translate the brand promise into expected behaviours. Whether this is

---

[17] Employee Satisfaction Proves Crucial to Shareholder Value – www.vault.com

something employees are allowed to work out for themselves (e.g. in a branding workshop), or are provided with (e.g. through roadshows), it needs to be tailored to the particular needs of the company, the brand, and the target audience. Story-telling is often helpful at this stage; letting gossip and fantasy create corporate myths that perpetuate and add to the cache of the brand. Inviting informal ways to share and discuss the brand are very important. Employees need to be able to talk about the brand promise among themselves, working out any difficulties and developing attachment and excitement.

Manner, the famous Viennese maker of wafers and chocolates, found that sponsoring the Austrian ski jumping team really engaged their employees. Frequently they would gather in front of the television to watch together how their beneficiaries would fare in the ski jumping competitions. Similarly, product placements in movies like *The Terminator* or TV shows like *Ally McBeal* and *Friends* were primarily directed at employees. Otto Riedl, Head of PR, explains: "To see our little Manner products in such cool movies and TV series made employees really proud."

Kneipp, the well-known German maker of herbal medicine, beauty and wellness products, for the first time featured employees in their advertising campaign. The campaign is comprised of several stories taken from everyday life where employees rely on the power and efficacy of Kneipp products, telling the audience how well they work (see Figure 3.13).

For example, one employee recommends an ointment for the bruises he suffered from playing sports, while another suggests a relaxing massage with warm arnica oil to recover from work stress. Angela Kreipl, Head of Communications at Kneipp, explains: "Employee engagement was not the primary motivation to feature employees in our ads; we were looking for authentic, real-life endorsements of our products. That is when the idea to feature our own employees emerged. But employees seem to like it, and it definitely had a positive impact on employee motivation."

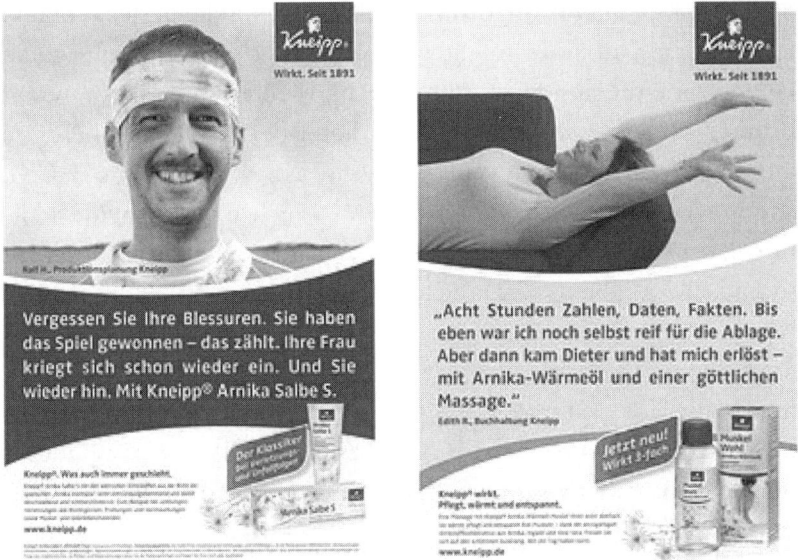

Figure 3.13 Kneipp employees featuring in the new ad campaign

In order to keep employees engaged, dramatic and surprising little things typically have the most impact. Spending a few hours in a different world – like the call centre listening to customers complain, or rotating jobs, or helping out in the retail store or on the shop floor – might be just as impactful as getting access to senior leaders. Away-days, events, unusual shared activities are all good ways to remind employees of the brand. For example, the Italian retailer for sporting gear and clothes, Sportler, invites their employees for a major journey every five years. For example, they climbed Mount Mero (4600 m) in Africa to remind everyone of the team spirit, the importance of human beings, and their commitment to sports which are the foundation of their brand. Incidentally, they have recently launched a new product brand called Mero.

Also, looking for opportunities that provide the perfect context for the brand message might pay off – these opportunities could come from the inside in terms of big events, relevant news or planned activities, or from the marketplace. Typically, there are a number of regular events like the Xmas party, the AGM, announcement of financial results, etc. which might provide additional trigger points for employee engagement. For example, it should be a given that the brand is discussed in the annual report.

Keeping the CEO and senior management engaged is just as important. For example, UBS, the global financial institution based in Switzerland, introduced a new brand in 2003 with significant senior management support. Employee engagement has been an ongoing initiative for several years now, but slowly management is directing their interest and attention elsewhere. "Management has different pressure points now, in their mind branding has been successfully completed. So they focus their attention more and more on new issues and challenges that need to be tackled," says Beni Eggli, Head of Global Brand Management at UBS. "But as the person responsible for the brand, I know that the brand needs constant engaging with the employees; it is never done and dusted. If top management take their eyes off the brand, employees will notice quickly and brand equity will erode."

Induction for new hires

New hires need to undergo brand training as part of their induction training. It serves as a basic orientation that provides important cultural and behavioural clues with regards to what is important in a company, what is expected in terms of behaviour, what is accepted and what is not. Francesca Karpel, Senior Manager Internal Communications at NetApp, a fast-growing global software brand, has moved from the HR team to the marketing team while keeping the same role of making sure that business and brand drivers are understood by the employee community:

> We have experienced phenomenal growth since our foundation 15 years ago. Our success is built on strong values and a unique culture. Our two founders, Dave Hitz and James Lau, are still with the company and very engaged, lending our brand significance and energy. Our executive team wrote the values – they spent a lot of time developing them. Our values are honesty, integrity, and teamwork, which are more common; however, they also include simplicity, getting things done and going beyond. We are a team of self-starters and people who have high goals. The stated purpose of our company is to build a model company. We have a very strong internal brand, people who share our values love working here and we are recognized as a great place to work in several geographic regions, including being recognized among the top 50 best places in the Fortune Magazine Best Places to Work list the past 6 years. It is important that new hires absorb our values immediately as they come onboard so that they can do well. Therefore, we designed a new hire program called T.O.A.S.T., when the company was still young. The acronym "Training on all special things" was intended to distinguish it from typical new hire orientation programs. It is kicked off by the CEO and closed by the President, and most new hires participate in the program. The program was originally offered only in our corporate headquarters. It is now offered in other locations in the U.S. and around the world so it is easier for employees in our rapidly growing global workforce to attend.

Connective brands work with the idea of a "signature experience" for new hires

For new hires, a signature experience is a "distinctive practice that conveys what it is really like to work at a company and what makes the company unique".[18] For example, all new Ducati employees are trained to properly ride a Ducati motorcycle. This has become one of the company's signature experiences and a major point of attraction for new hires. It signals the importance and obsession with the bike which is at the heart of the Ducati brand.

> **To conclude, we would like to share some thoughts**
>
> Employees are human beings with their own value system and needs. If they sense that the employee engagement efforts are genuine and authentic, they will more likely respond by engaging with the brand and acting in line with the brand. However, they are typically very sensitive to being manipulated and controlled, which might impact their behaviour adversely.

CUSTOMER ENGAGEMENT

Moving away from an understanding of brand building with customers that is founded on intrusive and manipulative communication approaches like the classical TV ad, companies need to reassess how best to engage with customers.

First of all, there are "natural" points of interaction between the company and the customer that occur as a result of doing business together (e.g. walking into a bank to open an account); these interaction points can be used for customer engagement by making them more appealing and differentiating.

Then, there are interaction points that are created solely to engage customers (e.g. an event or a PR stunt). These need to

---

[18] Erickson, T.J. and Gratton, L., What it means to work here, *Harvard Business Review*, March 2007: 1–10.

walk the fine line between being intrusive (like a pop-up ad) and welcoming (like a newsletter with appropriate and informative content). Companies are becoming more creative with these interaction points, both online and offline.

The opportunities to engage with customers are numerous, and creativity seems to be rewarded. One thing companies need to keep in mind, however, is that authenticity and transparency are key underlying drivers of whether an initiative will work or not. For example, sending your employees into the streets of New York asking passers-by to take a picture with their new mobile phone might not be the way to go, Sony.

Employing a multitude of different vehicles and channels will be key to the success of customer engagement, allowing customers to self-select the most suitable way to engage.

As discussed in Chapter 2, online customer engagement will become more and more important. Activities that invite the customer to engage at their own discretion, that are non-intrusive and genuinely interesting, will have a far greater chance of succeeding than strategies that simply take the offline print or TV ad online. It is very likely that companies will finally shift their marketing budgets such as to reflect the way media is actually consumed – making online an increasing contributor.

Blogs, online communities and social networking will likely be developed further by new technology that will emerge, but for the time being, they need to be integrated into every customer engagement programme. However, fake blogs ("flogs") that hide the commercial affiliation between the blogger and the corporation and pretend to be created by objective third parties will be damaging to brand (e.g. the exposed Wal-Mart travelogue that followed two hippies around the US as they parked their van in Wal-Mart car parks and raved about their service and food). Mobile phones are increasingly becoming a way to reach out to customers, but it is unclear at this point whether customers find it intrusive or engaging.

Connective brands engage customers along the loyalty pathway

The loyalty pathway is a well-established tool to describe a customer's journey from first contact with a product or brand all the way to purchase and loyalty. As customers move along this pathway and learn about the brand, their engagement and willingness to purchase increases (see Figure 3.14).

Companies can therefore tailor their engagement programme to the various phases of the loyalty pathway. It is important to understand that a customer engagement programme might help the customer move from one phase of the pathway into the next; however, there are also other factors that might have that same effect but are not under the control of the company or brand. For example, a customer might move from familiarity to consideration (of buying) for a number of reasons, including more information on the brand, an endorsement by a respected friend, more money to spend because of a promotion, or a great new product launch. By the same token, customers can also move down along the pathway, for example because the have heard bad things about the product quality, because a competitor launched a better product, because they no longer need the product due to a change of circumstances, or because they disliked the way the company interacted with them.

The fact that customers can move up *and* down along the loyalty pathway emphasises the need for continuous engagement. As companies track where the majority of their customers and potential customers sit on or move to the loyalty pathway (e.g. through identifying major drop-offs in conversion rates along the purchasing funnel), they can prioritise engagement activities accordingly.

As each phase along the loyalty pathway is characterised by a particular customer mindset and also indicates the degree of

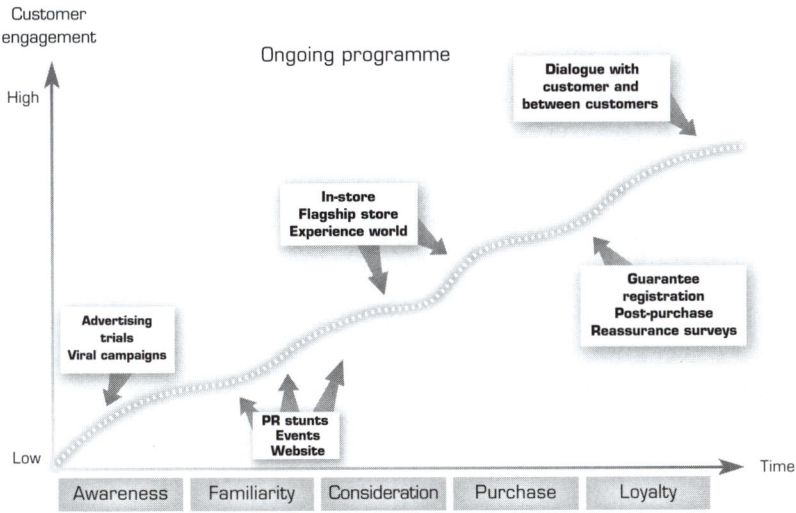

Figure 3.14 Customer engagement along the loyalty pathway

engagement, different ways of engaging are more welcome and more appealing.

Connective brands develop a systematic and strategic approach for customer engagement that caters to different phases of the loyalty pathway.

In the *awareness building phase*, brands need to get noticed by a large number of potential customers. While some brands achieve this without advertising, e.g. Google or Zara, others still rely heavily on advertising. As already pointed out earlier, advertising is less and less effective as a means of generating meaningful connections. However, it can still be very effective for creating awareness.

Connective brands make sure that their brand principles and brand promise are reflected in each element of the customer engagement programme. Ads that seek differentiation and attention at all costs without actually reinforcing the brand message will not engage the customer in the intended way. For example,

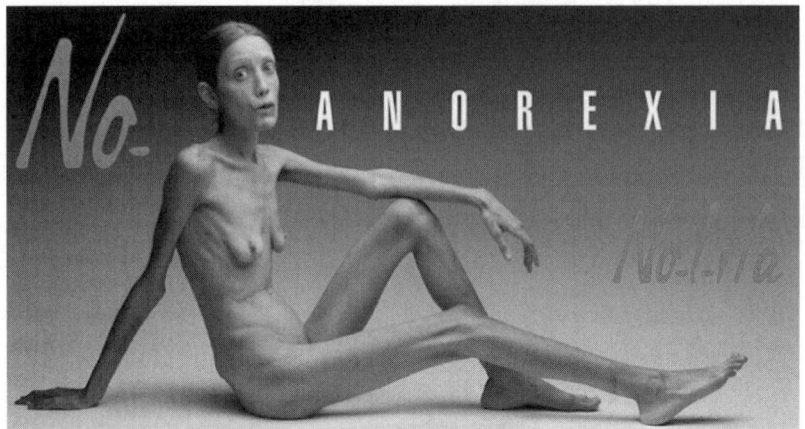

Figure 3.15 Shock-ad No-l-ita!

in autumn 2007, Italian fashion brand No-l-ita launched its "No-Anorexia" ad campaign (see Figure 3.15) shot by shock photographer Oliviero Toscani who was also responsible for the controversial Benetton ad campaigns of the 1980s and 1990s, including dying AIDS patients, a kissing nun and priest, a new born baby with the umbilical cord, and many more.

The No-Anorexia campaign was launched just in time for the opening of Fashion Week in Milano and – backed by the Italian Ministry of Health – officially aimed to draw public attention to eating disorders. While shock has been proven to raise awareness,[19] it is less clear what it does to customer engagement beyond the initial exposure. Very likely, this ad raises expectations for No-l-ita not only to draw attention to but also *to address* the issue of eating

---

[19] Dahl, D.W., Frankenberger, K.D. and Manchanda, R.V., Does it pay to shock? Reactions to shocking and nonshocking advertising content among university students, *Journal of Advertising Research*, 43, 3, 2003: 268–280. Using shock in advertisement is a trend so prolific that it even has its own name, yobbo advertising, which is about shocking the audience by whatever means it needs.

disorders. If they are able to meet these expectations, this could be a highly effective strategy for customer engagement; however, if it proves to be only a disruptive strategy to catch attention, it will most likely result in customer backlash.

Building *familiarity* can be achieved through a multitude of activities, most likely a combination of offline and online media. For example, the website typically is a great source of information if customers want to learn more about a brand. Therefore, the website also needs to reflect the brand promise and brand principles, in terms of design, layout, look-and-feel, user-friendliness, appeal, etc. For example, if customers of the No-l-ita brand want to find out more about their involvement in addressing eating disorders, they would naturally go to the corporate website. While the corporate website has an opinion poll assessing whether or not viewers are in favour of the campaign (last time we checked, of the 6000 viewers 78% were in favour[20]), there is no additional information on anorexia. This may discredit the efforts of the campaign and reduce customer engagement.

Sponsorship is an activity that has gained in importance in trying to engage customers. Connective brands understand the contextual values a sponsorship programme can provide and select their sponsorship activities in order to maximise support of the brand promise. For example, Red Bull, the famous Austrian energy drink, sponsors extreme sports like air racing, ski jumping, base jumping, etc. This allows them to connect with "cool" scenes and "in" sports, reinforcing the coolness and high energy of their product brand.

Connective brands aggregate sponsorship activities and develop strategic frameworks that avoid fragmentation. Peter Mayer, Director Sponsoring at WWP, an Austrian sport sponsorship consulting firm owned by famous skiers Harti Weirather and Hanni Wenzel, says:

---

[20] As of 2 March 2008; www.nolita.it

We have observed at least two trends in the recent past – one, clients are concentrating their sponsorship activities into fewer and more targeted initiatives to improve impact and at the same time ensure better alignment with brand goals, and two, there is a noticeable shift with larger, more established firms to direct some of their sponsorship budgets away from sports and towards both the CSR arena and activities with an educational or science/research related focus.

CSR can in fact be another way to engage with customers. However, this should not be the primary motivation for undertaking a CSR initiative. As discussed earlier, CSR programmes only have positive impact on employees, customers, and other stakeholders, if they are genuine and pervade the organisation. CSR can be an effective way to increase customer engagement also for low involvement categories. For example, soaps and shower gels typically would be characterised as low involvement, but the Dove "Real Beauty" campaign and programme – aimed at breaking down stereotypes and helping women everywhere to realise their own inner beauty – have facilitated entirely new dimensions of customer engagement.

Many of the traditional programmes for building familiarity can still be applied in today's environment; however, they might have to be augmented with online activities. For example, press releases, news, events, white papers, conferences, trade fares, etc. all help to learn more about the brand; however, connective brands need to allow for customers to use different media to get to the same information. Customers who could not attend an event might like to see the video clip online; customers who want to read the white paper might subscribe to the newsletter or download it directly from the website, etc. Linking all activities, also online and offline, is very important in all phases of the loyalty pathway, as already demonstrated in the No-l-ita example earlier.

In the *consideration* phase, customers are thinking about purchasing the product and are evaluating a number of alternatives.

Depending on the nature of the product, this could be a spontaneous decision or there could be quite a lengthy research phase involved. In the latter case, customers might consult online forums to exchange information with other users and look for recommendations. Connective brands find a way to engage with customers even if the engagement is initiated by the customer; for example, some companies bring the conversation back into the offline world: "For example, Panasonic parks a truck in various retailer's parking lots that showcases its electronic products, and invites customers to experience the Panasonic brand. Those experiences create impressions and conversations," remarks Danielle Blumenthal, a brand expert and blogger.[21]

Many brands do still not engage with the many social conversations that happen online and contribute to the development of their brands. Failing to engage in these activities could lead to the development of a parallel brand which would ultimately fragment and dilute the intended brand promise.

But it is not only the online world that can create such sentiments. Lonsdale, a high quality clothing company founded in London (UK) in 1960, was discovered by right-wing extremists for one reason: if a jacket is carefully placed over a LONSDALE T-shirt, it reveals only the letters NSDA; one letter short of NSDAP, the German language acronym for Hitler's Nazi Party. The more popular Lonsdale became with its unwanted fans, the more its reputation got tarnished with associations of racism and fascism, in particular in the Netherlands, Belgium and Germany.

The negative impact on the brand was considerable: many representatives in the affected countries, for example the German mail order company Quelle, refused to stock Lonsdale. Then Lonsdale launched a counterattack – they got involved in several

---

[21] Blumenthal, D., Sneak preview: new John Wiley book on branding, Jan. 2008, accessed: http://blumenthalonbranding.blogspot.com/2008/01/sneak-preview-new-john-wiley-book-on.html

anti-racist initiatives, sponsored an African soccer team that played under the slogan "Lonsdale loves all colours", and actively distanced itself from the "wrong" target group by cancelling contracts with dealers who were directly associated with the right-wing scene. It looks like Lonsdale has won the battle – representatives of anti-racism initiatives in Eastern Germany reported incidences of right-wing extremists burning Lonsdale clothes.[22]

The case of Lonsdale demonstrates the importance of staying in touch with the various brand dialogues that are going on outside the company. Connective brands use customer engagement as a way to anticipate such developments and proactively address these issues.

Arthritis Ireland, the national charity dedicated to improving the quality of life of people with arthritis, found another interesting way of engaging with their customers: they worked with the creators of one of Ireland's most popular soap operas, *Fair City*, to write arthritis into the script of the show. "Arthritis is still a condition that is not fully understood by the general public," said CEO John Church. "Most people believe that only the elderly can get arthritis. However, that is not true. We have worked with the producers of *Fair City* to develop a story line where one of the characters develops a form of osteo-arthritis. It will be very educational and will hopefully raise people's awareness and willingness to donate to the cause."

In-store engagement is another important category of customer engagement, important for both the *consideration and purchasing phase*. Whether in a brand-owned store, a retailer's store, or a flagship store, they all provide opportunities for companies to engage with the customer. For example, Manner, the famous Viennese wafer maker, was looking for ways to engage with their customers. Although the brand has acquired cult status in Austria,

---

[22] Flacke, M., Lonsdale loves all colours, *Stern*, 30 Sep. 2004, accessed: http://www.stern.de/lifestyle/mode/?id=530510

BRAND FRAMEWORK 193

Figure 3.16 Manner and its stores

there is very little interaction between the customer and the organisation behind the brand; this is primarily because Manner was sold exclusively through third parties for more than 100 years. Understanding the important shift in customer–brand interactions, Otto Riedl, Head of PR and also great-grandson of one of the founders, created the first flagship store in Vienna. Since the Manner brand is all about conveying a mixture of Viennese kitsch and tradition, that is exactly what the store exudes. "Engaging" are not only the sweets but also the wide variety of souvenirs ranging from T-shirts to backpacks to umbrellas, all in the characteristic and typical salmon shade of pink.

Nivea, the popular German beauty and body care brand from Beiersdorf, has taken a similar route to engaging with customers. They built "Nivea House" which offers beauty treatments, spas, and Nivea products on three floors, allowing customers to get enveloped in the world of Nivea experience.

The product itself and product packaging are very powerful ways of engaging customers. For example, innocent drinks not only make delicious "tasty little things", they also have very

Figure 3.17 Nivea House

engaging product labels that invite their customers to give them a ring on the "banana phone" to have a chat and be entertained. The banana phone is not a hotline, it is designed as a way to break down the barrier between the customer and the company, a way to engage customers more deeply. Calling the banana phone, the nice people on the other end might tell a joke, sing a song or simply share what's going on. innocent also invites customers to "pop into" Fruit Towers, their lofty headquarters in Shepherd's Bush, London, if they are ever in the area.

The actual experience of consuming the product or using the product is one of the single most important ways to engage with the customer. Guarantees, product registration schemes, labels to ease post-purchase cognitive dissonance are all ways to engage with the customer directly after the purchase and can combine online and offline initiatives.

Once customers are becoming more *loyal*, they are starting to engage more deeply with the brand. This is the phase where customer engagement turns into a meaningful dialogue between brand and customer. For example, customers in the sporting industry tend to be enthusiastic and passionate about their sporting equipment and like to contribute to developing new products. Companies can engage this creativity either online or offline. The same is true for online communities that involve machines and more or less technical goods such as espresso and coffee makers. The customers in these communities like to "tinker" and often exchange ideas on how to improve the performance of the underlying product with very simple changes. Connective brands find a way to engage these customers not only to work with the ideas of product improvement and product innovation, but also to build meaningful relationships with them. It is important to understand that online communities have their own set of rules and employees who barge into online conversations without understanding these rules will very quickly create negative brand impact.

Loyalty cards have been around for a long time and exist in many different ways: there are account cards for single providers (like the Boots card), loyalty cards combined with credit cards (e.g. Lufthansa Credit Card), cards that bundle the benefits of a number of different providers (like the Payback card in Germany or Nectar in the UK), etc. The principle is always the same, though – customers collect points with every purchase which they can redeem against cash, special offers, or even donate to charities.

The question is whether loyalty cards work in the context of brand building or not. Are they an effective way to build and maintain engagement? Do they really result in loyalty as their name suggests?

Caroline Papadatos, Chief Knowledge Officer for the AIR MILES Reward Program and Alliance Data Loyalty Services, explains:

> Depending on the loyalty strategy and market conditions, retailers who launch a loyalty scheme usually look for either a lift in customer acquisition, same store sales growth or holding EBITDA and/or revenue stable in the face of strong competitive pressures. If a company does it well, they create an experience for their customer that is

aligned with their needs and wants. Companies invest at a level that is commensurate with that customer's present and future value.

What are loyalty cards good for?

At one level, they replace the sort of personal service provided by the old Mom-and-Pop store who knew their partners' names, knew whether they had kids or not, knew which sort of pears they preferred – and therefore gave a pear away for free here and there or offered a product at discount prices. This is hardly possible for companies in today's anonymous shopping world. And yet to turn customers into loyal customers it is crucial to know what they want and like. Customers want to feel appreciated and expect added value for repeated patronage. This can either be offered through instant discounts or give-aways. The prerequisite of such a "quality strategy" is to know what customers really want. Loyalty cards are able to deliver such data.

In the long term, retailers will have to focus more on the ability of loyalty cards as a source of collecting customer data to help personalise the shopping experience, rather than on their original function as discounting cards.[23] It will help target customers with relevant information and products.

However, says the warning of Papadatos, companies need to know how to collect, analyse and transfer data effectively: "Loyalty programmes are a device to collect behavioural data which can be used to define pricing, to define locations, range of products, and much more – in theory. In practice most marketers do not fully utilise the data. In fact, most companies do not recognize the full value of this data – there is still a long way to go."

---

[23] Davies, F., Points mean prizes, Extended Retail Solutions, no date indicated: 130–132, accessed: http://www.gdspublishing.com/icpdf/ers/gds3.pdf

CASE STUDY: ARAL – THE LARGEST FILLING STATION NETWORK IN GERMANY

Imagine you are the marketing manager of a filling station company and responsible for developing loyalty programmes: what a difficult task! Especially today when you feel pure horror as the numbers of the small digital display soar up and the euros disappear in a small dark hole.

BP's Aral has the largest filling station network in Germany. If trust were an indicator of the degree of loyalty, then BP's Aral is a success story: with approximately 2400 stations and roughly 600 million customer contacts each year. Aral has a market share of around 23%. "We won the most Trusted Brand Award 2008 presented by *Reader's Digest*, one of the most widely read journals in Europe. This is the seventh time in a row," explains Dirk Sauer, Brand Manager of Aral. Also the readers of the journal "*Auto, Motor and Sport*" have rated Aral as one of the best known and best liked brands in the fuels category in 2008 for the third time in a row. Asked for the secret of their success, Sauer answered:

> Among many other initiatives, we commenced our cooperation with the German loyalty card provider programme, PAYBACK in 2006. We have two types of cards, one is the regular PAYBACK card with which customers earn PAYBACK points at the service stations when making fuel, car wash and shop purchases.

Figure 3.18 Aral – largest filling station network in Germany

These are redeemable with any of the 17 programme partners. The PAYBACK plus card has an additional payment function. I believe this programme helps to communicate and positively transmit our brand values exceptionally well. Hence we have seen an increase in our brand image since 2006 and the launch of the PAYBACK scheme at Aral. It even exceeds our prior "collecting points" scheme in many ways. Both in terms of sustainability and getting deeper customer insight the PAYBACK participation is the better solution for us.

How the Aral loyalty card reinforces its brand values

The Aral brand values are *Genuine – Together – In-Touch*. Sauer explains:

> The value *Genuine* is a mark of our personality. The customers are more critical than ever. They do not want an advertisement that promises too much. The loyalty card sends a clear message: the more money you spend on our forecourts or in our shops the more you will be rewarded. This is the promise – no more, no less; the card is simple to use, everybody knows how they work. We know that customers quickly recognize brands that do not fulfil their promises. Customers make quick decisions which have long-term consequences. If a brand does not keep its promise customers are usually not up for giving a second chance – not in our competitive market anyway.
>
> The value *Together* reflects an attitude through which we aim to reach joint goals. Acting together ties our employees together which is the basis for outperforming our already very high standards. This will ultimately benefit the development of strong relationships with our business partners. Our loyalty card is a good example of a holistic approach as well: it combined our different ways to reward customers into one, easy-to-understand loyalty scheme.
>
> The last value is about being *in touch*. That we are close to our customers is shown by the high density of filling stations. Closeness also refers to the way we communicate with our customers: through commercials, through ad material shown at the

filling stations or personally. The loyalty card enables such close communication with our customers – we know what they prefer, where they buy and how. We use this information to design our convenience stores, make decisions about the product range we offer, and many more. It is really the little details that count and make customer experience a worthwhile one. For instance, our data showed that there is an increasing portion of women who visit our filling stations. That is something we need to keep in my mind for future marketing activities.

Data resulting from customer satisfaction research which is measured quarterly shows that Aral meets their clients' needs by offering an attractive combination of product and service. In terms of points redemption Aral has seen two developments. Sauer clarifies:

> Firstly, you will always need to have an attractive reward palette on-site so that customers can see and instantly redeem their points for the products they desire. Secondly, we found out that collection periods of customers are longer in the Payback scheme than in a single-partner scheme. They often collect their points for months and months without redeeming.

Some brands manage to create a myth or cult like the Ducati motorcycle brand. In these cases, the customer engagement programme extends far beyond the actual product in order to feed the user culture. This could include the meeting of other owners in a convention, a museum of bike racing, bike racing events, meeting a racing legend, etc. See Chapter 4 for more detail on the Ducati case.

Connective brands make customer engagement a priority and do not outsource such an important brand building element to third parties. For example, large consumer brand companies sometimes entrust parts of their stakeholder engagement to their PR firms. This has the effect that stakeholder engagement is reduced to a superficial communications exercise.

Similar to the employee engagement programme, several approaches of segmenting customers can be used to design a customer engagement programme. In addition to the loyalty pathway discussed above, traditional segmentation approaches (e.g. demographic, media consumption, attitudinal) may be used as a basis to identify interaction points for engaging customers and are an effective means of doing so.

Engaging other stakeholders

Beyond employees and customers, a number of additional audiences need to be engaged that vary by industry sector, nature of the brand promise, particular goals, and specific situation a company or brand is in. For example, in the oil industry, a critical stakeholder group would be NGOs and special interest groups who are very critical of and vocal about everything an oil company does. If an oil company claims to be "green" like BP, this will further amplify the need to engage NGOs and special interest groups so that they can validate the claims. Or if an oil company just had an accident that resulted in a major oil spill, this might be the case as well.

NGOs

With the growing CSR imperative, many companies have started to engage NGOs and special interest groups by inviting them to work on joint projects, be it in order to validate the authenticity of their CSR efforts or to mollify their critical voices.

Partners and suppliers

Yet other companies have started to engage their suppliers and partners more actively in order to ensure that they also contribute to their brand delivery. For example, Aveda works with their suppliers and partners to ensure that they keep to the same environmental standards. They are also prepared to pull the plug if they don't change their practices; Aveda allegedly retracted all ads from the *Yoga Journal* when they found out that they no longer used recycled paper.[24]

Retailers

LEGO, the Danish toy company, is engaging their retail partners through brand training, making them wear LEGO T-Shirts and work with them on joint CSR initiatives.

Shareholders and financial community

Another important stakeholder group are shareholders and the financial community. They generally thrive on information and transparency, therefore adequately engaging them means giving them access to the CEO and the senior management.

Engaging other stakeholders can serve a multitude of different reasons:

- To offset negative associations (e.g. in the case of stigma industries or post scandals)
- To communicate and anchor the brand promise
- To build relationships and loyalty
- To get feedback and information

Multi-stakeholder engagement

Sometimes it can be beneficial to bring together several stakeholder groups in one initiative. For example, Nestlé CEO Peter

---

[24] How Aveda is Changing the Complexion of Magazines, accessed: http://makower.typepad.com/joel_makower/2005/10/how_aveda_is_ch.html

Brabeck-Letmathe talks about the pressures resulting from Nestlé's quest to analyse how the company affects the world and could operate in a sustainable manner. "You are, as a CEO, under pressure from 180 degrees – fundamentalists on one hand and fundamentalists on the other. You have financial fundamentalists wanting a say in how your company is run. On the other side you have social fundamentalists who say the company should not make a profit and that the company is only here for social values."[25] Multi-stakeholder engagements could be a solution to this dilemma.

Multi-stakeholder engagements of companies, governments and NGOs can contribute to greater transparency of the value chain, satisfying customers desire to know, for example, how and where a product is produced or social innovation that benefits both the company and society through new products or services that address CSR issues.

An excellent combination are programmes that allow to engage both customers and employees at the same time. For example, Maggi, the German provider of ready-made meals and the famous liquid seasoning of the same name, has created a cooking studio where employees and customers meet to eat, to cook, to shop, and to discuss. This provides employees with the opportunity to engage with customers and get direct feedback. At the same time, it provides customers with the opportunity to engage not only with the product, but also with the employees behind the product brand. This is a mutually enriching experience (see Chapter 4 for case details).

The BMW Group expects their marketers to seamlessly transfer between their three brands including BMW, MINI and Rolls-

---

[25] Interviews/Q&As: The big interview – Peter Brabeck-Letmathe, Nestlé CEO – Values and the value of water, Ethical Corporation Interview, 10 Oct. 2006, accessed: http://www.ethicalcorp.com/content.asp?ContentID=4544

Royce in order to keep them engaged and also to ensure that they are all aware of what makes each brand unique and different. Not surprisingly, their brand training is very exciting.

The BMW Group Brand Academy is an institution designed around management seminars where a mix of people from within the company, dealerships and agencies experience the three brands first hand through all five senses. For example, learning about the MINI brand might involve a dialogue about "What makes a MINI a MINI?", the experience of the "go-cart" feeling typical of the MINI, getting to know the MINI customers by walking around in a room decorated in a style deemed typical for MINI owners[26] and making a movie from a library of clips that are tailored to express the brand essence. All activities are designed to engage participants in a process to discover and understand the brands and what makes them so unique. The BMW Group Brand Academy is quite popular and is almost constantly booked, although it is a voluntary activity. So far over 10 000 people have gone through the Brand Academy in Munich. In addition, there are mobile Brand Academy units in the markets to promote a uniform brand perception worldwide.

Conclusion

There is no limit to creativity when trying to engage employees, customers, and other key stakeholders. However, the programmes need to reflect and embody the brand promise and brand principles. In order to build strong brands, stakeholder engagement needs to be genuine, non-intrusive and interactive. Engaging

---

[26] Grauel, R., Marketing-Kolumne: Gebrauchsanweisungen zu Lehrplänen, Brandeins, Dec. 2006, accessed: http://www.brandeins.de/home/inhalt_detail.asp?id=2172&MenuID=8&MagID=81&sid=su6624966162952

employees and customers is an absolute priority for all connective brands; additional stakeholder groups can be prioritised based on business and brand needs.

> **Key questions to be answered**
>
> - How can employees be engaged in a meaningful relationship, considering their diversity?
> - How can customers be engaged in a meaningful relationship given the emergence of new media tools?
> - Which other stakeholders should be engaged and how?
> - Which multi-stakeholder engagement programmes should be pursued?

BRAND BUILDING THROUGH ALIGNMENT OF PROCESSES AND STRUCTURES

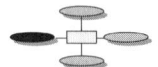

In order to enable consistency in the delivery of the brand promise across all stakeholder groups, all enabling processes and structures have to be changed or revamped in a way that creates the intended brand experience for all key stakeholders. Brand experience is ultimately defined by the sum of all interactions a stakeholder has with an organisation. Considering our networked world and the blurring of boundaries between stakeholders (e.g. an employee may also be a customer and a shareholder at the same time), it is important to define consistent brand experiences not only for the customer, but for all key stakeholders.

A tool that is often used in consulting practice to define and improve customer experience is the plotting of the so-called stakeholder journey. The idea is very simple – on a large piece of paper, all typical interaction points between the customer and the organization are plotted in chronological sequence (as much as possible), usually using four phases; interactions before a product is bought or a contract is signed, interactions relating to the actual purchasing process or contracting phase, then the product experience, contract fulfilment or project delivery, and finally interactions in the post-purchase or post-delivery phase. This tool works for all industries, be it B2B (business to business) or B2C (business to customer), and is very intuitive but powerful. An example of such a stakeholder journey is shown in Figure 3.19. As you can see, it is possible to plot the interaction points not only on the time axis, but also against their power to add or subtract brand equity. This is an easy way to prioritise interaction points by stakeholder relevance.

Take, for example, an IT services firm with expertise in installing and tailoring software for business clients on a global basis. The pre-contract phase could start with a booth at a trade fare where the IT firm presents their competences and skills. Many industries have a couple of trade fairs that are "the" exhibition to be seen at, making the interaction a key one. Next, a potential customer might check out the IT provider's website, learning more about who they are, what they do, what they have done, and getting a feel for what they stand for. They might then call up some peers to see if they have worked with this firm to get a reference. Depending on how much they value the opinion of peers, this could also be a very important interaction point. Next, the potential customer might choose to order some marketing materials relevant to what they are looking for. Timeliness and friendliness of the response, the actual collateral and quite possibly a proactive follow-up could all be part of this interaction point.

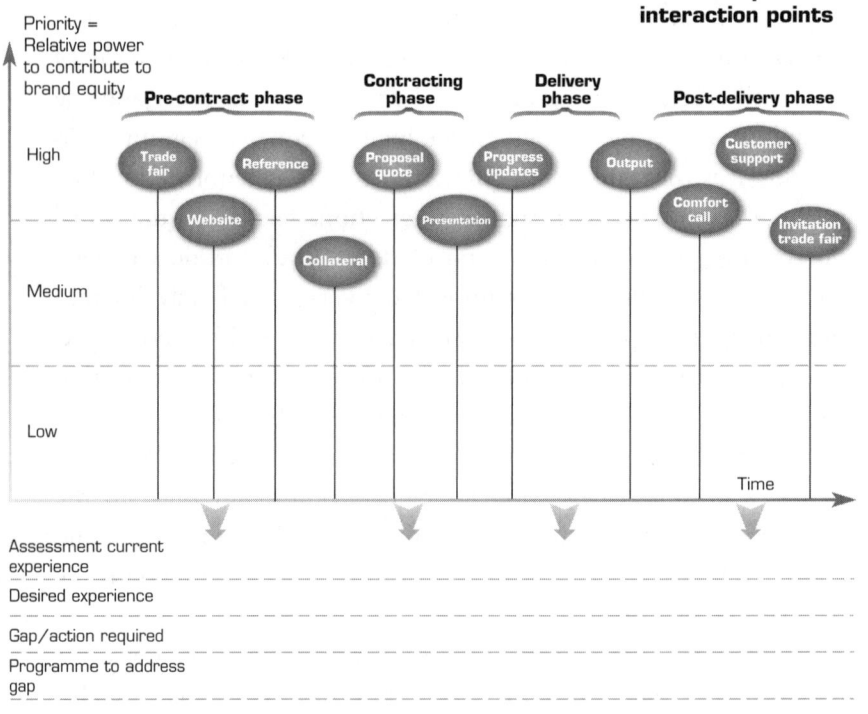

Figure 3.19 Stakeholder journey

If the customer then asks for a proposal (or a quote), it will be important that all documents are in order, the prices and solutions offered are competitive, and the negotiations are pleasant. Once the customer has agreed to sign a contract, the actual contracting process might constitute another important interaction point. At this point the potential customer has turned into a customer. Now the phase of project delivery starts. This phase will have many interaction points, starting with kick-off meetings, progress updates, actual work being carried out, workshops, presentations, and a final output which ideally is on time, on budget and to specification. If not, expectation management would have hopefully prevented a big interaction point where the ugly truth finally surfaces. After conclusion of the project, many firms actually end the interaction with their customer right there. However, post-purchase or post-delivery interaction points can be of tremendous value to both the customer and the provider. In the case of the IT firm, the global project leader might give the key client a comfort call to discuss how things went, what went really well and what could have been improved. Inevitably, there will be a point where the customer needs to call customer support. At this interaction point it will be really important that the support provided is fast, efficient and friendly. Then, when the annual trade fair rolls around, the customer might get an invitation as a VIP to come and see what's new. Of course, the actual stakeholder journey will be much more detailed than this high-level summary.

Once the typical stakeholder journey is plotted, a number of analyses can be conducted to work towards the desired brand experience blueprint:

- First, a holistic view across all touchpoints is taken. Keeping in mind the nature of interaction the brand wants to create, superfluous touchpoints are removed (some can be annoying, e.g. several points of contact in order to get the contract sorted) and missing ones are added (bearing in mind that they

have to be welcome and appealing) in order to improve stakeholder engagement.
- Then, for each interaction point, the current stakeholder experience is assessed. This should be a description plus an evaluation.
- Next, for each touchpoint the "ideal" or "desired" stakeholder experience is described. This should be a creative exercise where different teams can think about how the brand can be manifested in each interaction point. It is amazing how employees get into this exercise; it really helps them to understand what the brand is all about and at the same time gives them a sense of creating and designing their own brand expressions in a way that would make them proud, engaged and committed.
- Finally, programmes are designed that can or could close the gap in each interaction point between actual and desired stakeholder experience. For practical reasons, it sometimes pays to focus on high relevance interaction points and quick wins in a first step.

This exercise is repeated for all key stakeholders; sometimes it makes sense to segment stakeholder groups further and to create a separate journey for them. For example, if a company serves a number of clearly defined customer segments with very different needs, it pays to draw a separate journey for each segment.

- The last step in this process is to bring all the stakeholder journeys together and to look for consistency. Now you also know why we recommended to do this on large sheets of paper! Looking for interdependencies and cross-checking all journeys against each other is necessary in order to avoid contradictions and maximise alignment. When satisfied with the alignment, programmes can be bundled together, e.g. by impacted department(s) and integrated. For each programme or programme bundle an activity plan and/or business case has

BRAND FRAMEWORK

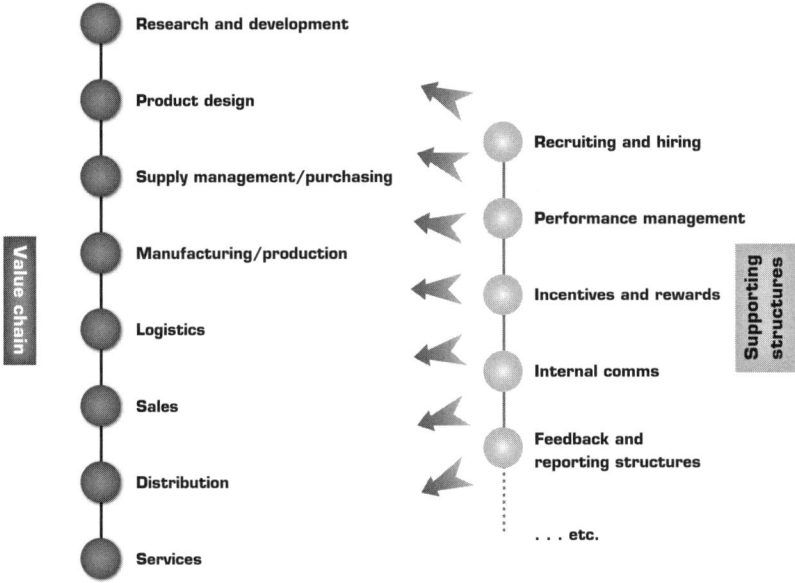

Figure 3.20 Enabling processes and structures

to be created, detailing expected timing, resourcing, budgets, key responsibilities and anticipated impact.

In the case of the IT service company, major programme bundles could include stakeholder engagement (e.g. more seminars, more keynote speeches by their thought leaders, more white papers published), product development (e.g. a more modular approach to programmes delivered), logistics, flow of information within the company (e.g. creating an intranet for programmers to exchange tips and tricks), hiring and recruiting (e.g. only experienced programmers who love to travel and have an affinity with the company culture), incentive and reward structures (e.g. incorporate customer satisfaction), contracting (e.g. reducing legalese) and customer service (e.g. operating on the basis that the first point of contact resolves the issue). See also Figure 3.20 for examples of relevant processes along the value chain or supporting structures.

210 CONNECTIVE BRANDING

Key questions to be answered

- Which interaction points are there? Which ones are most impactful on employees, customers and other stakeholders?
- Which processes and structures need to be aligned to improve stakeholder experience?

PART III

CRITICAL SUCCESS FACTORS FOR MAKING IT HAPPEN

Chapter 4 Practical applications – stakeholder engagement

We look at issues encountered when engaging employees, customers, and other key stakeholders across cultures and situations. We discuss the critical success factors and illustrate key points with case studies.

Chapter 5 Practical applications – the process of alignment

Here we turn our attention to the challenges of aligning brand promise and brand experience. We summarise critical success factors and illustrate key points with case studies.

CHAPTER 4

PRACTICAL APPLICATIONS – STAKEHOLDER ENGAGEMENT

In Chapter 3, we introduced a framework for how to build connective brands. When applying this framework in practice, brands and businesses are faced with a multitude of different challenges and issues. In Chapters 4 and 5 we will explore some of these in depth.

We will focus on critical success factors, present illustrative examples and case studies, and provide some tools that will be helpful in framing and addressing the issues particular to your own business, brand, and competitive context.

As discussed in Chapter 3, the two key drivers of brand equity in the connective brand framework are (i) the strength of the emotional connection with key stakeholders (engagement), and (ii) the alignment of brand promise and experience across all stakeholder groups. These relate to the elements that define a brand and facilitate its delivery. If a brand fails to connect with key

214 CONNECTIVE BRANDING

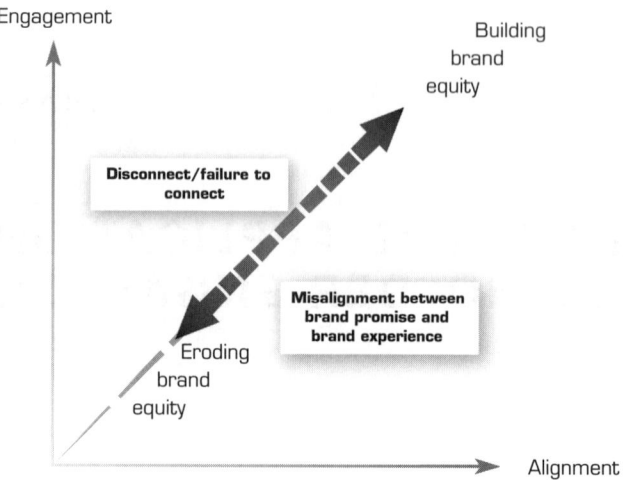

Figure 4.1 Key issues faced by connective brands

stakeholders and/or fails to align brand promise and brand experience, brand equity will erode (see Figure 4.1).

Brand alignment ensures that there is no disconnect between the brand promise and the actual brand experience. Over time,

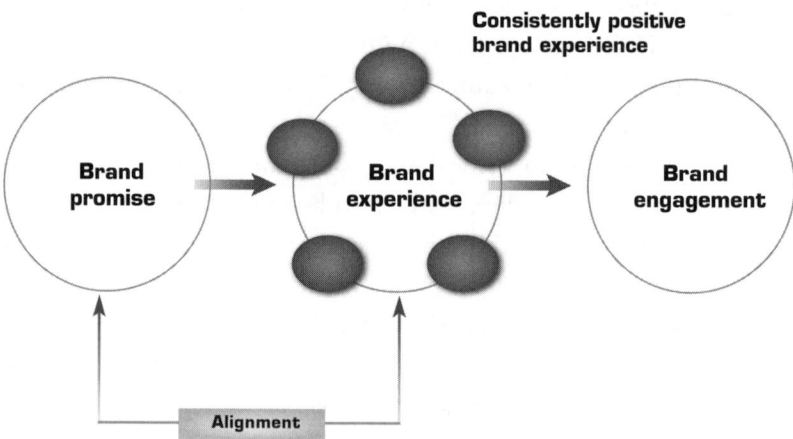

Figure 4.2 Conceptual model

consistent experience of positive interactions with the brand will gradually become increasingly emotional, before turning into brand engagement (see Figure 4.2).

We will first address stakeholder engagement in Chapter 4 and then the process of alignment in Chapter 5.

Creating and maintaining emotional connections with all employees, customers, and all other key stakeholders is a very challenging task. Not surprisingly, many brands encounter difficulties in this area.

EMPLOYEE ENGAGEMENT

In Chapter 3 we described the typical journey employees go through when starting to engage more deeply with an organisation or brand. As employees move from being informed, to understanding, embracing and eventually living the brand, their commitment to the brand and hence their willingness to enact the brand increase (see Figure 4.3). Each of these phases, however, has its own challenges and obstacles that need to be overcome.

In the following section we will first highlight a number of critical success factors, and then provide examples that are meant to inspire our leaders to master the issues particular to their business and brand.

As employees are moving through the different phases of engagement, a number of factors will determine both the speed and direction of the movement. First of all, personal circumstances may distract the employee (decreasing commitment and willingness to enact the brand) or strengthen the engagement; the same is true with any employee's basic affinity with the brand promise. Finally, the key interaction points between the employee and the brand can be disappointing or reinforcing, again driving engagement up or down.

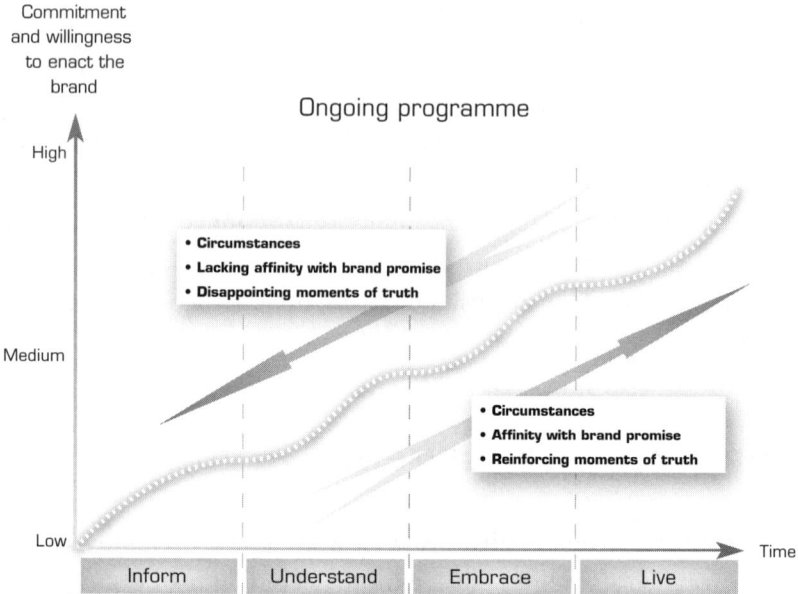

Figure 4.3 Employee engagement programme across phases

Critical success factor #1: Engaging top management

Some companies and brands are lucky enough to have brand-savvy top management. For those that do not, it is often up to the branding team to push the branding agenda up the list of management priorities. Although this may often seem like an uphill battle, it is the single most important critical success factor for employee engagement. Employees need to be inspired and motivated, and nobody can ignite this fire better than top management. If top management does not live the brand, employees will not either. Employees are typically the first to notice if top management lacks enthusiasm and conviction, which will negatively impact their morale and attitude towards the brand.

Figure 4.4 shows some simple statements to help determine how engaged top management is in the brand. Only if the major-

	I agree	Not sure	I agree	
Top management has a vague idea what the brand values really are	☐	☐	☐	Top management knows what the brand values are and communicates them explicitly and implicitly when interacting with employees
When the CEO speaks to employees he never mentions the brand	☐	☐	☐	When the CEO speaks to employees he talks about the brand and its importance
Top management does not seem to be particularly proud of the organisation, products/services or culture	☐	☐	☐	Top management makes it a point to demonstrate their commitment and pride at every possible opportunity
Top management hardly gets involved in branding decisions	☐	☐	☐	Top management drives all branding decisions
Branding is restricted to the middle management level	☐	☐	☐	The brand is represented on the board (e.g. CMO)
The annual report never mentions the brand	☐	☐	☐	There is an extensive brand section in the annual report
Getting budget for the brand is nearly impossible	☐	☐	☐	The brand is properly funded and has to meet strategic goals
Brand is seen as "fluff" and primarily communications based	☐	☐	☐	Brand is seen as a strategic asset and is anchored in business processes
Branding is dealt with when nothing else of importance is on the agenda	☐	☐	☐	Branding is seen as a strategic priority and part of the growth strategy

Check the box most applicable in each line

Figure 4.4 How engaged is top management?

ity of the boxes ticked is in the right-hand column, is top management truly engaged.

Living the brand and demonstrating that brand is "not negotiable"

CEO and top management need to demonstrate to employees that they care about the brand and become role models of enacting and transmitting brand values. There is no better way to motivate employees to live the brand than showing them that the brand is simply not negotiable. Every CEO and top management has to make difficult decisions. Sometimes they are more visible to employees and sometimes they stay within a close-knit circle; but every time such a decision is taken, it will communicate their stance towards the brand. Alex Batchelor, Marketing Manager at Royal Mail, points out: "Many brands set out their philosophy, their mission, etc. But living it is an entirely different challenge. Just like nobody sets out to be a bad father, it all usually starts with great intentions. In the end, it all comes down to making the right choices. Every decision that needs to be made translates into a choice – the choice to do the right thing or the choice to do the easy thing." This is exactly what it came down to at Orange, the UK mobile communications provider who was later acquired by France Telecom. Orange had entered an already crowded marketplace in 1994 but quickly built up a strong brand around the brand values of innovation and fairness. In particular the value of fairness was meant to set Orange apart from incumbent providers. One way the value of fairness manifested itself was a new way of billing – instead of using devised units, the standard industry practice at the time, Orange introduced "per second" billing which Orange believed was the most transparent and fairest way for the consumer. In addition, most mobile phone packages at the time offered free minutes which were rolled over into the next billing period if not used up; however, most providers would impose restrictions on how free minutes could be used, often resulting in the expiration of unused minutes which rendered them useless. By contrast, Orange's new billing scheme ensured that free minutes would always be used up first, without any restrictions, and also never expire. In 2004, Orange came under quite a bit of profit pressure and began identifying ways to save money or increase revenues. One of these initiatives determined that changing the roll-over minute policy could save Orange £30–40 million, thereby considerably easing the financial crisis they were in. It was suggested that they make the required changes, put the necessary fine print on the bottom of a letter to their customers, and not make a big deal out of it. Alex Batchelor, ex-Orange brand manager, recalls: "Orange had a very strong brand at the time. We *all* worked there because we believed in it. So not surprisingly, this idea of corrupting our value of fairness would not fly. Interestingly enough, it was a senior *finance* manager at the time who was the first to stand up for the brand and recommend we stick to our principles instead of compromising our biggest asset, our brand, for a short-term gain." This really demonstrated to everyone within Orange that they mean it when they talk about fairness and motivated employees across the entire organisation to live the brand. Sometimes, these little stories turn into corporate myths that become part of the social fibre of an organisation. They have the power to convey both the importance of branding in the organisation and the nature of brand values.

Brand decisions and projects

Engaging top management is also of critical importance when reviewing and redefining a brand. Lack of top management engagement can severely limit brand impact. This can be seen in the case of a UK-based international technology company which had a proactive and savvy branding team but a CEO who focused solely on technology and neither understood nor valued branding. After years of trying to persuade the CEO that the company could benefit greatly from investing in a brand repositioning project, the branding team was finally granted the funds and resources required to put a small project team in place and start the work. The branding project served three major goals:

- The company had grown through a number of significant acquisitions but integration of the various firms and cultures had never really come to fruition. A new brand was thus thought to serve as a vehicle to unite the separate cultures and facilitate integration.

- Partly due to the silo mentality and partly due to a general lack of direction, employee morale was low and needed a boost. A new brand was thought capable of injecting energy and motivation into the organisation.
- The company had low visibility and presence compared to other companies its size; again something the marketing team hoped to address with a new brand.

After thorough analysis of customers, employees, and other key stakeholders, as well as the competitive landscape and relevant market trends, the branding team defined new brand values, a brand essence and a brand vision. However, since the CEO was known not to be in touch with the brand, he had not been kept in the loop during the various stages of the project. When CEO sign-off could no longer be postponed, the branding team gathered once again for a meeting and looked at their brand proposal with the CEO's eyes. The proposed new brand contained some functional elements and some emotional elements and was quite aspirational in nature, requiring a departure from the current technology focus and a shift towards genuine customer centricity. It became apparent very quickly that nobody wanted to present the intended new brand to the CEO – partly in fear for their job and partly in fear for the project being stopped. So the branding team started to "adapt" the intended new brand to what they thought the CEO might want to hear and therefore likely approve, disregarding the fact that their brand proposal was based on rigorous analysis and solid business reasons. What was left of the bold, inspiring brand proposal was a diluted, generic concept that was focused heavily on functional aspects and did not present a (much needed) stretch for the organisation. The brand was signed off by the CEO, but needless to say, none of the three strategic goals were achieved. Worse, the CEO was affirmed in his view that branding is little more than wordsmithing and generally a waste of money.

This example is interesting on several dimensions. First, the situation where branding is not seen as worthy of CEO or top management attention is quite common. Unfortunately, this can lead to a vicious cycle where an erosion of talent in the branding department due to a lack of career prospects results in further downgrading of the brand's standing within the organisation. This cycle can often only be broken if leadership changes. Second, when finally granted the necessary resources the branding team did everything right – except engage the CEO from the outset and take the hard decisions early on. By postponing the decision making to the last possible point in time they had manoeuvred themselves into a corner. And lastly, none of the branding team members were willing even to present the original proposal to the CEO – their boldness had been reduced to a mere whisper when about to enter the lion's den. All this translated into a lost opportunity for the company to pull everyone together and push ahead of competition.

If the CEO or top management simply cannot be brought on board, no matter how hard the branding team tries, an alternative strategy has to be developed. One strategy the technology company in this example could have pursued is to find a powerful and brand-savvy sponsor outside the top management team who was willing to endorse the new brand and present it to the CEO.

Critical success factor #2: Engaging role models

The branding team carries significant responsibility as role models. Their enthusiasm for the brand, the product or service, the people, and the organisation needs to ignite excitement at all levels of the organisation. If *they* don't live the brand, then nobody else will. At Lacoste, the famous French polo shirt maker with the crocodile logo, the management is well aware of their responsibility to spark brand engagement. Stephanie Medioni, Global Marketing VP for Lacoste-Clothing, explains:

> We all are very excited about our products and very proud of them. We have been able to keep the same quality standard and brand promise for 75 years while also staying current and relevant. To me there is no doubt that you cannot ask your employees to give their best if the leadership is not proud and enthusiastic about what they produce. Therefore, the board of Lacoste should always have a "croc" on them. Of course, this is not always easy to do and sometimes requires a good deal of resourcefulness. For example, when I went to the Berlinale, I was determined to wear a polo shirt but still wanted to dress very elegantly. So I went for a black polo, combined with an elegant black skirt and silver shoes. I think it got the message across.

In some companies, founders play a significant role in defining, communicating, and evolving the brand promise, in particular if their personality has shaped the company and the brand. In companies where the founding fathers have long passed away, they are often kept "alive" through stories about how the company was founded. For instance, talking about the origin of the crocodile logo Lacoste himself liked to recount:

> The American press nicknamed me "The Alligator" after a bet that I made with the captain of the French Davis Cup team. He had promised me an alligator-skin suitcase if I won a match that was important to our team. The American public stuck to this nickname, which highlighted my tenacity on the tennis courts, never giving up my prey. So my friend Robert George drew me a crocodile which was embroidered on the blazer that I wore on the courts.[1]

Such stories nurture the brand and are an intuitive way for employees to engage with it.

Some companies still live by the values written down by their founders (for example, Marriott Corporation or Merck),[2] yet others resurrect them for advertising campaigns (for example, the

---

[1] www.lacoste.com
[2] Collins, J. and Porras, J., *Built to Last: Successful Habits of Visionary Companies*, New York: Collins Business Essentials, 2002.

current "Siemens Answers" campaign and the current Lacoste campaign). Founders who still run their large and successful enterprises usually can inject energy and motivation into the organisation, but often also raise questions and doubts about whether anyone will be able to fill their shoes one day. If a succession plan is not in place, this could create a significant void not only for the business, but also for the brand.

In smaller companies the role of the founder is typically even more pronounced. Very few smaller companies have a branding or marketing department and often the founder takes on these tasks intuitively and without much formal training. Successful founders tend to have a strong personality, and are authentic and very determined to implement their own values and vision, all traits which bode well with being a brand role model. For example, Josef Zotter, the founder of Austrian-based chocolate maker Zotter Schokoladen Manufaktur GmbH, produces hand-scooped chocolate with a kick. Some of Zotter's flavours are quite adventurous, like chocolate with banana curry or caramelised bacon bits. "Keeping an open mind is part of my own attitude towards life and has helped the chocolate creations to become a success," says Zotter. The chocolate producer currently employs 80 people and is one of the few European companies who produce in organic and fair quality. Zotter continues:

> I have always valued *Organic* and *Fairness* as two prerequisites of achieving sustainable business success. This is why we engage in several activities like working with Fair Trade[3] which we have established

---

[3] Fair Trade certification is a market-based model of international trade that benefits over one million farmers and farm workers in 58 developing countries across Africa, Asia and Latin America. Fair Trade certification enables consumers to vote for a better world with their dollars, simply by looking for the Fair Trade Certified label on the products they buy. Fair Trade principles include fair pricing, fair labour conditions, direct trade, democratic and transparent organisations, community development and environmental sustainability.

Figure 4.5 Chocolate role model Josef Zotter

in 2004, or the support of three cocoa cooperatives in Nicaragua with knowledge transfer. Our employees experience Fairness in the way they are treated. For instance, most of our workers are women with a family at home and of course we try to be as flexible as possible to make sure that both family and work can be combined. We embrace the value Organic in many different ways, from cooking with organic food in our canteen to eating out in organic restaurants for company events; the canteen will shortly also be equipped with utensils like flour mills and pasta machines which our employees can also use.

Critical success factor #3: Networked collaboration

Connective brands rely on the networking talent of the core branding team members. The core branding team does not work in isolation, but strives to continually expand and build on a network of brand enthusiasts and role models. As described above, these role models can be located on any hierarchy level and are often self-selected. For example, Helen Casey, Head of Brand with financial

STAKEHOLDER ENGAGEMENT 225

	I agree	Not sure	I don't agree
We have identified role models for all strategically important positions	☐	☐	☐
We have role models on all hierarchical levels of the company	☐	☐	☐
Our role models solicit feedback on brand engagement and brand alignment	☐	☐	☐
Our role models help to reduce anxiety and fears	☐	☐	☐
Our role models have access to detailed information about the brand promise and anchoring initiatives	☐	☐	☐
Our role models take every opportunity to discuss the brand promise	☐	☐	☐
Our role models know how the business strategy relates to the brand promise	☐	☐	☐
Our role models actively recruit more role models	☐	☐	☐
Our role models get together regularly to discuss what works and what doesn't	☐	☐	☐

Check the box most applicable in each line

Figure 4.6 Assessment of the role model network

services provider Old Mutual Group, says: "Based on my previous experience with implementing a branding initiative with Old Mutual in South Africa, you need to identify people with enthusiasm and to get them involved in what the brand is all about. Sometimes it happens that they identify themselves, through their own initiative." The development of such an informally appointed network is one of the crucial factors for anchoring brands within an organisation. In addition to self-selected role models it is also important to specifically engage opinion leaders and other influential employees across the company. Typically, these people serve as multipliers and add tremendous value to the network.

The questions in Figure 4.6 will give a good indication of the quality and nature of your role model network. If most answers are "not sure" or "I don't agree", you do not optimally leverage the role model potential inherent in your company.

Critical success factor #4: Building brands on simple and powerful ideas

For a large majority of employees the brand is not the key priority in their day-to-day tasks and responsibilities. When asking them to enact the brand, this often means adding extra effort or additional complexities to their daily routine. The likelihood of employees internalising the brand promise is not only driven by how attractive it is and how good the role models are; it is also driven by the extra effort required to absorb and implement it. Therefore, simple ideas and messages are most suitable for employee engagement. However, this can depend on the make-up of an organisation. For example, an engineering company comprised of technically focused employees, a manufacturing company with a large number of blue collar workers or a consulting company with conceptual thinkers will all vary with regard to how intuitive branding is for their employees – as well as the complexity of the brand promise itself. This reality needs to be considered when defining or redefining a brand promise. Simplicity is especially important in companies with flat hierarchies and a large number of contract, part-time and semi-skilled workers. This is, for example, very prevalent with large retail chains where employees constitute a major interaction point between customers and the brand, whether they are helping patrons find their way around the store, stock the shelves or operate the register. Austria-based XXXLutz, the world's second largest full-service furniture store chain, has been working hard to address this challenge. Thomas Saliger, Head of Marketing and Communications XXXLutz, explains:

The trick is to define the brand in a way that is simple, easy to understand, easy to communicate, easy to act upon and still able to be infused with emotions. This allows *all* employees, regardless of their hierarchy levels in the organisation, to live the brand. And only then will the brand become a behavioural guideline for the entire organisation. Our mission is to become the number 1 whilst staying light hearted [Translation: "mit Sonne im Herzen gemeinsam zur Nr 1"] – a very simple concept that all our employees are familiar with and can relate to. We also believe that we are XXXL, that we are great but can always improve, and that every day is a new beginning with new opportunities.

While Saliger concedes that employee engagement might be easier and more effective in the senior management realms, he also emphasises that continuous and disciplined work on all levels shows amazing results. Saliger explains:

Other key ingredients for successful branding are pride and self-confidence; our values are not only very simple, but also very

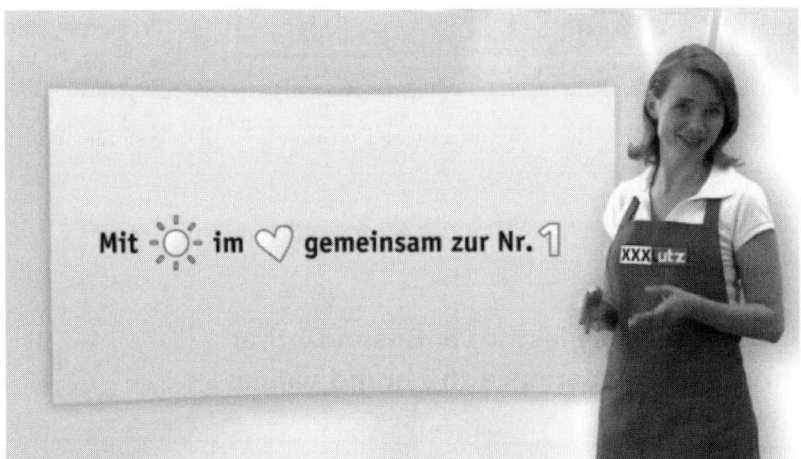

Figure 4.7 XXXLutz – our mission is to become the number 1 while staying light hearted

positive and very powerful. A shared belief system coupled with feeling valued will increase employee commitment and motivate employees to enact the brand and without making everybody sing anthems when they arrive at work every morning. Joke aside, but you do need to put in place a number of elements that demonstrate the importance of the brand to everyone. For example, in our case we do not hire senior people from the outside – we recruit them exclusively from within the company. By putting people through the ranks internally we make sure they are steeped in our culture and in our brand values. There is no greater tribute a company could pay to employee commitment.

While many companies are designing programmes that reward brand-conform behaviour, XXXLutz takes the stance that if a brand is truly lived within an organisation, brand conformity will follow automatically.

Figure 4.8 XXXLutz – Austria-based world's second largest full-service furniture store chain

Critical success factor #5: Ensuring that employees experience the brand values first hand

In order to enable employees to live and enact the brand promise, not only do they need to understand it; they need to embrace it.

Allowing employees to experience the brand first hand will facilitate the move from understanding the brand to embracing and living the brand.

The earlier case of Hollard insurance in South Africa demonstrates how effective it can be when management treats employees the way they expect employees to treat their customers. By adopting a "sorted" attitude towards employees they made it much easier for employees to adopt a "sorted" attitude towards customers.

First hand experience is particularly important in smaller companies where strong cultures are being formed more easily. For example, Germany-based Nostalgic was founded in 2003 and organises private or incentive self-drive trips with classic 1950s Alfa Romeo Spiders, primarily in Italy. Nostalgic promises its guests a taste of the glamorous Italian lifestyle of the 1950s. "Driven by Style" is the mantra for their branding decisions and in order to communicate this message, all employees are taken at least once on a client journey. This allows them to experience first hand what it is their customers buy – driving the old cars, staying in small and beautiful hotels, enjoying the Tuscan countryside, using the road book that plots the trip, etc.

In service-based industries employee engagement and consistent delivery of customer experience are vital, but there are fewer tangible brand elements that can be standardised and quality controlled. Nevertheless, they can be used successfully for employee engagement. For example, in the hotel industry, the building itself, the room design and furniture, as well as staff uniforms are all tangible elements that can be used to express the brand promise and create employee engagement. One of India's up-and-coming upscale hotel chains that intend to fill the gap between luxury hotels and value accommodation, Lemon Tree Hotels, illustrates the point. Lemon Tree Hotels aims to create a memorable brand experience for its customers through its unique brand proposition of being fresh, fun and spirited, that is "refreshingly different".

Figure 4.9 Lemon Tree Hotels in India – brand expressions that ignite

Their customer insight is that the business traveller who returns to the hotel from a hard day of work requires an environment that is uplifting, a place where s/he could unwind – not one that is stiff and boring. A number of brand elements have proven effective for Lemon Tree Hotels in stimulating employee commitment and identification, thereby instilling a certain brand culture. For instance, its senior employees are encouraged to sport ponytails, making this unusual hairstyle a symbol of youthfulness, high energy and fun.

Vice President Rahul Pandit explains: "It's very aspirational in the company. When people say they want to get promoted, they are not saying: 'Hey, I want the next grade. It is hey, when can I get a ponytail?'" Managers at the hotel believe the sight of senior staff with ponytails makes customers feel more relaxed. Gaurav Pallial, another manager, said: "Whenever you visit a five-star hotel, people are hesitant to approach the man on the desk as he looks too busy. Here, people walk up and the first question they ask is, 'What's with the ponytail?' So it's a nice ice-breaker." The hotel's grooming manual stipulates a maximum length of three inches for ponytails for male executives.[4]

The walls of the hotel are not lined with tasteless reproductions of art as in many other hotels, but with crazy jokes to brighten up the mood of the guests. Sharanita Keswani, Director of Marketing, explains:

> All the little design and visual elements that we have introduced energise our employees and make them proud to work for Lemon Tree Hotels because they see that they make our hotel chain really different and appealing. Our employees are totally aware of their crucial role in enabling customer experience as promised by our brand. Our motto is to have "People with Zing", meaning that our staff is ready to serve customers by going the extra mile. Like the fruit they are named after, Lemon Tree Hotels are fresh, cool and sparkling with zest.

Critical success factor #6: Demonstrating relevance to employees

Not all employees are in direct contact with the customer, often drastically reducing the relevance of the brand promise to their job. For some companies, like third party suppliers or fast moving consumer goods sold through major supermarkets, there is often very limited to no interaction with the end customer. This can be detrimental to employee engagement and the brand. Some companies are trying to remedy this by specifically creating customer interaction points that demonstrate the relevance of employees' attitudes and behaviour to the customer experience. This approach was taken by a German manufacturer of car and bus parts. They invited customers to the production sites on a regular

---
[4] Pony express! 19 Sep. 2005, access: http://www.management-issues.com/2006/5/25/blog/pony-express.asp

basis and asked them to describe the end product for which the car parts were used. The marketing manager remembers: "One of our customers very drastically described what would happen if our product was not manufactured properly – the bus would drive into the wall." This interaction with customers will help demonstrate the relevance of living the brand, in this particular case of delivering high quality products all the time.

Maggi, one of the biggest Nestlé brands and a synonym for high quality products in the "fast and easy-to-prepare category", has identified several touchpoints through which customers can give feedback to employees directly.

One of the interaction points Maggi has created is the Maggi cooking studio which has proven very popular in Germany. "The concept is based on a combination of demonstrating how to use the product and offering a wide range of value-added services to

Figure 4.10 The Maggi retro bottle with cult status

the customer, like soup bars, daily cooking classes or the Maggi shop. We work to continuously innovate and refine these services," explains Andreas Peters, Chief Marketing Officer, Maggi GmbH, Germany. Today there are already four Maggi cooking studios across Germany. From a branding point of view, the Maggi cooking studio is an invaluable point of interaction with customers; like most packaged consumer goods, Maggi employees traditionally have little direct response from customers.

Maggi cooking studios are exclusively run by Maggi employees. In 2006 more than 900 000 people visited the Maggi cooking studios in Frankfurt, Hamburg, Dortmund and Leipzig. People go there to eat, to shop, to get involved in discussions or to take part in cooking classes. "Observing these live experiences allows us to understand how consumers get actively engaged in a two-way relationship with our brand and our people. It is a phenomenal opportunity to better understand our customers and their needs. In fact, in some cases the experience of talking to customers turns itself into an immersive experience," reports Peters.

In order to get a more structured and representative view on how customers experience the Maggi brand and the cooking studio, they work with an external agency. Peters explains:

> We really want to get further insight on certain brand elements, for example quality, hygiene, service orientation, friendliness of our employees, etc. The participants of cooking classes are called up by our external research agency after the opening of a Maggi cooking studio and asked to evaluate these dimensions. Every time we make a significant change to the Maggi cooking studio, e.g. if it is refurbished, we also conduct market research.

The offline cooking studio has been augmented with a virtual version in the 1990s, and provides a database of more than 6000 recipes, with short films, information about nutrition and products, an online shop and raffles.

With their experiences in the cooking studios employees support the detection of trends for further product development. Peters continues:

> Actually our employees are real trend scouts. The key is to create research opportunities in a natural environment that add to the consumer's experience rather than detracting from the experience of visiting the Maggi cooking studio. All too often traditional techniques see consumers being sidetracked from the live experience to take part in research activity – often by clipboard wielding researchers.

With more than 70 000 written inquiries and 80 000 telephone calls, Maggi employees have "an ear into their customers". All comments, inquiries, and questions from the real and virtual Maggi cooking studios are reported in a monthly newsletter to their marketing colleagues. Through telephone conferences and "Jours Fixes" the Maggi cooking studio employees are integrated in the new product launch process and advertising activities. Also, job rotations help those sitting in the "second row" to give them a breath of exposure to how customers feel, what they think and how they experience the brand Maggi. "At the moment this is still in its infancy, but we aim to enhance this practice," explains Peters.

Research data gathered from analysing the brand image is also forwarded to employees, in particular to those working in the Maggi cooking studio. Peters describes: "To know how customers rate and evaluate our brand is really important to our employees. It confirms the great work they do, and at the same time it motivates them to look for ways to further improve the customer's brand experience." And Maggi employees can be really proud: independent research as carried out by *Reader's Digest*, one of the most widely read journals in Europe, confirmed Maggi to be – third time in a row – the Most Trusted Brand 2008 in the food sector. More than 25 000 people – of those about 8000 are from

Germany – participate in this written survey. "The survey tells us how the brand Maggi is anchored in the minds of consumers and purchasers, which criteria are most relevant for forming opinions, and to which degree the trusted brands are really purchased," explains Peters.

By using customer feedback as a way to instil employee engagement Maggi is able to integrate the "external and internal Maggi world". "We know that achieving such alignment is not a one-time event, rather an ongoing process. Through evaluating how customers experience the Maggi brand we have input that helps to build employee commitment to our brand strategy. At the same time this ensures that employees understand how they can help achieve this strategy," says Peters. This statement further supports the premise behind the importance of engagement which is based on a correlation between customer satisfaction and employee engagement.

Critical success factor #7: Translating the meaning of values

Employees have different interpretations of what a brand is and what brand values mean in their particular context. Differences relate to, for example, gender, functional background, age or culture. Especially when going international, someone needs to translate the brand values to employees' specific context. For Robert Hirsch, owner of HIRSCH Armbänder GMBH, headquartered in Klagenfurt (Austria), it is the leaders who act as "translators" of brand values across geographical and cultural distances. "The ideal leader should 'have charisma and be visionary', be 'dynamic' and have 'intellectual capacity' in addition to traits like 'decisive', 'mobile' and 'vital and persistent'. Unfortunately – I have to say – such socially competent leaders for intercultural work areas are almost never found," Hirsch points out. His view is that leaders need to examine first to what extent brand-related rules, norms and guidelines applicable in a western European environment can be transferred to other cultural contexts. Hirsch explains:

> This starts, for instance, with the reward system for employees which should be different in western countries compared to those within Asian contexts. Primarily, the reward system should be perceived as fair by all employees, despite their cultural diversity. A typical problem though is that there is no universally valid and "objective" standard of fair measure. Therefore you need to do your homework by finding out what "fair" means in each cultural context. Equally, we needed to evaluate the five dimensions that make up our HIRSCH brand culture. What does innovation mean in an Indian context? For instance, innovation is manifested by paying our employees salaries which are not mere weekly fixed payments but payments consisting of a fixed base and with additional opportunities to earn more based on quality produced. How can the thought of "networking" be adapted to local needs and expectations? What does "adhering to high production standards" mean in an Indian context? To ensure high quality standards we regularly invite production workers to our main production site in Klagenfurt. They receive intensive material training as well as culture training, are introduced to our locally established network such as retailers. I personally use such opportunity to explain to our Indian visitors the HIRSCH philosophy, the HIRSCH culture and the HIRSCH brand.

Critical success factor #8: Maintaining employee engagement

Engaging employees is not a one-off event, it is an ongoing process. Frontline employees who are in direct contact with customers, suppliers, retailers, and other key stakeholders on a daily basis need to fully understand what the brand is all about. They embody the brand and need to know what behaving in line with the brand means for their day-to-day working context. For these employees, a continuous brand engagement programme needs to be designed, which ensures that their understanding of the brand is up to date and their motivation remains high. The marketing manager of a global financial services company explains:

> A lot of people want to be served well. Fewer people actually find it fulfilling to serve. It is important that you search for those and then give them a company and a brand they can be proud of. But employee engagement can't be a one-time event where you walk away being certified. You need to get to the point where employees own the brand and are excited about it. Ultimately, this should be viral and result in a positive loop where employee enthusiasm sparks positive feedback from customers which creates more enthusiasm.

How can engagement be maintained on a high level throughout?

Google has just landed the top slot of the *Fortune Magazine* "Best Places to Work" ranking for the second time in a row. They have been able to create and maintain a strong and thriving company culture despite phenomenal growth. Google's culture is very strongly driven by the iconic nature of their products; they drive everything – the product is the brand. This creates immense pride and a real sense of belonging among the Google workforce.

"Google's culture is one of the reasons why Googlers are passionate about working here. The company early on recognised the importance of recruiting the right people not just in terms of skill set but also cultural affinity," explains Obi Felten, Head of Consumer Marketing at Google UK. "The recruiting process is stringent and tough – we have high standards in terms of background and experience, but we also place a lot of emphasis on cultural fit." Candidates have to demonstrate a certain

"Googliness": they need to be ambitious, self-starters that roll up their sleeves and get things done, independent thinkers, and able to work well in a collaborative team-based environment where priorities and projects change frequently. In most companies cultural fit is an intuitive assessment by the interviewer, but Google uses a more data-driven approach: they surveyed current employees to work out which characteristics make a successful Googler and apply this to candidates.

Google thrives with its creative and innovative workforce; there is a strong emphasis on collaboration and making best use of employees' ideas. In order to put this creativity to work and to ensure that there is a constant stream of new products and features in the pipeline, Google allocates a significant amount of time and resources to innovation while never losing sight of their core products, search and advertising. Its 70-20-10 management principle allocates 70% of company resources to search and ads, 20% to new businesses adjacent to search and ads, and 10% to truly new things.

Google drives employee engagement through the principles of ownership and meritocracy. Every employee sets their own quarterly goals which are then cascaded upwards, and aligned with top-down company strategy. The self-set goals are then visible to every Google employee on the intranet. Engineers are encouraged to allocate 20% of their time to experimental projects, so they are free to work on what they are really passionate about. "Twenty per cent projects" are evaluated on whether they contribute to Google's mission of "organising the world's information and making it universally accessible and useful", rather than directly commercial considerations. While the experimental projects carry no immediate expectation for revenue generation, they have been a driver in developing key products. For example, Gmail and Google News were created this way. The approach works well for Google not just to generate ideas but also to keep employees engaged and excited about what they work on.

The principles of meritocracy are manifested in a number of ways, including the importance of peer reviews. Peer feedback is part of the annual review process; unlike most companies this is completely transparent so the reviewee sees who said what about them. On an ad hoc basis, Googlers can nominate fellow employees for a peer bonus to be recognised for doing things over and above the call of duty, for example someone from a different department or region helping out on a project. The peer bonus scheme is very unbureaucratic, proposals are quickly reviewed by the line manager and HR, and the beneficiary receives a congratulations email and a small financial reward in their next pay check.

On a much greater financial scale, Google introduced the Founders' Awards in 2005 which emulate the upside typical to Silicon Valley start-ups (the first two Founders' Awards consisted of $12 million of restricted stock).[5] The principle is simple – Google rewards teams who make a major contribution to the success of the company with millions of dollars in stocks, thereby creating a pay-off in line with selling off a successful start-up business to someone like Google. This programme is an innovative way to maintain employee engagement in a maturing business and a bold attempt to keep the start-up culture alive; this is appealing and motivating for both existing Googlers and new applicants.

With so many new employees coming onboard in recent months, there is a real danger that the culture is diluted. In order to counter these effects, Google has a chief culture officer, Stacey Savides Sullivan, whose responsibility it is to retain Google's unique culture, to facilitate cultural assimilation across offices, regions, and diverse cultures, and generally to keep Googlers

---

[5] Hafner, K., New incentive for Google employees: award worth millions, 1 Feb. 2005, *New York Times*, http://www.nytimes.com/2005/02/01/technology/01google.html?_r=1&oref=login&oref=slogin

happy. In a recent interview with CNET News.com, Sullivan, who is Director of Human Resources in addition to Chief Culture Office, explained: "I work with employees around the world to figure out ways to maintain and enhance and develop our culture and how to keep the core values we had in the very beginning – a flat organization, a lack of hierarchy, a collaborative environment – to keep these as we continue to grow and spread them and filtrate them into our new offices around the world."[6] Employee commitment and engagement are very important to Google, and it is part of Sullivan's job to find out what the company can do to keep commitment levels high:

> The last few years we've been doing a happiness survey as part of our annual global company survey. Four or five years ago, Larry and Sergey wanted to find out how happy people are and what it's going to take to keep them working at the company. We're trying to figure out how committed people are to the company, what's causing that commitment level to be high or low, what makes a difference to them and their management and direct managers. The results ended up being centered a lot on career development and growth. So career development is more of a focus than giving more stock options or increasing salaries.

In particular, Google is working hard to get the work–life balance right for their employees – they try to avoid early morning or late night meetings, they welcome working from home and pay for home broadband, provide massages and on-site gyms and doctors, they have a generous maternity and paternity programme in place, and even allow people to bring their dogs to work.

---

[6] Mills, E., Meet Google's culture czar, CNET News.com, 27 Apr. 2007, http://www.news.com/Meet-Googles-culture-czar/2008-1023_3-6179897.html

CASE STUDY: TED – HOW ORGANISATIONAL CIRCUMSTANCES IMPACT EMPLOYEE ENGAGEMENT

Continuously making employees feel committed to the essence of the brand is essential as it translates directly into customer satisfaction. However, keeping the level of engagement high at all times is difficult as the following case study demonstrates.

In February many 2004, United Airlines started a low-cost airline called Ted in the midst of bankruptcy proceedings. The new airline borrowed its name from the last three letters of UniTed and was designed to compete against successful discount carriers like JetBlue, Frontier, and Southwest Airlines.

The name Ted was chosen to personalise the airline, presenting it as a living being rather than an anonymous organisation. When United introduced its "Meet Ted" pre-launch campaign, it tried to reach people at a very personal level, providing gifts to people like coffee and newspapers, flowers, pizza, meals and drinks, all with the compliments of the mysterious Ted. They succeeded in building huge customer curiosity about who Ted was before they revealed and launched the new airline. The pre-launch campaign was not only successful in exciting the public, but also successful in gaining massive attention from the media. Consequently United smartly created immense brand awareness before the brand was even available

Figure 4.11   Ted – the low-cost airline of United Airlines

Figure 4.12 Ted – refreshingly different airplane

on the market. When Ted was finally exposed to the public, its physical brand attributes turned out to be refreshing: from the spacious comfortable seats of the new planes to the exterior design, with colours of bright orange and creamy-white on the tail.

United had put in place a launch team of six who had the challenging task to get Ted off the ground with very little budget and in a very short time. Anna van Exel was the launch team member in charge of internal marketing. She remembers:

> We had quite a few challenges on our hands at the time. United deemed it necessary to keep the planned launch of a low-cost carrier secret as long as possible, introducing a surprise element when we were ready to go to market. In the end, we had three months to get employees ready to embrace and live the new brand promise. In addition, we had to fight against the negative attitude of those who thought the launch of a new service was a waste of money and the wrong investment in a time of crisis. We also had to overcome the legacy of Shuttle, a service that had been launched on the West Coast and which had failed after initial success.

A further complication for Ted was constituted by the fact that due to union agreements Ted shared staff with United Airlines. Ted did not recruit its own new employees, but worked with a constant flow of employees that came from within United. In some locations, people self-selected to join

Ted. The Ted brand was all about being spontaneous, entrepreneurial, engaging, down to earth and resourceful, intending to make customers feel relaxed and to help them enjoy the flight experience. Everybody working with Ted had to understand the underlying mindset and intended customer experience. In "leisure hubs" like Denver this was easier to accomplish for the launch team, since Ted flights were in a separate concourse. In the other major hubs, however, where United and Ted would operate in parallel, for example Dulles or Chicago, this was more of a challenge. It was difficult to create real differences in both employee behaviour and customer experience between United and Ted, while at the same time sending a message that Ted was part of United. "This required both ultimate flexibility on the side of our employees, and a very simple and clear brand message from us," van Exel explains:

> Basically, our employees had to express the brand values of whichever airline they were serving – this might have been Ted in the morning and United on the way back home. The difference between the two brands basically came down to attitude and price – Ted was positioned to be cheaper and also to be more relaxed and fun. For staff, this meant slightly different (more casual) uniforms, different protocol on board, different catering options, and generally a more casual and relaxed style. The brand training had to make absolutely sure that employees understood these vital differences in intended customer experience between the master brand United and the sub-brand Ted, and more importantly, how that translated into different behaviours expected of them.

To ensure employees would engage in the Ted brand, van Exel made sure first of all that everybody involved in Ted understood the business reasons behind the decision to create a new brand in the midst of bankruptcy proceedings. Then, employees were informed about the brand promise of Ted and how this was different from United. This required translating the brand promise into relevant behavioural guidelines for each staff group, from in-flight service to pilots. A Ted aircraft was sent on a 12-city roadshow to engage with employees; selected frontline employees would "crew" the roadshow to demonstrate expected crew behaviour and to help colleagues understand the brand, while senior leaders were on board the plane both to signal top management commitment and to help answer questions. More than 1000 employees were able to meet with the top of the Ted organisation in this way. As more and more employees got excited about Ted and word spread, an overwhelming number of volunteers tried to get involved in making the new brand successful. Van Exel and her team were quick to use these volunteers as brand ambassadors, teaching them about the brand values and how best to communicate them to customers and colleagues. In addition, they tried to create identification with Ted through a number of activities, including a monthly newsletter called *Ted Times*, the *Ted Pocket Guide* with quick facts, and employee contests posted on the company intranet. "It was amazing how quickly Ted turned not only into a brand within the brand, but a subculture. Those involved in the launch really got the difference, and they were excited by the prospect to deliver something unique and of value to our customers," van Exel describes.

Against all odds, Ted turned out to be a big success at the time, not least due to the efforts of the internal marketing team. However, the launch team was dissolved shortly after the launch. "Since Ted proved to be such a great success, management assumed that it would run on its own by now," van Exel points out not without disappointment:

> Responsibilities were subsumed into the various divisions like airports, in-flight service, etc.; unfortunately, branding is not the top priority in these entities. At the moment, there is nobody for whom the Ted brand is the top priority – and it is starting to show. The customer experience is losing its profile, becoming more and more similar to the original United experience.

Customers will notice, but may not care if they only select by price. Employees on the other hand will care if they were part of the Ted launch and came to embrace the Ted brand. New employees will have trouble to understand the difference between United and Ted, the positioning has become diluted and has been reduced to little more than price. Although it is part of their training, they never were part of the Ted "subculture" that could have steeped them in what Ted is all about.

Ted certainly has the handicap that all its flights are operated by United Airlines crew flying under the United Airlines operating certificate; as Ted is not actually a certified airline but rather a brand name for its low-cost offering, it also happens occasionally that Ted and United aircraft are swapped for various efficiency and availability reasons. Let's hope that United understands that Ted is more than just a repainted Shuttle. Only time will tell whether Ted will in fact survive as a brand.

Summary: Critical success factors – engaging employees in the brand

- Ensure that branding is positioned as a serious force within the organisation (and not just one of many projects or functions) by getting commitment from the CEO/ executive team.
- Identify brand role models at all levels who will live the brand and help generate brand-buzz.
- Make your role models part of an enterprise-wide network.
- Reduce complex branding concepts with powerful and simple ideas that help employees to relate to the brand promise. Supportive brand-related communication helps to

> translate the ideas into easy-to-work-with guiding principles.
> - Create opportunities for employees to experience first hand what the brand is all about. Brand values need to be translated into tangible and visible manifestations employees can intuitively connect with.
> - Connect employees with customers. Feedback directly from the customer adds relevancy and excitement.
> - Translate the meaning of the brand to employee's specific working context. Consider different mindsets due to cultural difference, functional backgrounds, gender, etc.
> - Maintain employee engagement by developing incentive mechanisms, such as career development pathways, learning opportunities, and generous reward and bonus structures. Such tools need to fit with the cultural values and need to be updated on a regular basis.

ENGAGING CUSTOMERS

In Chapter 3 we talked about customer engagement as a new way to interact with customers, which is neither intrusive nor manipulative, and over time results in meaningful relationships. Customers typically follow the phases of the loyalty pathway (see below) from first contact with a product or brand all the way to purchase and loyalty. As pointed out earlier, they can move up and down along the pathway, motivated by a change in circumstances or the nature of interaction with the brand (disappointing or reinforcing moments of truth). For example, Volvo has become more or less synonymous with safety. However, in a recent ad campaign Volvo created a fictional character whose body tattoos spelled out the coordinates of an undersea location of $50 000 in gold coins and

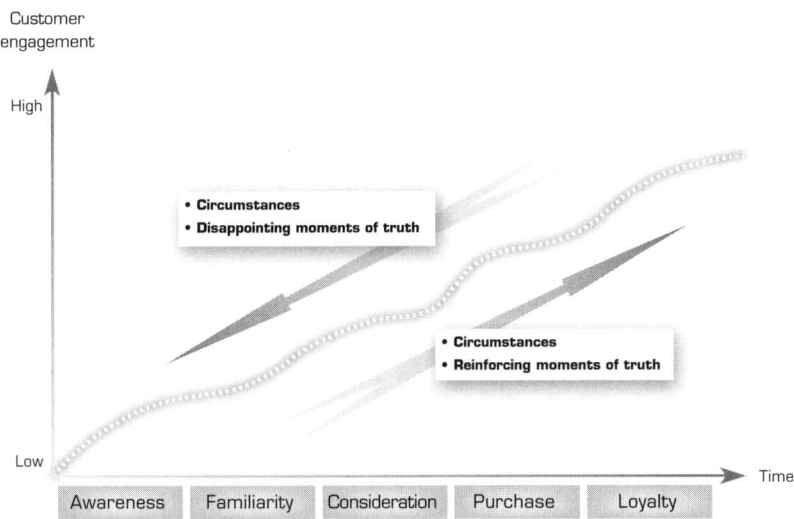

Figure 4.13 Customer engagement along the loyalty pathway

the keys to a new car. Linda Gangeri, national advertising manager of Volvo Cars of North America, said the tattoo man was a way to get people to think differently about the Volvo brand. This message might increase customer engagement with a younger and more adventurous audience that is not necessarily driven by "safety"; at the same time, it may reduce customer engagement with the loyal, more safety-driven Volvo customer base.[7]

Each of the phases along the pathway comes with a particular set of challenges and obstacles that need to be mastered. In the following section we will discuss a number of critical success factors that make sure that each moment of truth is turned into an opportunity, illustrated by examples and case studies that are meant as food for thought.

---

[7] Williamson, R., Checking out the Volvo XC90, Scripps Howard News Service, Saturday, 11 Aug. 2007, accessed: http://www.venturacountystar.com/news/2007/aug/11/checking-out-the-volvo-xc90/

Critical success factor #1: Authenticity (Do as you say)

As pointed out in Chapters 1 and 2, a focus on CSR has become quite popular as a means of engaging customers. However, as also discussed, this strategy bears significant risks for the reputation, the brand, and ultimately the business, if it is a mere communicative ploy and not followed through in every aspect of doing business. Sony, for example, started a global "green" programme several years ago. The programme aims to reduce negative environmental effects of all Sony products and impacts the entire product life cycle, from procurement of parts, the manufacturing process, product use, disposal and finally recycling of discarded products. For instance, Sony purchases components only from suppliers rated as Green Partners. Suppliers acquire this status if they meet Sony's strict requirements on avoidance of hazardous substances and can also provide proof in an audit. Now Sony also launched a new advertising campaign with the aim to get consumers to recycle their outdated or broken electronic gear. Cleverly, they are recycling old advertising spots as part of the campaign, featuring video cameras, portable stereos and other "amusingly clunky" equipment. The vintage ads are run ahead of supporting events as part of the Sony Takeback Recycling Program where consumers can go and drop off their old tech for recycling.[8] Martin Micko, responsible for marketing at Sony Austria, knows how important it is to live what is communicated and promised:

> Although we are still in the initial stages of observing what people talk about us out there, we are well aware that the internet forces us to make branding decisions much more carefully. Our vision is to develop innovative digital products for entertainment while continuously rethinking and improving processes with regards to their impact on the environment. This is what we communicate to the

---

[8] Metzger, P., Kickin' it Old School: Sony recycling hardware, ad campaigns, *Green Daily*, 6 March 2008, accessed: http://www.greendaily.com/2008/03/06/kickin-it-old-school-sony-recycling-hardware-ad-campaigns/

marketplace, this is what our top management team supports – and this is what NGOs such as Greenpeace evaluate: they rank leading mobile phone, game console, TV and PC manufacturers on their global environmental policies and practice, their use of harmful chemicals, and their willingness to take back discarded products from their consumers for responsible disposal and recycling. In 2008 Sony has surged ahead to occupy the fourth position in these rankings out of 18 top manufacturers. This means that our "green" project is starting to show results. As part of the project, we educate and sensitize our employees towards the environmental impact and launched several activities including environment days, etc. If we do not live up to what we communicate to the outside world this would be picked up very quickly by critical consumers and other stakeholders and discussed on the web.

Micko also points out that bigger, internationally operating companies have worse hands if compared to smaller and locally operating companies when it comes to being critically evaluated in terms of what is communicated versus what is kept. "This is like David against Goliath – the smaller ones enjoy higher likeability values," says Micko.

Critical success factor #2: Focusing on the most important moments of truth

Customer engagement programmes need to ensure that every interaction point between customer and brand contributes to a positive customer experience. Although ideally this means that every single interaction point is optimised, in practice this is next to impossible. Therefore, it is important – as a first step – to focus on those interaction points that are most important to the customer and real moments of truth. Disconnect between customer expectations created by the brand promise and actual customer experience in those moments of truth are most damaging to the brand. By the same token, living up to or exceeding expectations in these moments of truth will propel the brand into a new league.

What is considered a moment of truth depends on the nature of a product or service as well as the brand promise. For example, it is generally true that for retail chains the shop environment – including the building, the parking lot, the interior design, the way the products are presented, etc. – constitutes a moment of truth; this is further amplified by a brand promise that alludes to exclusivity, and becomes slightly less important for price-driven discounters. For example, architecture can be a means of customer engagement – the interplay of form, colour, material and lighting helps to create a certain atmosphere that appeals to all senses and sets the tone for a customer experience, potentially leaving a lasting impression. Carefully designed rooms and settings can create an emotional connection between a company and its customers. MPREIS, for instance, a supermarket chain in western Austria, bills itself as "The Seriously Sexy Supermarket". The company's stores literally stand out – they all share an unusual and progressive architecture. Realising that retail space is their major customer interaction point, MPREIS has been commissioning up-and-coming architects for the last 15 years, encouraging them to design buildings that make the most of their settings in the Tyrolean Alps. While other retailers build their brands around the consistency of near-identical outlets irrespective of location, MPREIS builds its brand around extravagant and unique architecture. Anton Mölk and Hansjörg Mölk, the CEOs of MPREIS since the late 1980s, have a strong affinity for design: "Generally, a brand is recognisable through uniformity. At MPREIS, we take an entirely different direction. Our trademark is the variety of different ways in which our architecture is expressed – each store is designed specifically for its location, but it is still recognisable as part of the MPREIS brand."[9]

Anton Mölk further explains:

---

[9] What's in store? Commercial Design Trends, 23 Sep. 2007, accessed: http://trendsideas.com/ViewArticle.aspx?article=9602&region=3

Typically, when new supermarkets are opened customers discuss special offers. At our openings, they discuss more the building, the architecture and how it all blends nicely with the surrounding spaces . . . of course our modern buildings also spur controversy. But this is what we are aiming for because with conformity no discussion would arise. People start being more aware of the quality of the room they enter. For us, investing in architecture means to create value for our co-workers, our customers and the general public living in the area.

The design experience continues inside the stores which promotes a market-style layout: natural lighting has been maximised, opening up the views to spectacular scenery; space permitting, typically a café and an outdoor terrace are provided in all stores. "Many of the MPREIS supermarkets are positioned on the outskirts of towns and villages, a long way from main streets," says Koberl, one of the assigned architects. "Traditionally, villagers like to be able to shop and stop for a coffee. In many areas, the MPREIS coffee shop is the only meeting place for miles. Compared to the typical, modern supermarket, these stores have taken on a very different, and much more social role in the community."[10] Clearly, MPREIS understands the role the retail environment can play in customer engagement and has successfully used this moment of truth to engage their customers on many levels.

Contact points also need to be welcome and provide a benefit or added value. For example, the well-intentioned call of a junior banker to the unsuspecting customer on a Friday afternoon to alert the customer that action had to be taken urgently due to the underperformance of invested funds does little more than create aggravation. It is an unwelcome, disturbing, and therefore unnecessary interaction point that destroys brand equity. The junior banker is neither equipped nor authorised to do something about the situation, the senior banker is not available until Monday

---

[10] What's in store? Commercial Design Trends, 23 Sep. 2007, accessed: http://trendsideas.com/ViewArticle.aspx?article=9602&region=3

morning, and the customer is left in limbo all weekend long, only to find out that things are really fine when finally talking to the senior banker.

Critical success factor #3: Bringing "online" into the brand

Successful customer engagement facilitates customer self-selection and uses the possibilities of the virtual world to engage customers at their own discretion – when they want, where they want, and however they want. As seen in the LEGO example earlier, even for products that are firmly rooted in the offline world, a meaningful online dimension can be developed and used for customer engagement. Unfortunately, many companies are still afraid of getting involved with all things virtual and, worse, others fail to understand that simply transferring offline communication to online without making the shift from monologue to dialogue does not work.

For example, Kraft Foods launched a new programme where the innovations team is turning to customers for inspiration. However, the tone of the website does not suggest that this is about co-creation at all; not only are they "most interested in ideas that are more than a concept, in particular new products and packages that are ready to be brought to market (or can be brought to market quickly)", they also make it very clear that Kraft pretty much knows everything already:

> Each year, Kraft receives many ideas from people and organizations outside our company. While we are always interested in new ideas, you should know that most of what we receive (or will receive in the future) is not (or will not be) new to us. This is because, as you might guess, Kraft has a large staff of scientists and marketers who are continuously working to develop and improve our products, packaging and processes. Therefore, many submissions from

"outside" Kraft actually duplicate Kraft's current or past research and development efforts. Many other ideas simply fall outside the scope of our business interests.[11]

This initiative fails to recognise the basic dynamics of the online world – it is a one-way dissemination of information, it is non-interactive, and does not sound like an invitation for a dialogue or collaboration.

Critical success factor #4: Retaining relevancy to core users

The luxury industry has undergone quite some transformation. In order to make luxury both more accessible and more profitable, it has jeopardised everything that makes it special. For example, Burberry encountered a loss of luxury appeal when expanding their product range to go more mainstream. In the UK, a working-class subculture called "chavs" (derived from the Romany travellers' word chavi, meaning child) emerged a few years ago; they are young, hang out at small-town shopping centres, intimidate passers-by and dress in baggy track suits, clunky gold jewellery and anything featuring the famous black, red and beige plaid, but in particular the Burberry baseball cap.[12] At the same time, football hooligans in the UK became as loyal to the Burberry brand as they are to their sport,[13] reportedly causing a pub chain in the UK to ban "design hooligans" from their properties.[14] When Burberry

---

[11] http://www.kraftfoods.com/innovatewithkraft/readmore.aspx
[12] Thomas, D., *Deluxe – How Luxury Lost its Lustre*, UK: Penguin, Allen Lane, 2007.
[13] O'Brien D., Burberry Square, Brand Channel, 16 June 2003, accessed: http://www.brandchannel.com/features_profile.asp?pr_id=130
[14] Menkes, S., Out of control? Managing success, *International Herald Tribune*, 28 Sep. 2004, accessed: http://www.iht.com/articles/2004/09/28/rsuccess_ed3_.php?page=1

finally ceased production of their baseball cap in 2004, the unwanted fans replaced them with counterfeit versions. Although Angela Ahrendts, the new boss of Burberry, downplayed the company's reputation as the brand of choice for "chavs",[15] it is no secret that mature luxury brands have to steer through treacherous waters – avoiding overexposure which could alienate a loyal high-end customer base and staying clear of underperformance, which is not tolerated in listed companies. While Gucci and Burberry are both seen to send unrestricted signals, thereby engaging wanted and unwanted customers and quite possibly losing relevancy to the target group in the process, Ralph Lauren and Chanel are seen to give more controlled signals, thereby restricting engagement and exposure in a way that primarily the wanted user is buying and loving the brand.[16]

Key success factor #5: Engaging different cultures

All brands dealing with international or even global markets need to walk the fine line between staying relevant to local customers while staying true to their brand promise. Customer engagement needs to sufficiently account for cultural and situational contexts, trying to anticipate what customers feel, think, and want.

Germany-based global financial institution Deutsche Bank pursues this goal by staging the Deutsche Bank brand icon as the carrier of its core brand values *Pursuing excellence, leveraging unique insights, delivering innovative solutions,* and *building long-term relationships.* Since the launch of the new brand values in March 2005, Deutsche Bank has made an ongoing effort to find a balance

---

[15] http://www.fashionunited.co.uk/news/burberry.htm, 9 July 2006.
[16] Menkes, S., Out of control? Managing success, *International Herald Tribune*, 28 Sep. 2004, accessed: http://www.iht.com/articles/2004/09/28/rsuccess_ed3_.php?page=2

STAKEHOLDER ENGAGEMENT 255

Figure 4.14 Deutsche Bank – winning with the logo

Figure 4.15 Adaptation to different cultural context and target groups

between global coherence and local adaptation. In the "Winning with the Logo" Brand communications concept Deutsche Bank leverages the power of symbols: they establish the logo as the global symbol for passionate performance.

Created by Anton Stankowski in 1974 as a classy signet of "minimal art", the logo is now given a third dimension. Deutsche Bank transforms the logo into a physical as much as a metaphorical corporate brand statement.

Christofer Habig, Global Head of Brand Communications with Deutsche Bank explains: "Unlimited connectivity and immediate accountability are intrinsic to the concept. We consider this essential to communicate brands in a diverse, constantly changing world. And the 'Winning with the Logo' concept works for us in two ways: (1) as the global brand messenger of Deutsche Bank, and (2) as the global 'hero' or our 'one bank culture'."

The concept has brought forward more than 1000 different executions in just two years. "The multitude of executions do contribute to brand fragmentation in a certain way, yet this is what we want to enable – but in a channelled approach. So far, we have been able to keep up the momentum to bring our brand values alive across businesses, regions, and culture," says Habig.

Key success factor #6: Paying attention to detail

Louis Vuitton, the French luxury leather and travel goods maker, currently runs a "Where will life take you?" campaign exploring the concept of a journey and its impact on the self, pondering the question "Does the journey create the person or does the person create the journey?" As part of this campaign, customers can travel to different cities with a number of celebrities on the Louis Vuitton website, including Steffi Graf and Andre Agassi as well as Catherine Deneuve. Interestingly, there is also one episode with Mikhail Gorbachev, the last leader of the old Soviet Union, sitting in a limousine as it passes a remaining part of the Berlin Wall, an open Louis Vuitton bag beside him (see www.louisvuitton.com). Allegedly, the publication poking out of Gorbachev's LV bag carries a headline in Russian that refers to the murder of Alexander Litvinenko, the former KGB spy who died in November 2006 after being poisoned with a radioactive isotope.[17]

---

[17] Levin, D., Louis Vuitton ad shows Gorbachev and subversive text, *The New York Times*, 5 Nov. 2007, accessed: http://www.nytimes.com/2007/11/05/business/media/05vuitton.html?ref=business

According to *The New York Times*, a translation of the headline started to circulate on the Internet, provoking questions as to what the hidden (or intended) message by Louis Vuitton might be. Although both Louis Vuitton and their ad agency deny that this was an intentional placement and much more the result of an attempt to make the picture look authentic with the help of a (random) Russian magazine, the blogosphere has helped fuel speculations of all sorts, including that this might have been a ploy to generate buzz and attention.

This demonstrates again the scrutiny all company communication is subjected to in the current environment. For some brands like Louis Vuitton even the smallest detail can become important. Whether or not Louis Vuitton *intentionally* placed this magazine in their ad, the resulting speculations distracted from the core values of the campaign focused on the theme of a personal journey, thereby diluting the message and potentially creating a source of misalignment.

Key success factor #7: Find simple but powerful ways to connect

Many companies talk about "breaking through the media clutter". But connecting with your customers does not have to be painful – it can also be fun and playful. For example, Dutch Rabobank Group is the largest financial services provider in the Netherlands operating on the basis of cooperative principles: it is comprised of several hundred independent local cooperative Rabobanks in the Netherlands as well as a large international network. Founded in 1898 as two separate cooperative banks in Utrecht and Eindhoven by enterprising rural folk, their roots are in agriculture. Their ambition is to become the largest, best and most innovative all-finance service provider in the Netherlands, and the leading food and agri bank worldwide. With their cooperative structure and a current membership of almost 1.6 million, the local Rabobanks are firmly rooted in Dutch society, which is also expressed in their brand values of *involved, nearby* and *leading*. In 2006, the brand promise of Rabobank was updated. Joost Augusteijn, Brand Strategy, Rabobank Group, explains:

> When we redefined our brand promise, we worked with three very important inputs – the business strategy, our identity, and zeitgeist. With regards to the business strategy, it is clear that the brand has to support the business strategy and facilitate the goals set out by it. With regards to our identity, it was very important to us to express who we *really* are. We did not look to be someone different, but to take who we are and make it relevant in the modern world. Therefore, I personally do not like the world repositioning. That sounds contrived and artificial. This is not about inventing something new, but about working with what has grown and evolved over more than a hundred years. For example, emphasis on the human side is part of who we are. That is also why our logo shows a human being on a compass. And finally, understanding zeitgeist allowed us to express who we are in ways that are relevant in today's world.

The reformulation of Rabobank's brand strategy resulted in a rewording of the vision, mission and brand promise. Augusteijn continues: "For example, our vision expresses how we see the world: *together we can accomplish more*. Mutual cooperation – com-

Figure 4.16 Rabobank logo

plementing and compensating each other's strengths and weaknesses – that is the very reason for our existence and at the same time, the essence of our culture and brand, deeply embedded in our organisation."

In order to put the "new" positioning and promise into action, Rabobank developed new products, services, and communications. The new line of communication was to be more gutsy and spontaneous, but still maintain the story-telling angle. In order to bring the brand values to life in communications, they invented a charming fictitious character called Jochem de Bruin, played by actor Vincent Rietveld, who demonstrates in several short and humorous clips the stimulating and innovative (*leading*) role of Rabobank in client's social environment (*nearby*), with commitment as a key driver (*involved*). For example, in one episode, Jochem de Bruin speaks in front of a large business audience. When introducing the bank's agri history and commitment to ethical principles, his audience starts to laugh louder and louder, but as he continues unerringly to explain that Rabobank is the largest bank in the Netherlands, the only privately held bank with a Triple-A rating and also the largest Internet bank in Europe, they start to clap in awe.

Augusteijn remarks:

> Jochem signifies our ideal employee. He incorporates all the values we strive for and exhibits all the behaviours we expect of our employees. At the same time, he also promises a particular experience to our customers. It is a simple concept, but we really found it highly effective, both for external and internal communication. For example, we had a site for employees where they could post good ideas and become Jochem de Bruin of the month. We have now retired Jochem de Bruin (the story is, he moved to Sweden with his wife) and replaced him with the well-known hockey player Fatima Moreira de Melo in order to keep things interesting and to signify the refreshed positioning. We have also launched a new glossy employee magazine named Fatima (playing on the popular Dutch magazine Linda, named after Linda de Mol) and so far, the

new character, storyline and communication have been received really well.

Rabobank has won numerous awards for their campaigns, including a Golden Effie for the most effective campaign featuring Jochem de Bruin.

> **Summary: Critical success factors – engaging customers in the brand**
>
> - Promise only what you can keep. Customers quickly find out whether you are authentic or just pay lip-service.
> - Keep brand relevance high. Focus on customer interaction points that are welcome and attractive.
> - Find a way to integrate online into your brand in a way that is meaningful to your customers.
> - Be aware that parallel worlds of brand meaning can develop, both online and offline. Avoid overexposure, avoid alienation of loyal customers through radical changes in strategic direction, and be proactive about steering the brand.
> - Allow the brand values to adapt to cultural and situational contexts.
> - Pay attention to details. The Internet megaphone has no mercy.
> - Find simple and powerful ways to connect with your customers. Story-telling is a good start.

ENGAGING OTHER STAKEHOLDERS

In Chapter 3 we pointed out that a number of additional audiences need to be engaged. However, balancing their often contradictory interests is not an easy task. Disappointed stakeholders are likely to engage in undesirable behaviour such as negative word of mouth or activism (i.e. anti-brand campaigns). This influences other important stakeholder groups, e.g. consumers, who might boycott the brand or engage in consumer created resistance activities, ultimately resulting in brand proliferations. In the following we present critical success factors that support reaching out to influencers.

Critical success factor #1: Reaching out to other stakeholders

One company whose brand and reputation have been suffering tremendously in the past few years is Wal-Mart Stores, the Bentonville, Arkansas-based US discount retailer. The 130 million customers who shop at Wal-Mart every week in the USA save $2300 per year on average,[18] a much appreciated benefit to many and a necessity to some. While historically applauded by capital markets for its sheer unstoppable growth, Wal-Mart's reputation has come under a considerable amount of scrutiny. Although customer favourability ratings remain high, any number of different groups including opinion leaders, regulators, and unions have become very vocal about their points of disagreement with the big blue-and-grey buildings and the organisation behind them. The points of criticism are very consistent – low pay, insufficient benefits, less than desirable working conditions, and aggressive negotiation tactics. While other discount retailers face similar issues, Wal-Mart as one of the largest corporations in the world seems to stir more negative sentiments than any other.

While special interest groups have invested their powers and efforts to launch attacks on Wal-Mart, exerting pressure through

---

[18] Davis, N.D., Corporate reputation management, the Wal-Mart way, Senior Honors. Thesis, Texax A&M University, April 2007.

media, lobbying, and grassroots movements, as well as raising doubts about the nature and trustworthiness of America's largest company in the hope to force them to change their behaviour and their policies, Wal-Mart itself has been strangely silent, not equipped to deal with such onslaught. By contrast to the increasing sophistication of the activities and campaigns of Wal-Mart opponents, Wal-Mart's own reputation management has been somewhat non-existent until fairly recently. Negative attitudes towards Wal-Mart started to impact on their bottom line. For example, a study carried out by McKinsey & Company in 2004[19] revealed that up to 8% of shoppers discontinued their patronage due to negative press they had been exposed to. Wal-Mart's reputation had become so tainted that even their quick response and efficient aid to hurricane Katrina victims in 2005 was not accepted as an act of genuine kindness by everyone. While their generosity and efficiency were applauded by many, including some who might otherwise be against Wal-Mart, they were also accused of using hurricane Katrina as a PR coup. CEO Lee Scott was put in a position where he had to deny the fact that this was a move motivated by PR opportunities and the brain child of their PR agency Edelman which they had hired in 2005 to revamp their image by both fending off negative attacks and deliberately sharing positive contributions made by Wal-Mart. According to a 12 September story in *Investor's Business Daily*, CEO Lee Scott "told a Boston conference that the company reacted as it did because it was the right thing to do. Public relations were not a factor. Still, he admitted it gave Wal-Mart a real boost. 'When you do the right thing, good things accrue to you,' Scott said."

According to Cathy Halligan, CMO of the online division, Walmart.com, "doing what is right" is a value that goes back to

---

[19] Barbaro, M., A new weapon for Wal-Mart: a war room, *The New York Times*, 1 Nov. 2005.

founder Sam Walton. "The ethos of Wal-Mart is very much about treating the associates (the people who work at the stores) and customers well and the rest will fall into place. Sam Walton did not believe in bragging about things, he was all about just doing it," Halligan explains. This attitude has certainly been reflected in Wal-Mart's lack of telling a coherent corporate story. But, as they are finding out now, failure to actively manage the corporate reputation can severely hurt a brand. The hesitance to tell a deliberate story to both, the 1.3 million US associates and the 200 million customers who shop at Wal-Mart at least once in 12 months, has placed Wal-Mart under constant attack.

In 2006, they hired Leslie Dach, the former vice chairman of Edelman Worldwide and a former senior Democratic Party strategist as executive vice president of corporate affairs. For the first time, that job reports directly to CEO Lee Scott. Dach immediately instituted an aggressive, campaign-style PR operation, including a "war room", allowing representatives to respond quickly to attacks launched against the company. In an interview with *USA Today*, when Dach was asked what he intends to do to change the perception that Wal-Mart is a "bad" company that pays its employees poorly and does not provide good enough healthcare, he responded: "We have a great story to tell. We may have spent too much time responding to critics, because when we tell our story on (environmental) sustainability, on job creation, on $4 generic drugs, it's very persuasive. Our opponents look smaller and shriller. We want to run a relentlessly positive campaign."[20]

As part of their new strategy Wal-Mart also axed its 19-year-old slogan "Always low prices", and replaced it with "Save Money. Live Better". The new tag line is used in new television ads which

---

[20] Fetterman, M., 5 questions with Leslie Dach, 11 May 2006, accessed: http://www.usatoday.com/money/companies/management/2006-11-06-5questions_x.htm

aim to go beyond the mere focus on price and to inject a more emotional tone, emphasising Wal-Mart's values of improving quality of life to its associates and customers by providing affordable products. Halligan explains:

> Saving people money so they can live better has been the purpose of the company since it was founded in 1962. The new tag line articulates our company's purpose simply and powerfully which has further strengthened the Wal-Mart brand's relevancy in the marketplace. At the same time, it resonates internally which enables our 1.3 million US associates to deliver an on brand experience more readily. Of course what makes it really powerful is the fact that Wal-Mart has improved as a company, from merchandising to marketing to operations and communications. This will put Wal-Mart back on the trajectory of being a great place to work and a great place to shop.

With a PR agency and corporate reputation management in place, Wal-Mart is hoping to slowly change public opinion. Halligan highlights:

> Wal-Mart is the single largest US company that has grown entirely organically in the US. It is the sheer size of Wal-Mart that creates backlash and that needs to be off-set by means of transparent communication that reinforces our values and brings discipline and focus to our story. There are many positive facts that are not known about Wal-Mart, like the fact that all associates were awarded company stock creating a lot of wealth when the company initially went public.

Of course, there is also a flurry of activities that are aiming to create proof points for an improved Wal-Mart image. For one, Wal-Mart has subscribed to an ambitious CSR agenda. "We are constantly trying to improve. For example, we are working with our suppliers to become more environmentally responsible. We have found a way to take water out of detergent products in order to reduce storage and transportation costs significantly, benefiting the environment, our customers, our suppliers and our bottom line," Halligan points out.

So what is the lesson in all this? Wal-Mart's failure to systematically engage with key stakeholders – externally and internally – has hurt both its brand and its reputation. If a company does not communicate, the void will ultimately be filled by a small but vocal minority. While coordinated efforts of deliberating a coherent and consistent story will help to reclaim some of the territory that has been lost to this small but vocal minority, this will clearly not be enough. Wal-Mart will have to address the recurring accusations not only in terms of communication, but also in terms of demonstrating that their business policies and processes are changing. But – they no longer can afford to dismiss their critics as propagandists, and rely solely on "doing the right thing" and sporadic issue management. After all, a strong corporate reputation isn't a by-product of success, but a means to it.

Critical success factor #2: Translating the brand promise into engaging ideas for all key stakeholders

As outlined in Chapter 3, only if brand experiences are consistent in every point of interaction, brand engagement of various stakeholder groups will develop. However, as the needs and desires vary within and across these groups, the brand promise needs to be translated accordingly.

As was already described in the LEGO brand case, the core brand values of Fun – Creativity - and Quality serve as the shared brand platform. As part of the brand development process, the LEGO Group defined what they would like their various stakeholders to believe and feel about the brand.

For instance, they would like parents to have the following associations with the LEGO brand:

The brand strategy defines the brand promise for each stakeholder group as well

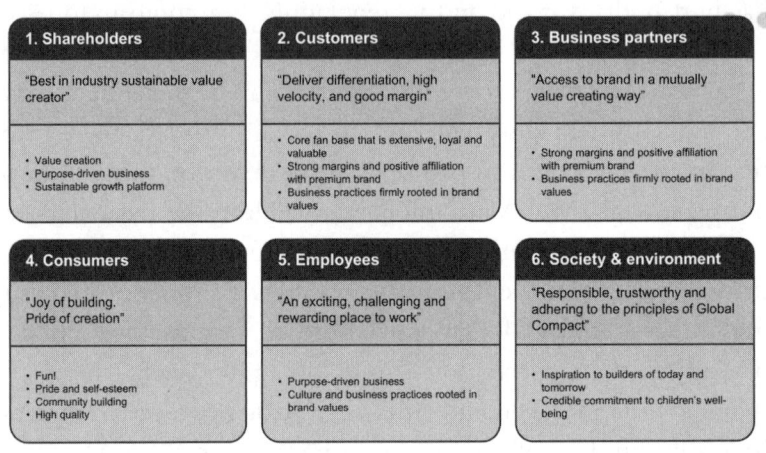

Figure 4.17 Translation of LEGO promise to various stakeholders

I know the LEGO toys will help make my child happy through creative, fun, and safe play. It will contribute to my child's development and well-being, both now and in the future. I love LEGO.

Shareholders represent another important stakeholder group. For this group they defined the following aspirational associations:

The LEGO Group not only delivers outstanding financial dividends, it also delivers emotional dividends from the profound and unique positive impact on children.

The "consumer" audience includes a number of different segments like parents, children, and AFOLs (adult fans of LEGO). Children are at the core of this group, and the aspirational emotional benefits the LEGO Group wants them to experience when playing with LEGO bricks or any other LEGO game are defined as follows:

> LEGO bricks are colourful, easy to put together and to take apart. They are fun to play with again and again. They are simple, intuitive, exciting and fun. I can create my own designs, play on my own or share with other children. It is never boring – every time I play with it, I discover new possibilities. I am very proud of all the things I can make with my LEGO toys.

"By visualising these aspirational associations, we were able to characterise the nature of brand relationships we aim to have with each key stakeholder group. We are then developing programmes and initiatives that help us turn these brand relationships into reality," Jacob Kragh, Senior Director at LEGO group describes. Take the example of the brand relationship between the LEGO brand and retailers. The LEGO group refers to its retailers and distributors as "customers". "We want our customers to be proud to be associated with the LEGO Group; we want the LEGO brand to enhance the quality image and hence also the success of their business," says Kragh. The LEGO Group is well aware that they compete with a large number of strong global brands for the attention of retailers and also for shelf space. While both LEGO employees and competitors bank on sophisticated performance scorecards and professional key-account management tools, the LEGO Group differentiate themselves through their brand values and the way business is done. So for retailers the LEGO Group is also designing a brand engagement programme. "We believe to be different along a number of dimensions, in particular, by providing high quality products that result in lower workload and costs due to fewer consumer complaints and returns," says Kragh. "In addition, retailers are currently being introduced to the LEGO consumer value proposition so that they can understand what we are all about and why we have such a large and loyal consumer base. Driving repeat purchases is among the key motivating factors for our retail customers," explains Kragh.

By translating the brand promise to particular needs and pressure points of each stakeholder group, the LEGO Group was able to increase relevancy and engagement.

> **Summary: Critical success factors – facilitating stakeholder engagement**
>
> - Recognise that other stakeholders also co-"own" the brand. Do not underestimate their powers and the way they can influence the way the brand is perceived by other audiences.
> - Define what the brand promise means to each stakeholder group. This ensures that the brand promise is relevant and meaningful to everyone.

We will now discuss a showcase for customer, employee and other stakeholder engagement. The case of Ducati illustrates that customer engagement cannot be successful without employee engagement; at the same time, engaged customers will dramatically improve employee engagement. The case also considers the importance of engaging other stakeholders and provides some interesting insights on what works and what doesn't.

THE CASE OF DUCATI – ENGAGING EMPLOYEES, CUSTOMERS AND OTHER STAKEHOLDERS

> The question is: How to entertain and how to excite the audience?
>
> David Gross, Creative Director, Ducati

Background

The Italian motorcycle maker Ducati Motor (DMH) was founded in 1926 in Bologna (Italy). When it was near insolvency in 1996, Texas Pacific (US) took a controlling stake. A former McKinsey man, Federico Minoli, was brought in to restructure the ailing company and to restore its legendary brand name. Since then, Ducati has not only completed a successful turnaround, but has come a long way to bringing its brand promise "Ducati turns dreams into reality" to life for all key stakeholders.

What Minoli and his team of international managers faced in Bologna was not encouraging and very culturally different: "Everyone was young at the company, with the exaggerated good looks of soap opera stars – no one seemed to be actually working. They were mostly posing at the water fountain trading gossip, in front of the coffee machine evaluating style," a tongue and cheek message of Gross in his book *A Memoir of Life, Love, and Motorcycles in Italy*.[21] Then there was a demoralised and defensive Bolognese workforce[22] who contributed their share to a not very welcoming atmosphere.

---

[21] Gross, D.M., *Fast Company: A Memoir of Life, Love, and Motorcycles in Italy*, New York: Farrar, Straus and Giroux, 2007.

[22] Turpin, D., Grand passion, *Business Life*, Nov. 2004: 20.

Creating a dialogue that engages

Engaging employees

"We were all aware that we had to inject energy into the organisation and spread enthusiasm to our employees in order to make our customers really passionate about our bikes," recalls David Gross, Creative Director. "We started to send our employees to customer events, and we offered bikes at discounted prices," says Gross. To show how serious Ducati was about engaging employees, all parking spaces in front of the main office block, which had always been reserved for the cars of the top management team, were allocated to employees who drove a Ducati bike.[23] For new employees instructors were employed to teach them to ride the bikes they made.

Ducati also launched a global corporate advertising campaign coined "Ducati People". The campaign featured Ducati employees riding their motorcycles in and around Bologna. While one objective of the campaign was to enhance brand awareness in the marketplace, the campaign was also seen as a way to instil pride and to better connect employees with the brand and its values. Gross describes: "Ducati employees are tremendously important in the Ducati business, they are our brand ambassadors – it is they who deliver the Ducati magic. Today, our staff, which ranges from highly qualified engineers to factory workers and frontline staff, show a real passion for Ducati. I even dare to say that Ducati makes work meaningful for them." When Ducati bikes were used in the film *The Matrix* employees got a real kick out of it.

Engaging customers

Ducati ownership penetrates social class and status. Ducati customers, or enthusiasts as the company describes them, range from

---

[23] Turpin, D., Grand passion, *Business Life*, Nov. 2004: 20.

well-off private bankers "who park their Ducatis in their living rooms, to simple assembly line employees who save up to pay for their Ducatis".[24] All of them are considered as friends or part of a family drawn together by the distinct Ducati myth, no matter where people come from, whether they are male or female, or speak different languages. Gross explains:

> We call them Ducatisti and speak about a Ducati clan or tribe – what connects them is the bike; this is what they have in common and it is a very strong bond. Ducatisti are very active, very energetic: they have developed their "own" language; some clubs have created their own logo. While some brand managers might see the logo proliferation as a threat for brand dilution we see this as an indication and vitality of our brand strength. We therefore do not seek to control the way our logo is manifested. Actually, we could not achieve that even if we tried. Just imagine if some Ducatisti tattoo the Ducati logo on their back – now that is not something we can control, is it?

Over the years, Ducati was able to create an experience world for their customers that is highly emotionally charged and rich of social fibre. The Ducati world consists of several elements:

The bike – an expression of design and innovation

With their flamboyant red or yellow bodies and high performance Italian pedigree, Ducatis are rivalling Harley-Davidsons as the motorcycle of fashionable choice.[25]

---

[24] Huber, D., Federico Minoli on the Ducati brand, Credit Suisse, 6 Aug. 2004, accessed: http://emagazine.credit-suisse.com/app/article/index.cfm?fuseaction=OpenArticle&aoid=66353&coid=72939&lang=EN

[25] Patton, P., DESIGN NOTEBOOK; as fashion on two wheels, it's a roaring success, *The New York Times*, 7 June 2001, accessed: http://query.nytimes.com/gst/fullpage.html?res=9B02EFDB113FF934A35755C0A9679C8B63&fta=y

Today, Ducati manufactures and distributes four high performance lines of motorcycles within the sport subsegment of the greater than 500 cc road market: Superbike, Super Sport, Sport Naked and Sport Touring. Multiple models within its four product lines are offered, which are differentiated primarily by their engine capacity, colour schemes and fairing.

The Ducati bike is famous for its Italian design, lightness, high performance and dynamism. The bikes are "an amazing product with a great history, culture and quality," says Gross. Design and continuous technical innovations are two features that help surprise and electrify customers. For instance, every Ducati bike has a Desmodromic valve control system, giving the bikes an unmistakable deep booming Ducati engine sound. All Ducati motorcycles share design features that are closely associated with the Ducati brand and serve to distinguish the company's motorcycles from those of its competitors.

In 2000, Ducati launched a hand-built limited-production Super Sport bike named MH900evoluzione. MH is the abbreviation for Mike "the Bike" Hailwood whose amazing racing career has been documented in countless books and films. A source of great pride for Ducati, many of Mike's career highlights have been astride a Ducati. The MH900e was the first bike to be exclusively sold on the Internet. In fact it was the first newly produced motorcycle ever sold on the Internet. The first year's production of 2000 units, priced at €15 000 each, was sold out in 31 minutes on the first of January 2000.

Ducati enables customers to personalise their bikes through acquisition of performance and custom-made accessories such as fenders and custom-painted gasoline tanks. "This meets the needs for Ducatisti to really immerse themselves with the bike; they know every part of the bike very well – some take the bike apart and put it together by themselves," explains Gross.

Racing

The extremely close bond with racing activities has led to the development of a profound synergy between the work undertaken on its competition motorcycles and its consumer products. "This is one of the fundamental reasons why racing is such an important commitment – it allows us to transfer the precious know-how gained through development on the racetrack directly to road bike production," says Gross.

In 2007, Ducati celebrated a historic success: the team secured Ducati's first MotoGP riders' World Championship, completing the hat-trick with the constructors' World Championship and also the team's World Championship. With Desmobid, an online memorabilia auction for fans who want to acquire parts used during a race and signed by the champion, as well as Ducati Corse, a portal for racing, Ducati reinforces the racing passion among Ducatisti (and those who are not yet part of the community).

Ducati Desmo Owners Club (DOC)

DOC's purpose is to connect members in sharing their joy in riding Ducatis as well as to give Ducatisti opportunities for entertainment under the Ducati trademark: members can socialise, build interpersonal relationships, participate in events and profit from exclusive services from DOC in both physical and virtual forms. With a free-of-charge DesmoCard introduced in 1999, members get discounts on Ducati products, Superbike Championship tickets and hotel rates globally.[26] There are more than 200

---

[26] Jelassi, T. and Leenen, S., Embarking on e-business at Ducati Motorcycles (Italy), Case study, 2001, accessed: http://csrc.lse.ac.uk/asp/aspecis/20010051.pdf

clubs spread out globally, for example in Australia, Japan and the USA among others.

While the real DOC physically brings people together, the online version *Ducati Community* is an essential way for Ducatisti to communicate anywhere and in real time. Offering subcategories like the Desmoblog, Desmo Women, fun (wallpaper, photogallery and screensaver) and newsletters, the community allows members to share their riding experiences, post messages and photos, access information on DOC activities, engage in video games and online racing, bet on motorcycle races and create their own Ducati websites.

Ducati Museum

When 55-year-old turnaround manager Minoli came to Bologna, his first priority was building a Ducati museum – to the astonishment of economic experts, and a move that sent employees on strike in protest.[27]

Located at the Ducati factory headquarters, the 1000 m² Ducati Museum highlights 50 years of racetrack heritage and also the history of the company (before it produced motorcycles) founded by the Ducati brothers in 1926. The Ducati Museum can be visited both on- and offline. Ducati has also cooperated with design museums such as the Guggenheim in New York or the Field Museum in Chicago to exhibit Ducati bikes.

---

[27] Huber, D., Federico Minoli on the Ducati brand, Credit Suisse, 6 Aug. 2004, accessed: http://emagazine.credit-suisse.com/app/article/index.cfm?fuseaction=OpenArticle&aoid=66353&coid=72939&lang=EN

Ducati University/Riding school

Ducati managers and technicians lecture at universities and polytechnic colleges on Ducati and its products. Riding courses at all levels are also offered.

Events

The World Ducati Weekend (WDW) is often referred to as the epitome of the Ducati experience. A veritable legion of motorcyclists and motorcycle fans from dozens of nations meet at the Misano World Circuit in Misano Adriatico, Italy, to have fun and celebrate their love for bikes. Since its first edition in 1998, the Misano World Circuit is the perfect backdrop for this celebration of everything that is Ducati. For the occasion, given the prevalence of the well-known main Ducati colour, the circuit turns red from tip to toe, reshaping itself into a "Red Planet" where Ducati fans feel completely at home. A lot is offered: one can sign up for the Ducati University conferences, held by managers and designers from Ducati; or book a trip to the past thanks to the second-hand market or the historical bikes' exhibition. There are stunts, a best custom bike competition, a charity auction, fireworks, music and much more – all to enforce the bond between Ducatisti and the brand.

Ducati stores

Ducati Stores are part of Ducati's own global distribution net and are set up on prime real estates from Manhattan to Tokyo and are exclusively run to distribute Ducati motorcycles, spare parts, accessories and apparel. The apparel that Ducati makes carries the Ducati signature: the material used meets race-driver standards, the design is clean with the typical Italian chic. The outfit contributes to the authenticity of a Ducatisti. The shops provide a high level of customised service and technical support. Among others, a "History Wall" shows images of the Ducati racing heritage; an "Engineering Wall" projects a large-scale drawing of Ducati's flagship motorcycle, 996.

Ducati Corners are set up in multi-brands shops in areas where the market size is not viable for establishing an exclusive Ducati store.

In order to ensure consistency in brand experience, presentation and marketing are pre-designed for both Ducati Stores and Ducati Corners.

Accessories and merchandise

Ducati managed to target the "lifestyle" segment by partnering with international designers like Donna Karan, high-end stores like Harrods and Macy's as well as Sotheby's, a top British auction house. At the same time Ducati established licensing businesses with Puma for the Ducati T-shirt, Oakley sunglasses, toys for children or bike models. As Gross asserted, licensing is "a 2 Mio business in profit . . . this number tells us that we are doing something right and it is an indicator of the health of our brand".

Engaging media, celebrities

Generally, Ducatisti have such a profound passion for their bikes that they are more than willing to show their strong love to the public. Even journalists are not immune. CEO Minoli states in an interview he gave in 2004:

> . . . we received major coverage on the front page of the weekend edition of the *Daily Telegraph*. The report covered the participa-

tion of an old Ducati in a vintage rally. In terms of PR, the article was fantastic and priceless. We would never have the money or the profile to be able to influence the placing of such a story. But there the story was, on the front page, because the journalist responsible was a Ducatista.[28]

Ducati earns frequent media coverage also through Formula One racers and their successes.

Achievements and challenges ahead

Today, Ducati enjoys a high level of customer loyalty with an estimated 60% of repeat purchase intentions. Customers are able to experience the Ducati passion because it is anchored in whatever is done at Ducati. Gross states: "Here at Ducati people do business for different reasons; a lot is done 'per fare una bella figura' (to look good). Our people show true attachment to motorcycles and they do things even sometimes against their economic interest – the passion is really strong."

The Ducati bikes and being part of the Ducati world is not "just a hobby". It is a lifestyle. Gross explains:

> To support this lifestyle, and to continuously fire the passion among your fans is exhilarating, yet very challenging. They put you on test in whatever you do. You have to execute really well. The fact that we are relatively small compared to our competitors might facilitate the creation of an authentic Ducati experience, both on the race track as well as on the roads. It requires different resources if you produce approximately 2 million bikes per year as e.g. Honda does compared to our output which is about 45 000 a year. In the case of Ducati, staying small and focused is certainly a crucial success factor in building a brand myth.

---

[28] Huber, D., Federico Minoli on the Ducati brand, Credit Suisse, 6 Aug. 2004, accessed: http://emagazine.credit-suisse.com/app/article/index.cfm?fuseaction=OpenArticle&aoid=66353&coid=72939&lang=EN

CHAPTER 5

PRACTICAL APPLICATIONS – THE PROCESS OF ALIGNMENT

The process of implementing a connective branding approach requires five key steps as depicted in Figure 5.1. We know from practical experience that most companies do not tackle branding issues in such a systematic and holistic way; therefore, the process is designed in a modular fashion, allowing companies either to work through the entire sequence or to focus on individual steps of particular relevance to their competitive situation and business goals.

Each step in the alignment process is characterised by a number of challenges and critical success factors which we will discuss in the following paragraphs. In addition, we will provide an activity guide at the end of each section.

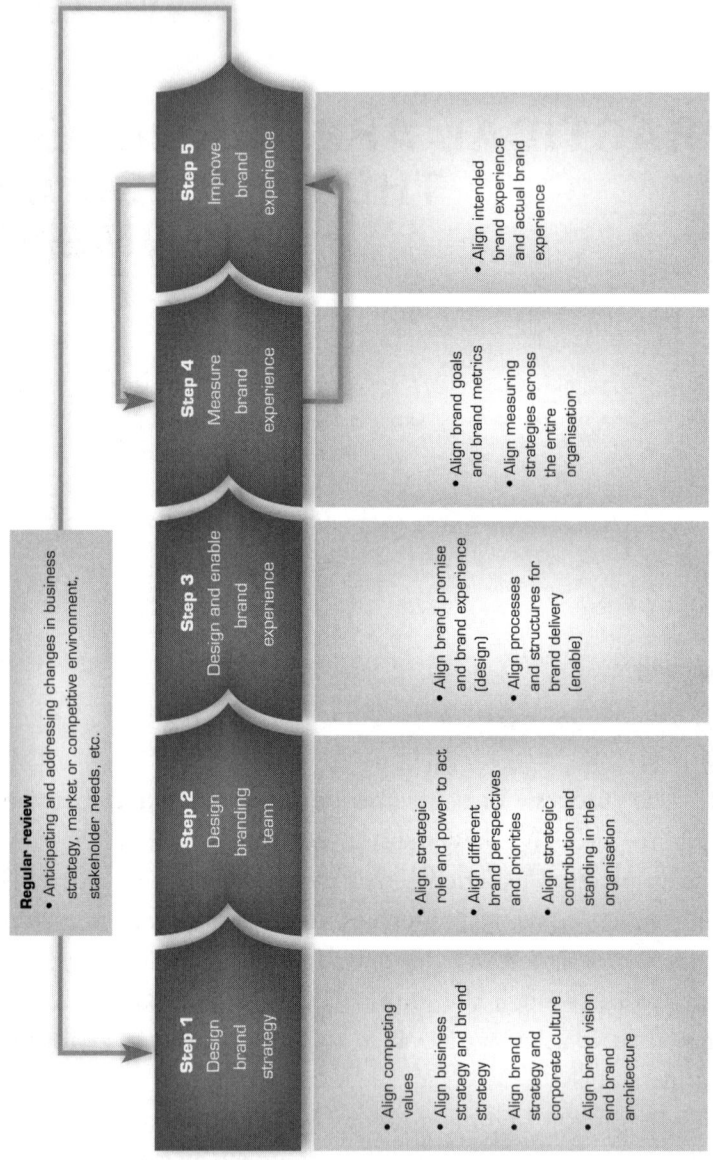

Figure 5.1 Connective branding – process of aligning brand promise and brand experience

STEP 1 – DESIGN BRAND STRATEGY

A new brand strategy is typically designed when a company has grown quickly and finds the need to formalise what they have done intuitively to date; or when more established companies see the necessity to inject new energy into the brand (e.g. to regain currency or relevance or to facilitate integration after a merger or major acquisition), respond to changing market dynamics (e.g. new entrants, new markets, or new products) or express a change in focus (e.g. new business strategy, new leadership, or repositioning).

For example, as jewellery brand Thomas Sabo accelerated their growth, they for the first time found themselves in a situation where it was no longer possible for the entire team to spend enough time with the founder Thomas Sabo to intuitively learn about the brand; they had to make sure that the values that make up Thomas Sabo were transferred to the entire team in a systematic way, thereby necessitating a more formal approach to defining the brand and setting up processes that directly impact and enable the brand.

Whatever the reason for embarking on brand strategy design work, it will typically necessitate the formation of a brand strategy development team which will most likely be temporary in nature, led by a core team of branding experts, and additionally draw on a number of departments and functions to make sure all necessary perspectives are covered. Including top management in the brand strategy development team from the outset is invaluable not only from an input and market intelligence point of view, but also with a view to getting early buy-in and significant support for implementation and ongoing management.

Critical success factor #1: Aligning competing values

Every company is shaped by a multitude of different values – some more prominent than others. For example, there are corporate

282 CONNECTIVE BRANDING

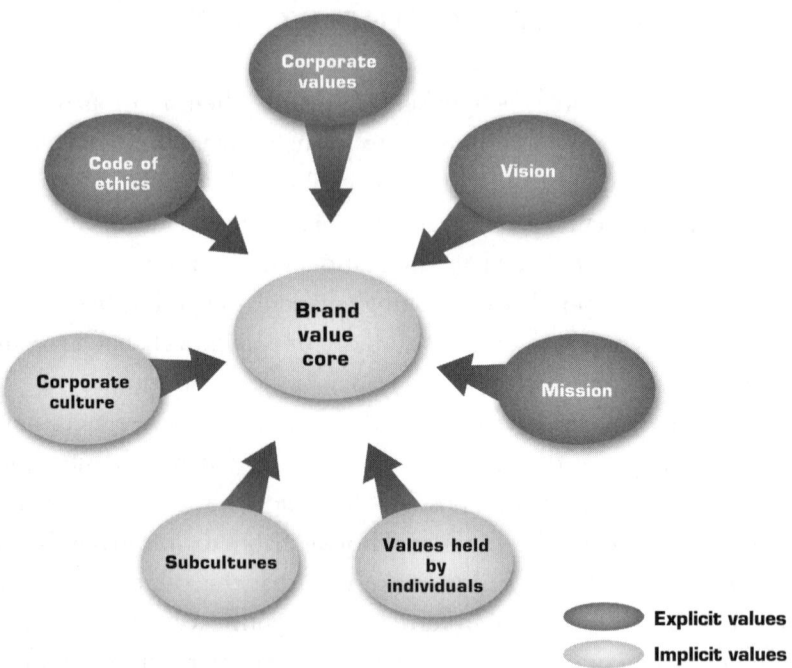

Figure 5.2 Competing sets of values

values made explicit in various official documents, but there are also implicit values that may manifest themselves in a particular corporate culture or even a number of subcultures (e.g. product design, the IT team or the "founding generation"). In addition, each individual employee subscribes to a set of values which will only partially overlap with those imposed by the corporation.

When designing or redefining a brand, all relevant sets of values – implicit and explicit ones – need to be surfaced and checked for coherence (see Figure 5.2). Corporate value statements, codes of ethics, behavioural guidelines, vision and mission statements are all important sources for existing values. In addition, a culture audit may help to surface the more implicit ones.

The brand needs to unify these different sets of values. If the brand does not rest on a shared platform of values, it cannot be translated into a coherent and unambiguous guideline for behaviour. The head of branding of a large global consulting company remarks: "Some people forget that the brand in a service organisation has to come from shared values that have emerged over a long period of time; it has to come from something that is already there – whether you call it values, culture, vision or something else."

The more strongly anchored this shared platform of values is, the more relevant the brand will be to internal stakeholders, thereby increasing the likelihood that they are able and willing to enact the brand and deliver on the brand promise.

CASE STUDY: OLD MUTUAL GROUP

> A London-based international financial services group originating in South Africa and offering asset management, life and general insurance as well as banking, recently went through a brand strategy development process. Increasingly, they felt the need to introduce a group brand that could bring together the many brands that make up their diverse portfolio (see Figure 5.3 with key brands by region).
>
> Each of the business units and brands are shaped by their own sets of values and had to be considered as an input for the group brand. To make things even more challenging, one of the key brands, Skandia, was undergoing brand development work at the same time, turning into a moving target. But this was not the only challenge that Nicholas Bicket, Director of Corporate Affairs at Old Mutual Group, encountered when developing the group brand with his team:
>
>> The first challenge was to get buy-in from the top management. This was a process that took about six months. As they provide and invest the financial resources needed, we developed

284 CONNECTIVE BRANDING

Figure 5.3 Overview Old Mutual Group key brands by region

a clear line of argument why such a project will be beneficial to our business. The pressure to develop a group brand initially came from the individual business units who felt the need to transform the complexity inherent in the old structure into positive management of diversity. This will make us more competitive and add value both to individual business units as well as the group. This was a great starting point for our branding initiative.

The development of the group brand involved representatives of all key business units and functions, including the Corporate Executive Team, Corporate Communications, Investor Relations, Public Relations, Brand Management and the Global Brand Forum (which is made up of the marketing heads of the key business units). Clearly, developing a brand promise that would be accepted across the various business units was a challenging task. Bicket explains (see also Figure 5.4):

> As a first step, we gathered all the key inputs. Very importantly, we used our corporate values of *Integrity, Accountability, Respect and Pushing beyond boundaries* as well as our vision to *become a premier international savings and wealth management group* as a basis for brand development, augmented by business strategy, our competences, and our ambitions, as well as competitive and market insights. Translating our aspirations and values into a brand promise was a lengthy and iterative process. At first, we landed on *Anchored Opportunism* and discussed this proposal with all key business units and functions in much detail. But our detailed discussions quickly surfaced serious issues; most importantly, it was not an intuitive concept that meant the same thing to all people, it basically needed a lot of explanation. So we went back to the drawing board and came up with *Sustaining Growth*. The positive response for this one was overwhelming.

In a next step, the brand promise of *Sustaining Growth* had to be explained in more detail. To this end, internal workshops were conducted to define the desired brand personality and further elaborate on it (see Figure 5.5).

286 CONNECTIVE BRANDING

Figure 5.4 Old Mutual Group brand framework

Bicket highlights:

The brand personality is characterised by five key elements: *Sharp to the opportunity*, *Free to perform*, *Bright*, *Thorough* and *Committed*. These elements are partly anchored and grounded in the culture of the organisation but also provide enough of a stretch to be aspirational. We are well aware that in a services industry like ours, our employees play a crucial role in delivering on the brand promise. In particular, the brand personality as it is perceived by customers will be shaped by the attitudes and behaviours of our employees. We believe that the brand personality of our new group brand will be able to direct and align all our culturally diverse members.

THE PROCESS OF ALIGNMENT

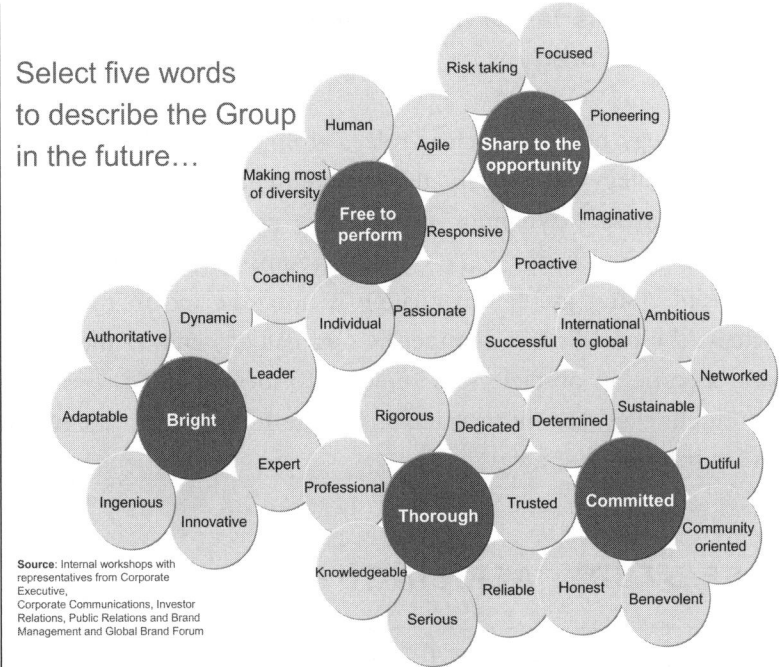

Figure 5.5 Explanation of brand promise

In a next step, Old Mutual will have to tackle implementation of the new group brand. Bicket continues:

> Commitment is only generated if the brand is perceived as relevant and of added-value by employees. This requires the translation of the brand promise into specific activities and messages. For instance, the brand element *sharp to the opportunity* indicates that we recognise and reward entrepreneurial thinking and proactiveness, that we have outstanding customer and competitor insights at local level giving our people a "first to market" capability, and that we are able to act quickly once parameters are agreed. The brand element *Bright* refers to our employees who are not only equipped with the right skills and excellent tools, but also switched on.
>
> The brand implementation process is expected to take roughly three years.

Critical success factor #2: Aligning business strategy and brand strategy

Brand strategy has a very clear role to fulfil – it needs to support business strategy and facilitate achievement of business goals. However, market dynamics, competitive contexts, or even business focus may change very quickly, requiring an adaptation of the business strategy. If this change is not reflected in the brand strategy, the brand can no longer be optimally leveraged and might even become an obstacle to achieving business goals. The case of Aer Lingus illustrates how a drastic change in business strategy can impact the brand strategy.

CASE STUDY: AER LINGUS

> Aer Lingus was established in 1936 as Ireland's national state-owned airline. It had been operating as a traditional full service airline since its inception, offering primary airport use, retention programmes, membership of an airline alliance, and short and long haul flights geared towards both business and leisure travellers flying to and from Ireland.[1] Although Aer Lingus did not manage their brand in a formal and structured manner, they developed significant brand equity with their customers and employees through their consistent delivery of great service. Customers returning to Ireland from abroad often recounted with pride seeing the shamrock emblazoned aircraft on the runway in some overseas airport.
>
> Emerging from an organisational restructuring that was known as the "Cahill Plan", Aer Lingus in 1995 decided for

---

[1] Wallace, J., Tiernan, S. and White, L., Industrial relations and conflict collaboration: adapting to a low fares business model in Aer Lingus, *European Management Journal*, 24, 2006: 338–347.

the first time to take a strategic approach to brand management. David Bunworth, then Sales and Marketing Director at Aer Lingus, remembers: "Aer Lingus was known and loved as a friendly airline; and while always being rated safe, in a professional context some of their standards could be improved." The arrival of no-frills, low-cost providers like Ryanair and easyJet had revolutionised short haul airline travel in Europe with their focus on price leadership, challenging Aer Lingus to clearly define their competitive positioning. Aer Lingus started by conducting market research with leisure and business travellers as well as cabin crew and ground staff. Bunworth explains:

> Market research had been conducted before, but there were no telling insights. So we decided to conduct large numbers of focus groups with all our key audiences. What we found out was that Aer Lingus had great strengths around the ability of connecting with customers, a strong intuitive sense to see beyond what is immediately visible. It became very clear to us that this was a great way to differentiate against low cost providers. We also discovered that professionalism was a bit of a recessive value, something we could improve and build on and which would be greatly appreciated by our customers.

The new Aer Lingus brand values were comprised of the core values *intimacy, intuition* and *professionalism*. While professionalism was primarily directed at the functional attribute level, addressing punctuality of departure and arrival, efficiency of check-in, on-boarding, and other processes, intimacy and intuition were aiming to create an emotional connection between Aer Lingus, its employees, and the customers. The marketing team was acutely aware of the pivotal role employees were to play in delivering on this high-touch brand promise through every point of customer contact, from reservations, to check-in, to the actual flight experience all the way to the frequent flier programme. Therefore, they made sure that every employee understood and supported the new brand promise.

The marketing team was very aware of how important it was that employees were informed first, before any other stakeholders. They allowed sufficient time for the new brand promise to be heard and understood by all staff, giving them multiple opportunities to ask questions, get involved in presentations and discussions and ultimately to adapt their behaviour, before external communication was started. To allow for the brand message to be embraced by all employees, they focused on personal communication with as many employees as possible, taking into consideration complications like shift work, and supplemented personal interaction with mail shots to their home. For example, every employee received a brand manual.

External launch – advertising campaign

When the advertising brief was developed, a good nine months after the internal launch of the new brand promise, the aim was to get a more emotional message across to customers. Ultimately, it was the combination of faultless performance (professionalism) with emotional connection (intimacy and intuition) that would position Aer Lingus successfully against low-cost providers like Ryanair. The customer facing advertising campaign centred around the message of "more than just an airline", supported by the song "True Colours". It also featured members of the cabin crew who had assumed the role of passengers. This not only instilled pride, but the switching of roles also facilitated an even better understanding of customers and helped to further improve the quality of employee–customer interaction. A series of print ads with well-known Irish celebrities highlighted the value-added services offered.

Challenges

One of the challenges Aer Lingus faced in building the brand internally was that operations saw the implementation of a new brand promise as an opportunity to get more staff. Bunworth remembers: "Their standard response was – yes we can do this, but we need 10 more people to do it this way. We quickly learned to communicate that the new brand was not negotiable and to teach every employee that the new brand was a licence to do things differently and better, with the same number of people." However, Bunworth is also quick to draw attention to the issue of overstaffing: "The cost base remained high in the organisation and overstaffing in non-customer facing areas remained a serious issue. High profits limited the negotiation potential with strong unions to take out non-value adding costs."

As with most organisations, Aer Lingus also faced some challenges in overcoming the cynical attitude of non-customer facing staff. Una Ryder, then part of the marketing team, explains:

> They simply did not see the point of it all. So marketing had to demonstrate how all their actions impacted on our customers in the end. For example, it was quite easy to create a link between bags not being handled with care, resulting in damaged or lost luggage, and our core value of professionalism. For the values of intimacy and intuition this was a bit more challenging; I do remember a meeting with the HR team responsible for recruitment who understood that by recruiting staff in line with the brand essence what we were looking for were people with an intuitive and empathetic style of relating to others. This enabled them to develop a brand competency framework that was just as relevant as the functional competences that had traditionally been recruited for.

Fate intervenes

The crisis post-9/11 that affected the entire airline industry and forced many of the airlines to rethink their business model and cost structure also hit Aer Lingus very hard. It nearly went into bankruptcy in 2001. No longer able to count on the financial support of the Irish government (allegedly as a result of EU policy),[2] Aer Lingus management saw no other alternative for a turnaround than transforming Aer Lingus into a low-cost carrier. Unfortunately, there no longer was a senior head of marketing in the organisation at the top table and so nobody spoke up on behalf of the brand. Bunworth explains: "Of course this is difficult to judge from the outside, but it appears as if for senior management at the time, the brand had turned from an asset into a liability, an obstacle to becoming a low-cost provider."

Very clearly, the brand had found its focal point in providing professionalism, intuition and intimacy. The values were anchored very deeply within the organisation, making it difficult for staff to shift.

Several rounds of cost reductions including personnel cuts, channelling sales through their website (they claim 95% of sales are now through the Internet),[3] a reduction in number of different types of aircraft used and a move from a hubs and spokes system towards a point-to-point service accomplished the transformation, together with a fare reduction. While this transformation was both commercially successful and necessary, this transformation resulted in a loss of brand meaning to both

---

[2] Wallace, J., Tiernan, S. and White, L., Industrial relations and conflict collaboration: adapting to a low fares business model in Aer Lingus, *European Management Journal*, 24, 2006: 338–347.

[3] Lonergan, F., Chief marketer Aer Lingus, Sunday Business Post Online.

employees and customers, making the Aer Lingus brand a "body without a core". Una Ryder remembers: "Full service was engrained in this organisation, it was at the core of its distinct competitive positioning and also one of the key sources of pride for staff. They were now asked to go from being a differentiated cabin crew to charging for food and drinks."

This created difficulties for staff, resulting in low morale and decreasing commitment. But it also created mixed messages for customers, since fares were ultimately not reduced enough to be on a par with the likes of key competitor Ryanair, although the offering had been stripped of every perk customers might have enjoyed before, including membership of the **one**world alliance. "Quite simply, the brand offering was slashed and dumbed down to become a low cost product but unfortunately this did not bode well with experienced cabin crew," Bunworth explains. "In addition, they were left out of a vital staff communications and education loop on the new brand promise. As a result, they failed to engage, causing inconsistent behaviours on board that confused passengers."

Today – Aer Lingus survived, but did its brand?

By moving the airline on the service spectrum from full service to "almost" no frills, Aer Lingus was able to re-establish its financial strength in a time of extreme turbulence. In September 2007, after successful completion of the turnaround and its flotation on the London and Dublin Stock Exchanges in 2006, Aer Lingus launched their first brand commercial on television since the turnaround. The campaign reintroduces a human face to the Aer Lingus brand after taking a deliberately functional approach to its branding over the past five years and again features members of the cabin crew, this time demonstrating the friendly care that Aer Lingus still promises to offer in contrast to more unambiguously no-frills rivals such as Ryanair and easyJet. This is an interesting attempt at picking up what might be left of connections with friendliness and warmth albeit under the new guise of a low-cost carrier.

Lonergan, current Marketing Manager at Aer Lingus, is quick to emphasise that the service-driven positioning will not be driven too far, since Aer Lingus does no longer want to position itself as a premium brand. "Our business is flying people from place to place. We've never forgotten that. In our view, low-fare air travel doesn't have to be a bad experience, and can be quite the opposite. I believe with this brand message, we are putting a clear space in our customers' minds between AerLingus and its rivals."[4] The future will tell us whether he is right, but the desired middle position of "low fares, way better" promises the best of both worlds while being in danger of disappointing everyone: those seeking great service and those seeking low prices. One thing is for sure – the middle position is difficult to get right. This may also explain the apparent contradiction in Lonergan's next statement: "This [Aer Lingus] is a 70-year-old brand, plenty of companies would kill for that kind of brand heritage. But at the same time, we have to make our brand relevant to the way people travel now and that's very different to the way they travelled 10 years ago. But our confidence is up now. We know we're established in people's minds as a low-cost operator." What was it again that put a clear space between Aer Lingus and its rivals?

---

[4] The Post.ie, Catherine O'Mahoney, Aer Lingus plans to build Tesco-like image, 30 Sep. 2007, accessed: http://archives.tcm.ie/businesspost/2007/09/30/story26973.asp

Critical success factor #3: Aligning brand strategy and corporate culture

If brand strategy and corporate culture are not in sync, confusing signals are sent to employees, customers, and all other key stakeholders, eroding brand equity as a result. While the brand is an explicit promise to customers, it is also a binding behavioural guideline for employees; at the same time, corporate culture informally orients employees and guides their behaviours and attitudes. As businesses grow, the brand strategy may have been adapted to changing circumstances with corporate culture still lagging behind, creating a disconnect between brand and culture (e.g. a business that is maturing fast but still clinging to a start-up culture). This tension between brand strategy and corporate culture can also translate into a struggle to stay authentic.

CASE STUDY: WIKIPEDIA

> For example, Wikipedia is facing some challenging choices at the moment. Wikipedia started in 2001 as a "feeder" project to the English language project "Nupedia" which was started with the aim of building an online library of articles written by experts. However, it became apparent very quickly that the system used by Wikipedia where anyone could write, review and edit articles was a more effective way of creating an online library. The viral idea spread rapidly, drawing people in who enjoyed connecting with like-minded spirits and who felt empowered by the idea of collecting and making available the entirety of knowledge in one single place (much in the spirit of the ancient and mythical library of Alexandria). As Wikipedia overtook Nupedia, it quickly grew into a significant global project. Today, Wikipedia includes millions of articles in hundreds of languages worldwide and is used extensively as a

reference source worldwide. Criticism with regards to currency and more importantly accuracy of information are constantly diminishing, as Wikipedia has proven at least as reliable as conventional encyclopaedias in many comparisons. As a result, Wikipedia is recognised as a source of reliable information by an increasing number of institutions such as universities, newspapers, and governmental bodies.[5] Quite contrary to intuition, the currency and accuracy of Wikipedia are hard to beat, although – or maybe because – anyone can edit the information. The editing system and ethos of the millions of contributors worldwide have made Wikipedia what it is today – namely one of the world's most popular websites.

Yet, what few people know is that Wikipedia is a trademark of the Wikimedia Foundation and hence a not-for-profit organisation. It relies primarily on volunteers and fundraising from philanthropists. In 2002, Jimmy Wales, one of the founders of the Wikimedia Foundation, announced that there will never be commercial advertisements on Wikipedia (as a result, the URL changed from .com to .org), thereby inscribing the ethos of non-profit in the organisation. This ethos, combined with the value of respect for others, has created a strong volunteer culture that binds the Wikipedia community together. Florence Devouard, Chairwoman of the Wikimedia Foundation, explains: "The community is our gold – without the community there won't be any content. Whenever an important decision has to be taken, the community will have a say. We will take great care not to upset the community. Sometimes, this makes it difficult to come to an agreement, since there is simply no top-down decision."

---

[5] For example, in 2007, Wikipedia was deemed fit to be used as a major source by the UK Intellectual Property Office in the Formula One trademark case ruling. Universities now accept Wikipedia as a source of research and benchmarks against conventional encyclopedias favour Wikipedia on a consistent basis.

One of the key principles Wikipedia operates on is that the information gathered is available to everyone for *free*. Unlike Google, who is digitising information and by this process creating copyrighted content, Wikipedia does not want to become exclusive. This is an important distinction and one that also is a key source of attraction and motivation for the community of contributors and editors. Florence explains: "The Google model is exclusive in a sense that their content is copyrighted, thereby limiting access and use. They are working towards a licensed model, whereas Wikipedia genuinely wants to make the world's knowledge accessible to anyone." And this is one of the key challenges Wikipedia faces today. Watching how Google is taking over larger and larger amounts of data, Wikipedia does not want to be left behind. "There are two camps within Wikipedia right now," highlights Florence. "There are the ones who cannot understand our hesitance to accept advertising money since they think that large revenue streams might help us speed up the process and grow faster. Then there are those who believe that money would spoil our unique culture and ethos that drive our brand and have created this amazing tool." As Wikipedia continues to grow, pressure on its management to accept advertising money will be mounting. However, changing the business model might have a number of severe consequences for the brand. The community of active contributors and editors might lose its lustre as they might increasingly be looking to be compensated for their work; after all, if money is introduced in the equation, some might want to capture a share of it. Yet to others, the new business model might simply signal that they are no longer required and Wikipedia might lose its attraction as the recipient of their contributions. It is difficult to assess whether a change in business model might also have an immediate impact on Wikipedia users, but it would definitely have a significant impact on corporate culture.

Critical success factor #4: Aligning brand architecture and brand vision

Many companies neglect the importance of assigning roles and responsibilities to individual brands in their portfolio. This usually becomes apparent when new brands are acquired and need to be integrated. Brand architecture makes sure that resources are allocated efficiently and in line with business priorities; it also ensures that each brand contributes to and benefits from the brand portfolio in an optimal way.

CASE STUDY: TUI

> The brand portfolio of the Germany-based global tourism company TUI (Touristik Union International) has developed into a highly complex structure due to a series of mergers and acquisitions in recent years. Aligning business strategy, brand architecture and brand vision can be a challenging task, as illustrated below with the story of Preussag, which turned first into TUI AG and then into TUI Travel PLC.
>
> Preussag – since 2002 TUI AG – has undergone a drastic transformation. The former mining company has evolved into one of the world's largest tourism companies in less than a decade. The reorientation began in 1997 when the management of Preussag made its first but far-reaching investment in the tourism business with the acquisition of Hamburg-based company Hapag Lloyd. A year later Preussag bought shares in Touristik International GmbH & Co., in short TUI, Europe's biggest travel company, whose name was later adopted by Preussag.
>
> In autumn 2001 Michael Frenzel, then CEO of TUI, launched a new brand strategy "World of TUI" which involved a bold step in terms of changing the brand architecture from a

house of brands to a branded house. The idea was to introduce a master brand that would bundle all group activities and could become the new "face" of Preussag for interaction with all key stakeholders, including employees, customers, travel agents, tour operators, and others. The master brand would provide a number of benefits – it would strengthen the feeling of belonging to the same company for employees of the various parts of the organisation, it would support the vertical and horizontal integration of different sub-brands and facilitate the integration of companies that had been acquired through a series of mergers. Most importantly, the master brand would enable a consistently positive brand experience for customers.

New brand architecture

"World of TUI" was established as the new master brand, becoming the key point of reference in all stakeholder interactions, including employees, customers, and other stakeholders such as travel agents and tour operators.

New brand vision, mission and values

The "World of TUI" was defined as follows:

- *Brand vision*. Become synonymous with "the most beautiful time of the year".
- *Brand mission*. "Putting a smile on people's faces".
- *Brand values to guide employee behaviour*:
    - "Opening doors" – adopting a welcoming, friendly, and positive attitude.
    - "Going beyond" – striving for excellence and commitment to always find a solution.

- "Enjoying life" – emphasising the enjoyment and fun factor of travelling with and working for TUI.

New logo

The smile inserted between the words "World of" and "TUI" is a visual expression of the brand mission ("Putting a smile on people's faces") and symbolises the emphasis on positive, enjoyment-driven interactions TUI is striving for with employees, customers, and all other key stakeholders.

The multi-colour concept and specially created typeface should bring the distinctive brand values to life across all linguistic and cultural boundaries for a consistent brand promise from the travel agency to the airline to the hotel.

Aligning brand vision and brand architecture

In order to ensure that all brands in the portfolio were properly leveraged with regards to the new brand vision, the brand portfolio was structured into three different segments (see also Figure 5.7)

- *Quality-volume brands.* The brands in this segment were all changed to include a direct reference to the new "World of TUI" master brand. This involved aligning the visualisation with a strong World of TUI endorsement. For example, tour operators Fritidsresor (Scandinavia), Thomson Holidays

Figure 5.6 World of TUI logo

THE PROCESS OF ALIGNMENT

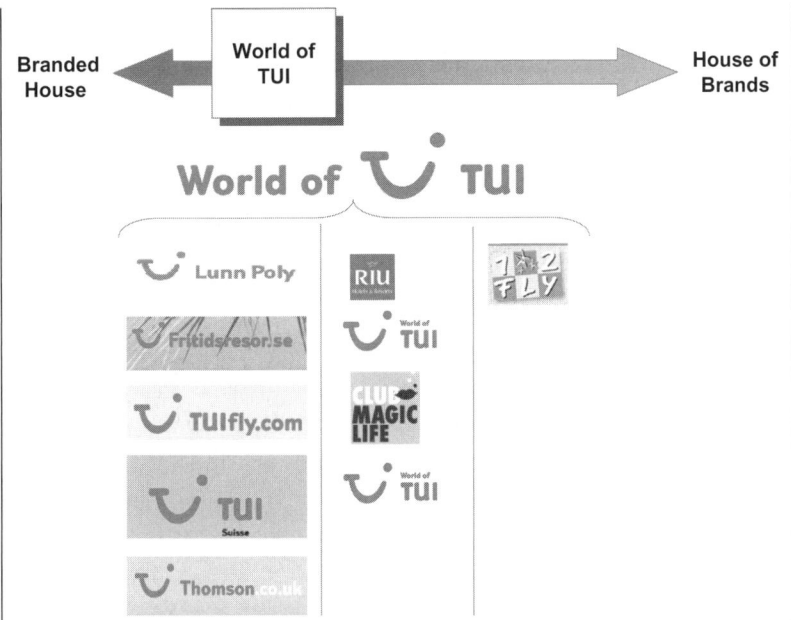

Figure 5.7 Brand management spectrum

(Great Britain) and TUI (Germany), as well as the airline companies TUIfly.com and Thomson Fly, or travel agency Lunn Poly were directly connected to the master brand (*called aligned brands by TUI*). World of TUI is used in the destinations as a master brand for all clients from Europe.

- *Specialist offers.* The brands in this segment retained their original visual manifestation and are only softly endorsed by the master brand, indicating that they belong to the family of TUI while allowing them a fair degree of freedom (*called endorsed brands by TUI*). For example, brands like Robinson, Airtours, RIU and Magic Life target more upscale and luxury holiday segments but can still benefit from association with the new World of TUI brand in the background.
- *Basic holidays.* Companies that focused less on the service aspect and more on price and hence have business models

and brands that are less compatible with the vision and values of "World of TUI" are not at all endorsed by the master brand and remain as standalone brands (called non-endorsed brands by TUI). For example, in the case of 1,2-Fly, a connection with World of TUI would create expectations that are not intended. By the same token, 1,2-Fly might infuse the master brand with associations around "basic, cheap and cheerful" that are not desirable for World of TUI.

Unfortunately, poor financial performance in 2006 prompted further changes in business and brand portfolio strategy. In March 2007, TUI Group announced a merger between its tourism division and the British provider of specialised holidays, First Choice Holidays PLC. First Choice is an integrated travel operator with its main strengths in specialist travel. This move complements the highly competitive and volatile mainstream packaged holiday segment with a more stable and profitable specialised travel segment. TUI CEO Frenzel commented: "With the merger we have forged by far the biggest and one of the most profitable travel groups in the world – with a customer base of almost 30 million. In the competition with low-cost carriers and online portals we are assuring and securing our Group and consolidating our position in the special travel segments that are associated with growth and profitability."[6]

The new company is named TUI Travel PLC, headquartered in the UK. TUI AG holds 51% of the shares and First Choice (FC) 49%. The former FC CEO Peter Long became the new CEO of TUI Travel PLC. As of 2007, with a brand portfolio that includes more than 200 brands, TUI Travel PLC generated a revenue of €18 billion, employs 48 000 people, and serves 27 million customers.[7]

---

[6] http://www.tui-group.com/en/pressemedien/hv/speech_frenzel.html
[7] http://www.tuitravelplc.com/

Aligning brand architecture and brand vision – again

The structure of the TUI Travel brand architecture is still organised around *Aligned*, *Endorsed* and *Non-endorsed brands* – but obviously with increased complexity. The new portfolio structure of TUI Travel PLC now includes five areas, including a mainstream sector comprising a number of vertically integrated tour operators across Europe, a specialist sector, an online destination services sector, an activity sector and finally a joint-venture cruise line.

In February 2008, the new vision, strategic goals and values were presented to the entire first and second level management (550 people) in Paris.

The new brand strategy includes the following elements:

- *Brand vision.* To make travel experiences special.
- *Brand values to guide employee behaviour.*

Figure 5.8 TUI Travel's strategic brand framework

- "Customer obsessed" – respecting customers and sharing the belief that there is no such thing as a mass market but a huge market of individuals.
- "Playing to win" – being passionate about being the best and about loving everything they do.
- "Value driven" – sharing an infectious entrepreneurial streak and a clear focus on the need for profitability; it is also about adding value to customer's experience.
- "Responsible leadership" – being committed to sustainable development and to making a positive impact on society; it is also about valuing each other, celebrating local differences and actively seeking to contribute to a better world.

Both the strategic goal and vision were formulated in a way "that international subsidiaries are accommodated," says zur Oven-Krockhaus, Head of Corporate Branding, TUI Travel. The strategic framework distils into *Winning Spirit*. The visual manifestation will remain the same.

Challenges ahead

TUI Travel now faces a number of challenges. First of all, the different corporate identities need to be aligned. Zur Oven-Krockhaus points out:

> While we have already shown that we can handle such complex projects, this time the situation is slightly different as more different businesses need to be merged – some with a highly entrepreneurial corporate culture and leadership style, some having structures of a big corporation with sometimes slower and less flexible decision-making processes. Both different corporate cultures and culture diversity need to be addressed. This is a great challenge.

Second, the values of "World of TUI" need to find a home in the new strategy. This is an issue that will be addressed bottom up.

Third, launching another set of brand values in such short sequence will very likely reduce enthusiasm for the latest brand strategy and generate cynicism, reducing the new efforts to "just another programme of many to come". This will have to be actively managed.

Activity Guide Step 1 – Designing the brand strategy

Working through the activity guide shown in Figure 5.9 will help set up a branding project to design the brand strategy.

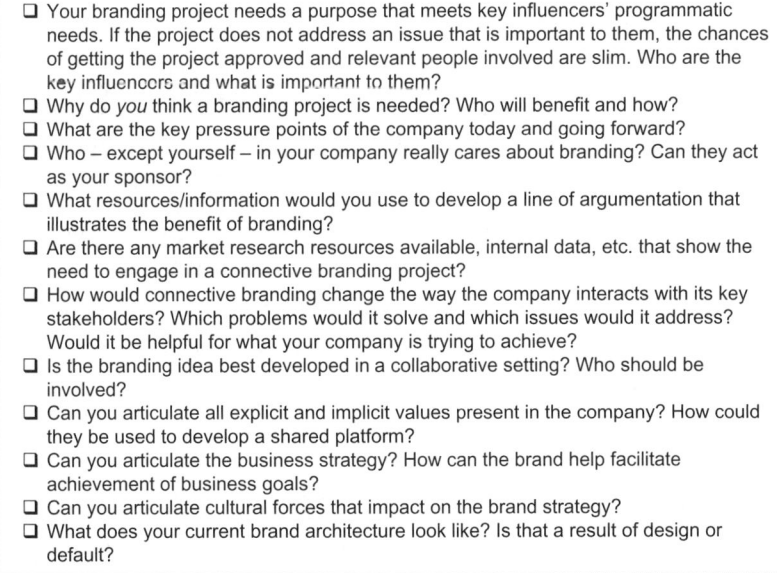

Figure 5.9 Activity Guide Step 1 – Designing the brand strategy

STEP 2 – DESIGN BRANDING TEAM

Once the brand has been defined or redefined, the core branding team needs to be established if it does not exist already. Ideally, for the sake of continuity, core members of the brand strategy development team also become part of the core branding team. Most likely, the branding team will embark on a lengthy process of educating the organisation on all levels about the value of branding, demonstrating that branding is a strategic contributor and worthy of a seat on the board.

Critical success factor #5: Aligning strategic role and power to act

In order to continually engage the organisation in the brand promise, the core branding team needs to be sufficiently empowered to facilitate alignment between brand promise and corporate actions, infrastructure and processes. This is only possible if the brand management team is furnished with sufficient power to act. In a networked collaboration model the core branding team will have contact with and influence on any process or structure that is seen as an enabler for the brand. For example, in the case of a large B2B technology company based in Austria, the brand manager participated in the presentation of the new HR strategy delivered by the HR department; they continually referred to "headquarters" and "subsidiaries" until the brand manager raised his hand and explained that the brand's value core centred on team spirit and hence did not lend itself to a separation into "us" versus "them". As a result of the ensuing discussion, the HR strategy had to be revised, better reflecting the brand.

Returning to the example of the UK-based international IT company with the technology-focused CEO discussed earlier, we have already seen how a lack of engagement of the CEO and top management team in brand building can limit its impact and potential. After the branding team had obtained sign-off for the new (and diluted) brand promise, there was a strong expectation that the new brand would raise employee morale, address attrition problems, and unify the separate cultures; however, these expectations did not come with the necessary power to act. While the marketing team wanted to properly launch the new brand across the organisation, they did not have a mandate to do so. Therefore, their internal implementation work was limited to producing a simple, one-page summary of the brand promise which was made available to all employees. It was easier for the branding team to brief an advertising agency to create a customer facing campaign, hoping that it would also raise awareness internally. They placed billboard ads at important business airports around Europe and ran full-page ads in business papers. However, they very soon noticed that nothing happened – employee morale did not change, integration was not facilitated, and even customer impact was lower than expected. Why? Well, the strategic objectives did not match the power to act. Had the branding team been furnished with sufficient power to act, they might have been able to leverage this opportunity for the benefit of the company; however, they ended up spending money without creating an impact.

Critical success factor #6: Aligning different brand perspectives

As discussed earlier, connective branding requires that corporate reputation, investor relations, public relations, human resources, centres of sustainability, communications, and any other functions which drive the brand and/or regularly engage customers, employees or other key stakeholders, become part of the core or extended branding team, or at a minimum collaborate closely.

However, the perspectives on branding and the importance of branding within these functions will vary greatly. Corporate reputation, for example, will be more closely aligned with branding than others. Sabrina Helm, Associate Professor of Retailing at the University of Arizona and a reputation management expert, explains: "Branding and corporate reputation are highly intertwined and as a matter of fact both aim to create the same effects on consumers and other stakeholders, that is facilitating favourable associations in order to differentiate from competitors. Over time this should result in trust, credibility, and integrity."

For those functions that interact with key stakeholders but are not (yet) focused on branding as a priority, an educational process as well as persistence are required. For example, the investor relations officer of a large global insurance company explained:

> Analysts are primarily motivated by numbers and financial performance. Therefore, to an investor relations executive everything else, including brands, will only be relevant as a means to this end. Of course there is always ambiguity around how valid and how solid future predictions are; in this context, the brand strategy could be of interest to them, but only as far as it helps them to interpret or even validate the business strategy and communicated business goals. While strong brands are known to facilitate growth through product and market extensions as well as increase staying power through tough times, it is still difficult to put all that into figures.

Similarly, human resources may not necessarily think about the brand when briefing an executive search firm in the process of personnel selection. Katrien Demeester, search executive at head hunting firm Russell Reynolds, explains the role "brand" typically plays in finding a suitable senior management candidate:

> We do not really use the word brand so much, but we work with the concept of company culture. "Cultural fit" is about how well the candidate fits with the company culture. We always ask our clients to describe their culture to us, but the answers are not always valid – sometimes there is an image gap between perceived culture and actual culture, and sometimes, the attributes managers use to describe their culture are quite generic and interchangeable, like collaborative or international, therefore losing their defining quality. In

these cases we will have to derive our information from alternative sources like teasing it out in questions about what drove recent hires to be more or less successful, and by ensuring we interrogate a large enough set of the client's managers.

The need for collaboration and aligning perspectives can also come from the desire to bring closer together a number of acquired brands in a portfolio. As the marketing director of a large global services company remarks: "I am a firm believer in using every tangible aspect of brands in particular for businesses with intangibles like a service organisation. So setting about a visual identity that puts a stake in the ground and sets out a singular future direction, can be a major step forward in aligning different brands in a portfolio."

CASE STUDY: GATEGROUP

For example, gategroup, launched in February 2008, is the result of a series of recent acquisitions by global airline catering provider Gate Gourmet and consists of 11 different companies (see Figure 5.10). While each of these companies has a specialist focus, they all work together to position gategroup as a comprehensive provider of flight services, including catering and hospitality, in-flight solutions such as design and food contact items, as well as aircraft provisioning and logistics. As a first step in bringing these companies closer together, a visual identity for the gategroup umbrella was developed which can serve as a shared point of reference going forward. Therefore, it was important that a symbol was chosen that can work with the brand values and culture of each of the 11 brands. "gategroup so far is mainly an empty construct that needs to be filled with life over time. We need to be aware that every customer interaction point pays in our brand account," remarks Bram Thissen, Creative Director of Corporate Identity and Brand,

310 CONNECTIVE BRANDING

gategroup™	Catering and Hospitality Solutions	Airport Handling and Logistics	In-flight Solutions
	Gategourmet *a gategroup member*	GATESAFE *a gategroup member*	Elan *a gategroup member*
	pourshins *a gategroup member*	Gate Aviation *a gategroup member*	Performa *a gategroup member*
	Supplair *a gategroup member*		HARMONY *a gategroup member*
			deSter *a gategroup member*
			potmstudios *a gategroup member*
			Gate Solutions *a gategroup member*

Figure 5.10 gategroup brand portfolio by business area

potmstudios, now also a gategroup member. In a next step, gategroup management will need to establish guidelines for the interaction with each other in order to ensure that all activities are channelled towards the objective of a relevant customer brand experience.

Critical success factor #7: Aligning strategic role and standing in the organisation

Not all companies believe in branding, and of the ones that do, not all give branding the standing it deserves. When companies "discover" the value of branding, for example as they experience accelerated growth and require a mechanism that helps preserve a certain culture and align employees behind a shared purpose, branding needs to be introduced to the organisation as a new discipline and strategic driver.

Traditionally, the branding team was located on the middle management level. Often seen as the department that organises events, arranges sponsorship contracts and produces marketing collateral, the branding team did not necessarily enjoy the standing in the organisation required to obtain a seat on the board. In order to be seen as a strategic contributor and driver, the branding team must develop and put forward a strategic programme that facilitates the achievement of business objectives. The branding team must seek participation in and contribution to discussions about strategic issues and try to create awareness and appreciation for branding as a strategic discipline. As already discussed in the engagement section, sponsorship of the brand in the C-level suite is very important, access to top management will not only benefit the brand, but also the standing of the branding team within the organisation; it will increase their clout and facilitate the alignment of underlying processes and infrastructures over time.

CASE STUDY: NETAPP

For example, in March 2008 NetApp, a fast growing global software brand based in the USA, publicly launched a new brand identity which was built on NetApp values and practices. This brand identity provided a consistent and systematic expression which had previously been lacking. In order to introduce the idea of branding to the entire organisation, Dave Hitz, one of the two founders of NetApp, used his blog called "Dave's blog" to explain in non-marketing terms (most readers are likely engineers) what a brand identity is, why it is important, why a new one was required, and how it impacts individual employees. Here is an excerpt:[8]

> At its heart, branding is about making promises. If you explain to people how your company can help them, the "brand promise", then they can figure out for themselves whether to buy from you. (I wrote this blog entry *about the idea of a brand as a promise*.) Based on past experience, I expect many readers – especially technical ones – to view this as so much marketing bullshit. Ironically, NetApp has never spent much on branding and awareness because our engineering-centric executive staff largely shared this view ... That's fair, but other aspects of branding are trickier to get right. I said earlier that if you tell people what you do, then they can figure out for themselves whether to be customers, but it's tricky to get the details right. Your explanation must be honest, clear, and relevant. If you aren't *honest* about what you can do, customers will figure that out, and you'll have a nasty backlash. If you aren't clear, then people won't understand what you are trying to say. Also, you must take a variety of audiences into account. Historically, we focused on the technical folks who use our products, but the higher-level business people who write the checks and make final decisions on vendor selection are equally important. Finally, you must be *relevant*. There are many

---

[8] http://blogs.netapp.com/dave/

> true things that we could say about NetApp, but we want to share the true things that customers care about, that will make them want to buy from us. (Just to be clear, there is a profit motive here.) For our top level messaging, we also want to say true things that are of interest to both technical and business people.

Francesca Karpel, Senior Manager Internal Communications at NetApp explains:

> The early focus of internal communications was on "why" the new brand identity was needed. Senior leaders in the company were briefed on the brand strategy through 2 global meetings in the fall of 2007 and provided with a toolkit so that they could talk with their teams about the "why" behind the brand strategy. At the beginning of 2008, the senior leaders were given an overview of the global roll-out plan as well as a sneak peak at the brand assets. Again they were asked to be advocates for the brand with their teams. [. . .] We solicited candid employee response to the brand strategy. We interviewed employees following both the Senior Leaders Meeting and the global roadshow sessions for an internal news program called Roving Reporter. Soundbytes from 27 interviews comprised a pre-meeting show for the global All Hands Meeting held a week before the public launch.

> Now that the brand has been launched, the corporate marketing and HR teams will partner on ongoing internal communications, training and events that will sustain the awareness of the brand and the standing of the branding team.

Activity Guide Step 2 – Designing the brand team

Working through the questions in Figure 5.11 will help you determine whether the time is right to adopt the model of networked collaboration in your organisation.

314 CONNECTIVE BRANDING

> - ❑ Can you articulate the standing of branding in your organisation? Do enough people care about the brand?
> - ❑ Do you already have a platform for starting or continuing the brand dialogue?
> - ❑ If you do not have a platform, how can you inspire the right people to discuss branding?
> - ❑ Who else impacts directly on the brand? Which functions regularly interact with employees, customers or other key stakeholders? Do they share your views on branding?
> - ❑ What are the strategic objectives of the brand in your organisation? Do you have the mandate to address them?
> - ❑ Who should be part of the team? Should there be a core team and an extended team? Who would represent the brand on the board? How is the branding budget allocated?
> - ❑ How can you best initiate collaboration? How can you make sure that the process does not stall?
> - ❑ Is this the right time to build a branding team based on collaboration? Or do you need to start off with something smaller to build trust among potential partners and to develop experience working together?

Figure 5.11 Activity Guide Step 2 – Designing the brand team

STEP 3 – DESIGN AND ENABLE BRAND EXPERIENCE

With the brand strategy defined and the branding team in place, the next step is to design the intended brand experience for employees, customers, and all other key stakeholders. The most systematic and holistic way to achieve this is by working through the interaction model; it allows companies to understand how a particular experience is generated and how to bring it in line with what the brand is all about.

Critical success factor #8: Aligning brand promise and brand experience (design)

Connective brands reflect the brand promise in every single point of interaction between the company or brand and key stake-

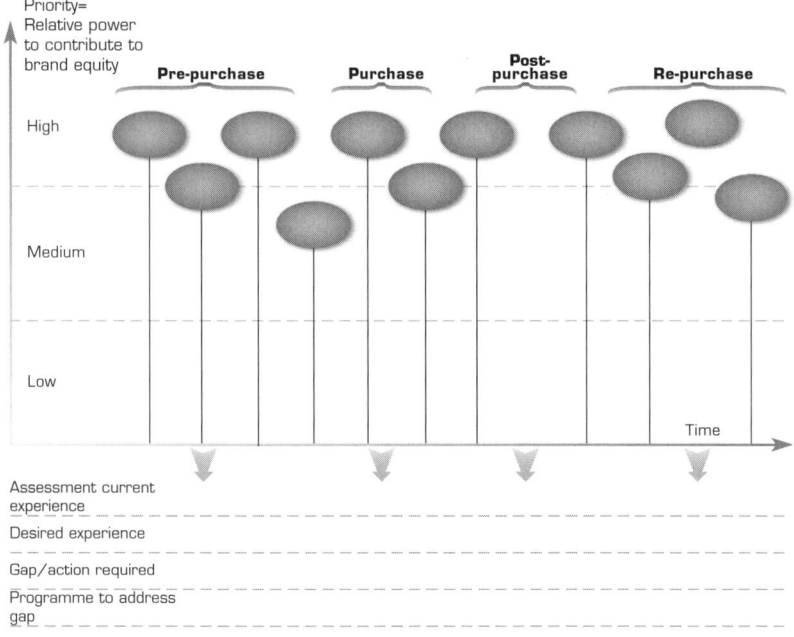

Figure 5.12 Key points of interaction

holders. Of course, not all interaction points carry the same importance and relevance, therefore it is important first to optimise the points with the biggest impact potential. For example, an Austrian jewellery brand knows that the actual purchasing situation is one of the key interaction points between their brand and their potential customers. They make jewellery with a difference – they recreate art from different historical periods in their exquisite enamel pieces. With ancient art being the very centre of their product and brand differentiation, it is not only essential that they can create and control the appropriate customer experience in the retail environment, but also provide sufficient information to potential customers. Therefore, they have decided exclusively to sell their jewellery through their own stores, all located in upscale neighbourhoods and following a particular design, and – most importantly – staffed by sales assistants who are passionate about art and hold a higher degree in arts. The head of marketing explains:

> What makes our jewellery valuable is not the use of precious stones and gold, but the artistic interpretation, celebration and recreation of historical periods. This is not necessarily intuitive and requires a good deal of explaining and educating. We really have to explain to new and potential customers how our jewellery is different from mass market fashion jewellery; that every piece is hand-crafted in our workshops in Vienna with considerable effort and skill, how we invest time and thought in extracting the most beautiful designs, how we create unique collections, etc. Interestingly enough, once this message has gotten across, many of our customers keep coming back for more. We also have to take into consideration that not all parts of the world appreciate the same forms of art. For example, one of our collections reproduces famous art from Klimt and Monet. While most of our European customers would instantly recognise these pieces, on the West Coast of the US Klimt and Monet are less well known, making it doubly difficult to explain the USP of the jewellery; other historical eras like the Egyptian, Greek and Roman art are more universally understood. Still, there is great emphasis on our sales staff to get across what makes us special as a company – our passion for art.

In service industries employees play an even bigger part in delivering on the brand promise in every interaction point. Coming back to the Aer Lingus example, the marketing team had to make sure that the intended brand promise of intimacy, intuition, and professionalism would translate into the intended customer experience; they rolled out an internal brand building programme over a period of roughly nine months. They gave around 40 presentations detailing the new brand promise and translating the core values into relevant messages for each audience. Whether they were talking to pilots, cabin crew or ground handling staff, they would make sure to give examples of how the brand promise would impact their tasks, their responsibilities, their expected behaviour, and the decisions they had to make. The translation of the core values into expected behaviours was particularly important in order to help employees understand when their behaviour was or was not in line with the brand. For example, the value of intimacy could be translated into preferential treatment of frequent travellers. "Roughly 35% of our customer base was frequent travellers at the time; these customers in particular were keen to experience a certain closeness, from having their personal details and preferences at our fingertips to knowing them by name," David Bunworth, then Sales and Marketing Director at Aer Lingus, highlights:

> Therefore, it was important for our customer facing staff to understand that. What worked really well to get this across was to combine cabin crew and customers for working sessions. For example, we once invited 50 cabin crew and 50 frequent travellers to the K-Club and asked them to discuss their experiences with and expectations of Aer Lingus. It was a real eye opener for our cabin crew to hear directly from our most valued customers how their actions would impact not only how they experienced each flight, but also what they thought about the airline overall.

For Thomas Sabo, a global silver jewellery brand, the product itself is one of the key interaction points. Their jewellery stands out through its unique and witty style, based on powerful symbols available as charms. The various collections pick up on the popularity of symbols across cultures and occasions, like pretzels and beer mugs for the opening of the Munich Oktoberfest, or provocative interpretations of love and relationship symbols like the snake and the apple (see Figure 5.13). The particular challenge faced by the company is to stay a step ahead in terms of what is trendy so that emerging symbols can be integrated into new collections in time. "While the popularity of symbols continually changes, a good example which may become important in the future is 'Great Blessing', a symbol which is already trendy in Asia and is about to be accepted increasingly in Europe and the USA," says CEO Bernd Stadlwieser.

Figure 5.13 Thomas Sabo Collier Seduction

Critical success factor #9: Aligning processes and structures for brand delivery (enable)

Once the intended brand experience is designed, all enabling processes and structures need to be geared for brand delivery. This requires prioritisation. The relative importance of interaction points represents a natural way to prioritise them; however, ease of change might also be a consideration. When Aer Lingus set out to implement their new brand, they prioritised the required changes to their offering partly by customer relevancy and partly by ease of implementation. For example, they revamped their frequent flier programme, invested in new aircraft to offer improved levels in time of comfort and an expanded network, upgraded their business and Gold Circle lounge network for frequent fliers, provided priority Fastrack security clearance at major airports for all Premier (business class) customers and bought new, more comfortable seating for high paying Premier passengers.

THE PROCESS OF ALIGNMENT

Employee behaviour is a key driver of brand experience. However, individual behaviour always carries some unpredictability and can never be controlled completely. Personnel selection processes have therefore received increasing attention as one way to increase likelihood of brand supportive behaviour. The hypothesis is: the more congruent the employee values are with those of the brand, the more likely he or she will be to enact the brand. However, companies increasingly outsource the personnel selection process to external partners. How can recruitment be designed so that it is still in line with the company's brand? Thomas Linquist, a consultant at international executive search firm Egon Zehnder International, explains:

> When searching for an ideal candidate, the required skills are of course the primary factor. In addition to technical and leadership competencies, cultural fit does come to bear in the selection process. Brand, however, is not a priority for every client. For example, in OEM driven industries where specialised companies supply components to large established manufacturers like in the automotive supply industry, a supplier's products are often not visible to the consuming public. As a result, the suppliers typically place little importance on brand building. In this case, the attributes of an "ideal" candidate tend to be predominantly functional or technical. By contrast there are other companies, for example in the luxury goods or also fast moving consumer goods sectors, where the brand seems to permeate all functions and the overall style of the company. This brand identity is intertwined in the culture and therefore by ensuring a candidate's chemistry and a cultural fit with the hiring managers we would be in effect supporting the brand through talent acquisition. In other words, key decision makers shape and perpetuate the corporate culture and the brand in very significant ways by deciding which new leaders will join the team.

While many companies employ highly sophisticated personnel selection tools, these often do not protect them from bad hiring decisions. Tim Leberecht, VP of Marketing and Communications of frog design, a worldwide leader in strategic–creative consulting, offers a more pragmatic point of view:

Potential frog design employees have to go through a rigid selection process which is accompanied by people from different departments to increase objectivity. While I believe we are pretty successful in finding the right people that match our value system, proven by low turnover rates and high degree of employee engagement, I am not sure it is the rigid process that achieves that. The personnel selection process develops its own dynamic, which is influenced by the activities involved, those who select potential employees as well as by the applicants themselves. In the end, you are never sure whether the applicant really fits your company until they start work there, and selecting people is always an intuitive decision.

Activity guide step 3 – Designing and enabling brand experience

Working through the activity guide in Figure 5.14 will help you to design and enable welcome and attractive brand experiences.

> ❑ Which key interaction points typically characterise the brand experience for employees, customers, and other key stakeholders?
> ❑ Can you rate each interaction point in terms of relevance to the stakeholder?
> ❑ How can you make sure the brand is reflected in each interaction point (design)?
> ❑ Which processes and structures need to change in order to enable the intended brand experience in each interaction point?
> ❑ Who do you need to collaborate with in order to achieve this?
> ❑ How can you cluster activities in order to maximise impact?
> ❑ Are there any quick wins/early successes you could leverage to keep motivation high?

Figure 5.14 Activity Guide Step 3 – Designing and enabling brand experience

STEP 4 – MEASURING BRAND EXPERIENCE

In order to validate that the *intended* brand experience equals what employees, customers, and other key stakeholders *actually* experience, regular measuring and subsequent fine-tuning are required.

When selecting a measuring approach, simplicity, effectiveness, and transparency are paramount.

Critical success factor #10: Aligning brand goals and metrics (measure the right things)

When setting up brand metrics, great care has to be taken to measure the right things and not the easy things. Measuring brand experience in every interaction point is highly effective (see, for example, the description of the SOPI method in Chapter 3). For example, UBS, the global financial services provider, have started to measure how important individual interaction points are with regards to the customer's purchasing decision as well as how attractive and how informative interaction points are in their current design. The applied method is based on assigning brand experience points to each interaction point, which are then distilled into an overall importance index. This will allow the marketing team to optimise the marketing mix and shift focus and resources to the most influential interaction points; provided interaction points have been identified correctly. For example, when UBS conducted their pilot study in the UK, it confirmed that advertising had very little impact on the purchasing decision for the tested target audience of wealthy individuals, whereas word of mouth carried a great deal of decision making power.

In the case of Aer Lingus described earlier, the marketing team conducted research pre-, during and post- the brand building programme in order to measure the impact of the new brand. This measured customer's perceptions of the brand values in action as experienced through the behaviours of employees. Each value – such as intimacy, for example – was translated into a number of expected behaviours such as responsiveness, overall cabin atmosphere and the sense that a passenger felt truly valued – these were then tracked and measured over time and used as a framework for measuring the brand's effectiveness.

Aer Lingus learned that while frequent travellers appreciated a certain closeness and connection with their preferred airline, there was a clear boundary that should not be crossed. Bunworth, former Sales and Marketing Director at Aer Lingus, explains:

> Some passengers felt patronised, or even smothered, by our staff. It was very helpful to be able to demonstrate cause and effect of their behaviour. Our co-invention workshops with customers, staff, and experts from a number of different fields were excellent for this. However, not all experiments worked out. For example, we also invited some of our most valued customers to come and help select the wine for our in-flight service. But they were intimidated rather than excited, resulting in anxiety instead of a feeling of real connectivity with the brand.

Similarly, professionalism was measured by speed of check-in, baggage handling and punctuality. Aer Lingus' level of delivery was benchmarked against key competitors like British Airways, British Midland and Ryanair. Over time, Aer Lingus would perform better against intimacy, intuition and professionalism than its competitors who were focused on different values and positioning strategies. Internal perception of brand performance was not measured, but might have provided a much deeper level of insight.

NetApp, the software company that launched their new brand identity as discussed earlier, measured the uptake of the new brand with employees. According to Francesca Karpel, Senior Manager Internal Communications, the early metrics within two weeks of the public launch showed global employee ownership of the new brand: "The brand enablement site for employees has received over 5500 unique visits within the first 10 days, which is over 75% of the total employee population. In addition, over 500 sales reps have actively participated in brand related forums."

Critical success factor #11: Aligning brand measurement strategies across the organisation

Large organisations often use measurement to get funding for a particular cause, to get political buy-in, and/or to create a sense of urgency. As a result, many people measure a number of things in many different ways. The lack of coherence and comparability seems wasteful and is not in the interest of connective branding. The approach of networked collaboration will ensure that the organisation develops a shared understanding of what brands are and can do. This will eventually necessitate alignment also of measurement strategies.

Helen Casey, Head of Brand at Old Mutual PLC, is well aware that they need to install a coherent brand measurement system that is shared by all business units, regardless of their particular focus or level of brand knowledge. She points out:

> Not only do we have to acknowledge that there are different levels of intensity with which we should communicate the new group brand identity, the measuring system also needs to be adapted. Currently, each business group has their own measurement tools, partly because the target markets are quite different and partly because they are in different branding phases. However, we still need to be able to understand how we are faring as a group against our targets for each of the target audiences, including our employees.

Bicket, Director of Corporate Affairs, adds: "Also, the various organisations should benchmark against one another, allowing ideas and processes to be exported from one organisation to the other within the group."

Activity guide

Working through the questions in Figure 5.15 will help evaluate how brand experience is measured in your company.

> ❏ Who in your company measures brand-related issues?
> ❏ Do you measure the right things?
> ❏ Is there a platform in place that pools all brand-related research? If so, do you have access to this platform?
> ❏ Are research results comparable across business units?
> ❏ How are research results communicated and to whom?
> ❏ Is there corrective action based on research result?
> ❏ Are there feedback loops in place? Who is involved?

Figure 5.15 Activity Guide Step 4 – Measuring brand experience

STEP 5 – IMPROVING BRAND EXPERIENCE

Brand experience is comprised of many interactions, each of which is an opportunity to build the brand. Measuring results provides the basis for continually improving and fine-tuning each interaction point in order to bring intended and actual brand experience closer and closer together.

Critical success factor #12: Aligning intended brand experience with actual brand experience

Aligning intended and actual brand experience requires the analysis of individual interaction points as well as a critical view of the entire system. Looking at individual interaction points will reveal opportunities to better engage employees, customers, and other key stakeholders, and to improve underlying processes. For example, a Germany-based online dating service present in many European countries noticed that the share of women in Germany dropped drastically over a very short period of time. Alarmed by this development, they measured customer experience and came to find out that their tone and style was not in line with the expectation of their target audience. Their managing director explains:

Our brand values are all about having fun while also being sincere and genuine. In Germany we started out by emphasising the fun element more, but soon noticed that female subscribers were declining rapidly, which of course could be disastrous for our service. We conducted research into the matter and found out that German women need a high level of trustworthiness and security from their online dating service. Our messages were too flirtatious for them, suggesting that our service might lack sincerity. With that in mind, we have revamped our site completely, changed our software, user interface, and communication style both in our ads and on our website, and it fixed the problem very quickly. In other countries, like France, for example, we are finding that a more flirtatious style is not only accepted, but wanted.

Looking at the entire system of interaction points will also help to determine whether any interaction points are missing (e.g. incomplete service) or superfluous (e.g. cumbersome process). For example, a German service provider measured customer experience in each interaction point and found out that they were excellent in the sales and project delivery phase, but still only got mediocre marks on overall customer satisfaction. After analysing their processes, they discovered that they lacked a substantial post-project interaction point.

Operational efficiency is sometimes imposed on an organisation without regard for the brand impact. For instance, the "commoditisation of the Starbucks experience" has been the topic of a now famously leaked memo by then Chairman Howard Schultz to his employees.[9] He has since been hired back as CEO and tasked with fixing the problem. But what is/was the problem?

Starbucks is modelled after the Milano coffee bar – a neighbourhood place (the "third" place) where the barista pulls every

---

[9] http://online.wsj.com/public/article/SB117234084129218452-hpbDoP_cLbOUdcG_0y7qLlQ7Okg_20080224.html?mod=tff_main_tff_top, accessed: 24 Feb. 2007.

espresso shot skilfully by hand, where the shop smells deliciously of coffee, and where people like to meet, not just drink coffee. In his memo, Schultz complained about the loss of all these qualities that made up the Starbucks brand. When Starbucks switched to automatic espresso machines – which have been used in some stores for at least five years and currently are in thousands of outlets – they solved a major problem in terms of speed of service and efficiency, but at the same time lost the intimate experience with the barista. In addition, when switching to "flavor locked packaging" for the coffee, this eliminated the task of scooping fresh coffee from bins in stores and grinding it in front of customers. "We achieved fresh roasted bagged coffee, but at what cost?" questioned Schultz. "The loss of aroma – perhaps the most powerful non-verbal signal we had in our stores." Streamlining the store-design process had eliminated another important interaction point, namely character. It created "stores that no longer have the soul of the past. . . . Some people even call our stores sterile, cookie cutter," says Schultz.

While Starbucks may have unintentionally eliminated key interaction points between brand and customers (and employees!), other companies may not be aware that too many interaction points can be equally damaging for the brand. For example, an Irish mortgage lender discovered that their mortgage application process contained several unnecessary steps, each of which were an inconvenience to the customer and actually took away from the overall brand experience. By streamlining the process and reducing the number of interaction points, they substantially improved customer relationships.

While feedback from regular measurement is the main source for improving interaction points, others like spontaneous customer feedback, customer complaints, online forums, and blogs as well as competitive benchmarking should not be disregarded. As shown in the case of Maggi, when employees interact with customers and other stakeholders they can collect a substantial amount of valuable feedback which helps to identify disconnects between intended brand experience and actual brand experience. However, this information needs to be forwarded to those who can take corrective action. While such feedback is crucial for connective brands, our interviewees have confirmed that such processes are rarely formalised. In addition, this kind of communication is often strained by the "mum effect", i.e. avoiding telling someone bad news.[10]

Activity guide

Working through the questions in Figure 5.16 will help you to get the improvement process started.

> ❑ Which interaction points are least aligned with the brand promise?
> ❑ Are any of the crucial interaction points misaligned?
> ❑ Are any crucial interaction points missing?
> ❑ Are there too many interaction points?
> ❑ How can you make all interaction points more engaging?
> ❑ How can you make sure the impact on brand experience is considered when important strategic decisions are taken?

Figure 5.16 Activity Guide Step 5 – Improving brand experience

FINAL STEP: REGULAR REVIEW OF BRAND STRATEGY

The brand needs to be in sync with all major strategic drivers within the organisation. In order to ensure alignment, attention needs to be paid to implicit and explicit changes, for example a

---

[10] Milliken, F.J., Morrison, E.W. and Hewlin, P.F., An exploratory study of employee silence: Issues that employees don't communicate upward and why, *Journal of Management Studies*, 40, 6, 2003: 1454–1476.

refocusing of the business strategy, presence of a new market entrant, transformational market trends, emerging new customer needs, etc. The impact of not responding to these forces can be detrimental to the brand.

CASE STUDY: SOS CHILDREN'S VILLAGES

> The case of SOS Children's Villages demonstrates how important such a regular review of the brand strategy is. In 1949, Hermann Gmeiner created the first SOS Children's Village in a small Austrian community called Imst. As a child welfare worker who had lost his own mother at the tender age of five, Gmeiner wanted to help homeless war orphans. He believed that all children should grow up as part of a family and so he designed SOS to provide a family for children in need, based on four pillars: a mother, a house, brothers and sisters, and a village (see Figure 5.17).
>
> The mother was the crucial figure in the SOS Children's Village. Gmeiner hired local women, who were unmarried and had no children of their own, to take on the role of "mother". They were expected to take care of several kids, not necessarily real siblings, but nevertheless called "brother and sisters", who constituted a small "family" and were provided with a "traditional Austrian" family house that symbolised a private place for the family, providing a safe haven for the kids to grow up. Each of the SOS children had their own bed, which was quite a privilege at the time. In fact, the idea of orphans getting this privilege created a fascinating tension in a society where customarily, after a long day out on the field, girls would retire to their sleeping room, while boys grouped in their own room, and babies shared beds with their parents.
>
> Grouping a number of SOS family houses together created an SOS village, a place where children found joy, goodness and a sense of belonging.

THE PROCESS OF ALIGNMENT

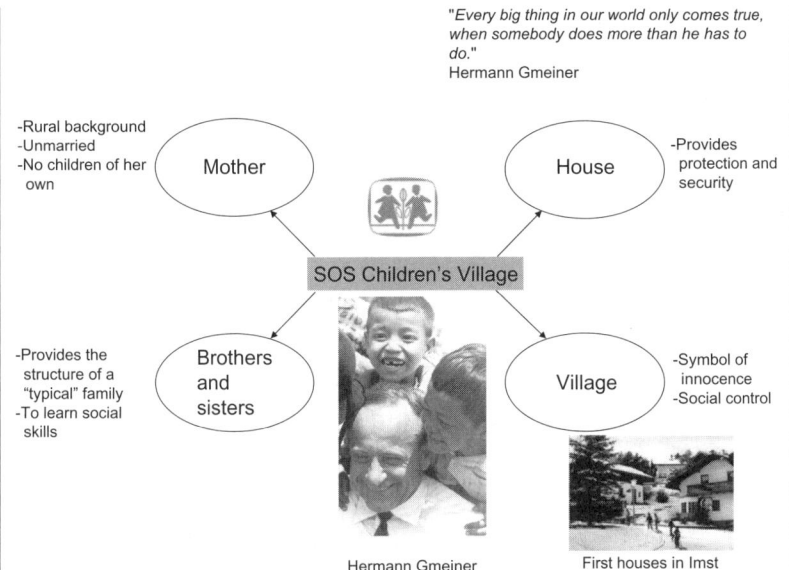

Figure 5.17 Pillars of SOS Children's Village

This proposition of providing orphaned children with an environment that was very close to a "typical family" structure was very appealing to the Austrian population, and so very quickly enough money was donated to build the first five houses in Imst, the first SOS Children's Village in the world (SOS Kinderdorf).

Changing society

From Imst, the SOS movement quickly spread to other places, first in Austria, and then over the entire world. However, the social and economic environment has changed dramatically, and with it society and the definition of what constitutes a child in need. As a result, SOS activities had outgrown their original scope. In the beginning, beneficiaries were children left parentless by the war. Over time, SOS began reaching out to a wider segment of children in need, slowly also including teenagers and whole families: today SOS takes care of orphans as well as non-orphans who cannot remain with their families for whatever reason, youths and families affected by health or natural catastrophes such as tsunamis and civil wars, as well as women in need. SOS has 766 facilities (including SOS Children's Villages, Youth Facilities, Kindergartens, Vocational Training Centres, Social Centres, etc.) in 132 countries around the globe.

Key issue – adapting to a new world

As society had changed, so had SOS – but not at the same pace. What was an appealing proposition to people wanting to donate money to a good cause was slowly losing relevance. At the same time, a myriad of competing projects and care organisations emerged, including global ones like UNICEF and World Vision and local ones like Kinderschutzbund or Barnardo's in Ireland, making it difficult for SOS Children's Village to differentiate and position themselves in the competitive environment. To make things worse, the donor basis was ageing at a worrying pace.

Therefore, in 2004, SOS Children's Village decided to revise their brand vision, mission and values to match the demands of a changed society and to regain relevance that would allow them to engage with their key stakeholders.

Approach

They embarked on a strategic process ("baking") in 2004 including an analysis of key stakeholders, a competitive analysis and a cultural audit. Parallel to the rolling-out process with approximately 500 SOS Children's Villages globally, the organisation planned to evolve into more than 1000 family-strengthening programmes ("FSP") to fight poverty in the SOS neighbourhoods. So, the term "SOS Children's Village" has been shifted from synonym to paradigm.

Getting everyone on board with these fundamental changes was no easy task. The key challenges were to get ready for that kind of brand extension, secure the necessary resources and have the FSP knowledge available at appropriate places within a suitable timeline.

The "new" SOS Children's Village brand

Reflecting the transformations in society, a new definition of what constitutes a child in need, and attempting to reconnect with their target audience, the new *brand vision* has become a great deal more empowering and includes a set of four fundamental ideologies:

- Every child belongs to a family;
- Every child grows with love;
- Every child grows with respect; and
- Every child grows with security

Their key insight evolves around "Giving childhood time and space". This vision is designed to be a source of energy and motivation for all key stakeholders.

The *SOS mission* evolves around building families for children in need, helping children to shape their own future, and to share in the development of communities.

As engaging *brand values*, SOS defined the following:

- Courage to challenge traditional methods of orphan care, and launch innovative child-care approaches;

- Commitment by stressing dedication to help generations of children to achieve a better life;
- Trust to highlight the practice of believing in each other's abilities; and
- Accountability that signifies SOS's reliability to partners by building a foundation of trust that dates back to 1949.

This set of values constitutes the core of SOS's strength, its spine.

Transforming the concept

Once the new brand vision, mission and values had been defined, SOS saw themselves facing an entirely new set of challenges: They had to relate the new concepts to the original SOS Children's Village, thereby creating continuity and a more relevant and differentiated proposition. The key was to avoid alienation of those who had been part of the "old" system for a long time.

The original pillars were updated in line with the new brand:

A. The SOS mother is replaced by parents wherever culturally appropriate

The SOS mother is no longer seen as the single heroic figure but she performs her job by being fully aware of the joys, challenges and complexities of present-day motherhood. Most importantly, however, SOS no longer neglects the roles played by both *father* and mother in the development of children. Therefore, SOS mothers are now invited to team up with their male partners. Depending on the cultural context, this is more appropriate in some societies than in others. Together mother and father face emotional and intellectual challenges, just like ordinary parents, and provide a more realistic environment in which a child can progress. Parents are provided with training in-house, for example through the Mother (Parent) Training Centers, where they can improve their social skills and knowledge to adequately prepare for their commitment as "parents" as well as to master their daily roles.

B. The family house turns into a home

Accommodation turned into a space where children feel that not only their basic needs are catered for but that they have a home where they belong. The house has turned into a home where the daily family life is shared in good and bad times, allowing children to return to even after making mistakes. Furthermore, SOS now also provides other types of accommodation such as rented apartments in cities.

C. The SOS village turns into a lively spot

The village is converted into a lively, socially well-integrated area. The unit is culturally diverse, giving kids a chance to open up to other cultures through exposure to an international network. The village ensures that children interact with open, trustworthy adults who care for their personal needs and foster their individual capabilities.

Most importantly, however, access to SOS is now open to *children* and *teenagers* in need, particularly those who have no parental care and those whose families have to live in difficult conditions.

D. Brothers and sisters

This is the only pillar that was not reinterpreted. Over the years, SOS has become a real advocate for not separating siblings. Wilfried Vyslozil, CEO of SOS International in Munich (Germany), says: "We have propagated the human right for siblings to stay together. It is important to assure that siblings are not split apart to provide stability and avoid further trauma."

Re-engaging with key stakeholders

The next set of challenges involved reaching out to key stakeholders such as donors, local authorities, media, spokespeople, etc. and communicating the changes in a way that highlighted the new contemporary context while still remaining true to the heritage of SOS. For example, donors – also called "friends" – are people and organisations who support SOS Children's Village. Originally donors provided merely financial support; today these friends also have the chance to play a meaningful part in the development of individual children, resulting in a deeper way of engaging and a more personal connection between the donor and beneficiary. For instance, donors can sponsor a child, an SOS Children's Village or a family strengthening programme, finance the construction of a football pitch, take on the running costs of a family house for a limited period of time or make a donation to one of the SOS Holiday Camps. Regular reports keep the donors informed of how the support is making a difference. Another innovative way is to support SOS Children's Villages in the form of pro-bono work as part of corporate giving.

As with any charity, one of the problems SOS faces is the fact that there is no tangible, physical "product". Many charities have found ways of acknowledging a donation in lieu of such a product. In the post war years donors received a brick as acknowledgement for their contribution, as a symbol for the houses that were built with the money given. Today donors receive more symbolic rewards that exemplify how their engagement leads to a better and fairer world for children like a "Rakhi-band" from India that stands for the love between siblings.

Results and challenges ahead

SOS managed to further increase the loyalty of their donor basis. Through telephone dialogue, web and media partners, they also managed to draw in a much younger target group. For example, by appealing to sports fans, they managed to open entirely new relationships like the FIFA who welcomed SOS as official charity of the 2006 World Cup (soccer) under the motto "6 villages for 2006". Thanks to the great support of soccer fans the six villages are already home to SOS children now.

Employees and donors have slowly come to embrace the now more realistic approach to problems in contemporary society. However, a fair amount of resistance among employees had to be overcome.

Three years after the process had been started acceptance was finally gained. Pilot projects and incremental changes have contributed significantly to growing faith into the altered brand identity.

We have now discussed the practical issues of achieving brand *engagement* and *alignment*. We will conclude the book with a showcase that hopefully brings it all together.

SHOWCASE: VAUXHALL

> Brand behaviours complement improvements to all our business processes by overlaying a Vauxhallness to the way we behave and act.
>
> *Paul Harrison, Vauxhall*

Background

Vauxhall was founded in 1857 under the name of Alex Wilson & Company by a Scottish engineer of the same name and sold its first car in 1903. Over time, Vauxhall had developed the image of an upper class British sporty car brand and was highly regarded. In 1925, Vauxhall was taken over by General Motors (GM), one of the largest automakers in the world.

Challenges

Right around the time of their centenary celebration, marketing managers Peter Hope and Paul Harrison, part of the marketing team at the time, noticed that customer feedback was showing serious dissatisfaction with the way the Vauxhall sales force and dealers treated them. At the same time, the company was suffering a slide in sales revenue and market share. Internally, there was a noticeable lack of understanding of what Vauxhall actually stood for — Vauxhall neither reinforced GM's values nor did it have its own identity. To make things worse, some retailers believed that the "Vauxhall difference" was dead — Vauxhall was perceived as boring, ordinary, and non-dynamic. It had lost the consideration it once had enjoyed, and therefore was not really attractive to younger and more affluent customers. To complicate things further, 90% of dealers are independently owned which means that one of the key points of interaction between the brand and the customer is not directly controlled by Vauxhall.

Approach

Hope and Harrison developed a strategy to address the pressing issues that included the following strands of work:

- Conduct a cultural audit to better understand the status quo in terms of current difficulties that needed to be addressed and strengths that could be leveraged
- Review and update the Vauxhall brand values in order to emphasise shared roots with GM, clarify Vauxhall's own identity and define a brand promise that can serve as a rallying point for employees
- Design a cultural change programme with the aim of improving brand understanding of employees, demonstrating brand behaviours required for delivery of the band promise and increasing employee motivation
- Measure progress and impact of the brand revitalisation programme

The brand revitalisation and cultural change programme aimed to turn Vauxhall into a 21st century, young, and inspiring brand that could facilitate penetration of a much younger customer segment while at the same reviving the existing, older customer base. In addition, the connection between GM and Vauxhall had to be clarified.

In addition to the internally focused activities, it was also very important to address the issues around dealerships and eroding customer connections. This resulted in the following initiatives:

- Understand key touchpoints between the customer, the brand and the company
- Understand key issues and key points where Vauxhall fails to connect
- Design a programme to rectify faults

1. Winning top-level support

Hope and Harrison were well aware of the difficulties and challenges that came with such a programme. Therefore, they sought and won the unconditional support of their managing director, Kevin Wale, who intuitively understood the importance of internal brand building. Senior management support did not only give them the mandate to carry out all the necessary work, it also provided them with an adequate budget. Furthermore, the support of Wale added energy, substance and significance to the brand revitalisation programme which was crucial in order to affect change in employee behaviour.

2. Establishing cross-functional collaboration

Getting the right internal stakeholders on board was another key success factor. Since finance had a huge impact on all business decisions, it had to be involved in the brand rejuvenation process. Also, it was clear that engaging employees for the new brand required the human resources and marketing department to be integrated. Hope and Harrison achieved all this by demonstrating the expected benefits to the particular concerns of each stakeholder group. For finance, they demonstrated the expected positive impact on the bottom line through increased customer loyalty, increased sales and increased brand value. For human resources, they emphasised how aligning the rewards and recog-

THE PROCESS OF ALIGNMENT

nition system with the brand promise would increase employee satisfaction, decrease attrition and ultimately also costs of recruitment and training. It was decided that particular attention had to be paid to contract workers since they had been neglected in the context of brand training, while winning their commitment in living the new brand values was considered equally important as that of regular employees.

3. Defining the Vauxhall values in line with GM

Now that all the basics were in place, Hope and Harrison carried out their cultural audit. They revealed a number of inconvenient truths, but also some strengths that could be leveraged. All the information was presented to the project team and discussed internally, which was important in order to gain a shared interpretation of the status quo. They then used the insights derived from their analysis and the GM values platform to derive the new Vauxhall values (see Figure 5.18).

This process resulted in the following four Vauxhall values, which would serve as the basis for the new brand:

- Create customer enthusiasm
- Environment of trust

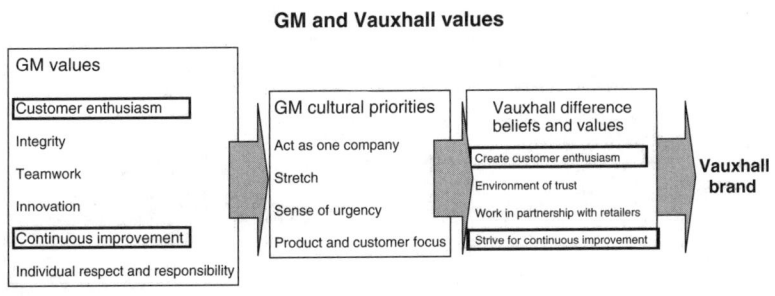

Figure 5.18 Changing the cultural environment

- Work in partnership with retailers
- Strive for continuous improvements

Two of these values – namely "customer enthusiasm" and "continuous improvement" – are shared with GM, creating a very clear link with the values and belief system of the parent company.

4. Redefining the Vauxhall difference

In a next step, the brand values were translated into a brand positioning consisting of the following elements (see also Figure 5.19):

- Product pillars – What we want to talk about
- Character – How we want to be perceived
- Benefits – How we connect and our communication style

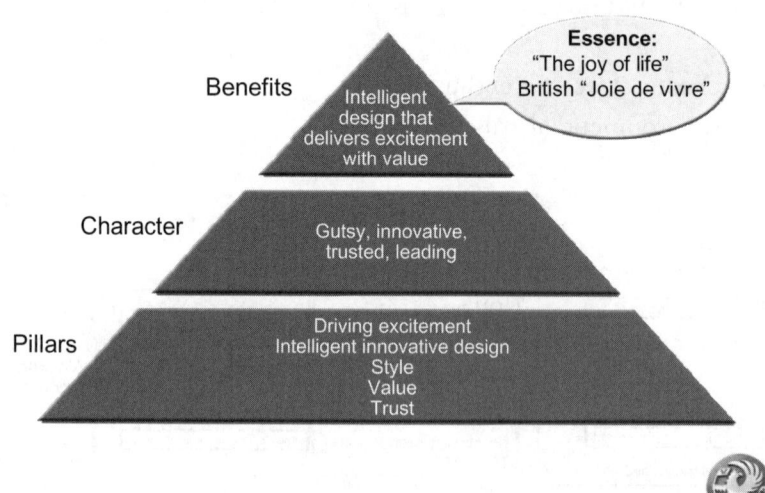

Figure 5.19 The Vauxhall brand positioning

The essence British *"joie de vivre"* was all about lust for life, 21st century Britishness and appreciating others and aimed at building a more emotional connection with key stakeholders (see Figure 5.20).

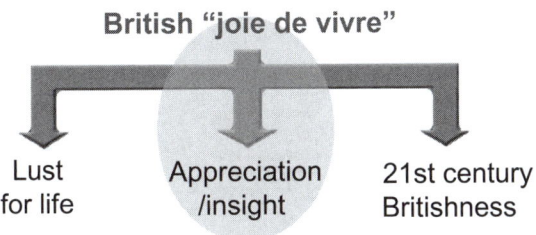

Figure 5.20 The Vauxhall difference

5. Internal brand engagement

One of the dangers many brand building programmes face is a focus on visual elements at the expense of behavioural elements. In order to counter this dynamic from the outset, Hope and Harrison highlighted that behaviours and actions deserved a great deal of attention (see Figure 5.21).

As Harrison pointed out: "If the actual customer experience and interaction with Vauxhall differs from the external communications and promise, there will be discord and ultimately our brand claims will be seen as shallow and false, resulting in no sustainable improvement in brand image." Therefore, Vauxhall took a great deal of effort to make sure employees understood the brand and related expected behaviour.

The internal roll-out had very clear objectives, namely:

- Create higher percentage of engaged employees with a clear understanding of Vauxhall's brand and business objectives

342 CONNECTIVE BRANDING

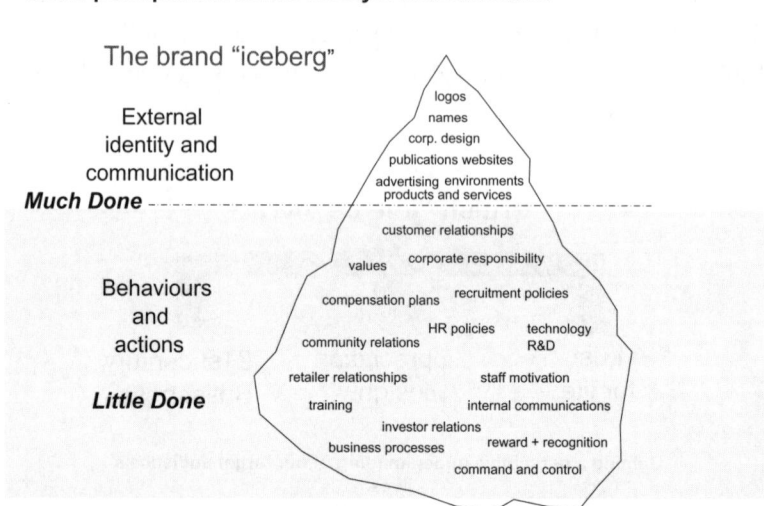

Figure 5.21 Importance of behaviours and actions

- Change behaviour and practices to deliver the brand promise
- Create an effective base for the retailer roll-out
- Create an ongoing process to eventually create the best automotive brand experience in the UK

However, one of the big threats to the success of the new brand promise was the cynicism and frustration prevalent among employees. Instead of celebrating "A Century in Motion", they were demotivated and anxious. Employees had been through several initiatives before, most of them amounting to no significant change at all, leading to a "just another programme" attitude. Being aware of this attitude and aspiring to ignite an effective process of change, Hope and Harrison decided to focus on "spiritual" engagement with a number of fast start actions that could create excitement about the impending change. Harrison highlights: "We needed to make people believe that this time round it was different. One way of doing this is through demonstrating change in leadership behaviour, but you also need to create something people want to be part of, something that makes them feel great." So they identified a number of "quick win" opportunities that would indicate that this time management was serious about the change. They focused on important employee-brand touchpoints like the canteen, reception area and ground floor meeting rooms where they would bring new and potential recruits as well as major customers. Harrison remembers:

> Looking at our physical environment with a critical eye, we quickly saw that it looks more like an insurance building than a company that sells exciting cars. Once identified, this was a fairly easy thing to change; first of all, we got our basic housekeeping in order and made a large number of small changes that accumulatively really spruced up the building. Then we introduced our "British joie de vivre" feel by displaying exciting vehicle images in all areas with high footfall, really making our cars "the heroes" and focal point of attention, supported by attractive backdrops with chromes and vibrant colours in sync with the colours used for external commuv nication. We also introduced natural lighting wherever possible by opening up the building, all of which added spark and energy to the physical environment.

These architectural changes were accompanied by posters that communicated the new brand message.

At the same time, they launched a major brand education programme. Starting with a series of brand trainings which were referred to as "mini GoFasts", they targeted groups of employees where a "quick return" was to be seen. In particular, the sales force was trained to understand the significance and implications of the new brand values in their work areas. The stated goal of the brand education was "to achieve a common minimum comprehension of Vauxhall's brand thinking – where and whom it affects the most," says Harrison. Hope and Harrison knew that they were talking to a wide spectrum of employees, with some of them possessing no knowledge of marketing or branding. Therefore, to reach and involve everybody of the organisation, a cascaded approach helped to disseminate the new brand values, using no marketing buzz-words or jargons, but a simple, to-the-point, clear brand message.

A key tool for shaping behaviour is role modelling. Employees always look to senior management to see whether they themselves live up to the brand promise. If they get a strong sense of congruency, this mostly encourages imitation. Consequently, Wale, the MD, did not only participate in workshops introducing the new brand promise to both employees and dealers, he also injected a bit of his personality into the organisation to make change happen. Harrison recollects:

> Wale was the kind of person that wanted people to stand up for ideas and fight for them. He brought to bear his Australian abrasiveness on an essentially British culture, thereby shaking up the tree a bit. Under his leadership, meetings became more aggressive, but also more engaging, real discussions started to happen and the up-turn increased tremendously. Very quickly it became clear that he genuinely cared about people coming on board the brand programme, he wanted them to actively partake, ask real questions and be candid. Within a few months, he had shifted our organisational culture from cautious to conservative risk taker, which is exactly what we needed in order to change. Of course, this also meant that some people became very uncomfortable, but if those who stand in the way of change start to feel out of sync with the organisation and are marginalised, then real change can happen. Once comprehension was achieved, we needed to focus on creating commitment to Living the Brand, i.e. define the relevance to individual employees and their day-to-day role.

They organised team sessions for each department and worked through the practical implications of the new brand promise, discussing the role of employees in the brand delivery, their contribution, and the impact of non-compliance, both to the individual and the company overall. The sessions were designed to create buy-in and excitement, while also deepening overall brand understanding.

6. Dealer engagement

As mentioned earlier, about 90% of Vauxhall's dealers were independently owned, placing a significant part of the brand–customer interaction in the dealers' hands. Although Vauxhall dealers in theory sign up to a franchisee standard, in practice it is very difficult to enforce. Harrison points out that "it is relatively easy to enforce the physical elements like the shop environment and visual presentation, but it is very difficult to influence human behaviour in this situation. In essence, we rely on the fact that this should be a symbiotic relationship." Unfortunately, dealers' loss of faith in Vauxhall did not bode well for this symbiotic relationship and the Vauxhall brand overall. Vauxhall had found out about this dealer issue primarily through customer research which showed that customers felt that they were not treated very well by the dealers, with issues ranging from the unwillingness to provide cost estimates for repairs, their failure to offer alternative transport while the car was being repaired and vehicles being returned to the customer in dirty condition. At the same time, dealers themselves complained that Vauxhall did not provide adequate support to live up to the imposed standards.

The challenge now was to find a way to maximise control of the dealer–end customer interface while at the same time engaging dealers in living the new brand promise. Historically viewed as an external audience, the situation forced Vauxhall to shift paradigms. By including dealers as an internal group that needed to be sufficiently educated about the new brand promise, its benefits and ways to be implemented, they were able to achieve a breakthrough. Hope and Harrison launched a wholesale brand roll-out programme following the same basic steps of Communicate – Comprehend – Commit as the internal brand building programme with the aim of bridging the gap that had gradually started to develop between employees and dealers. Harrison explains:

> We were very open and very honest with the dealers in explaining where we are coming from and where we needed to get to; we explained the problems around lost consideration and the perception of being "still trustworthy but dull" with great candidness, and even shared the findings of our market research. This created instant credibility and made it much easier to discuss how we planned to address the problems and what their role was in the process.

7. External communication

Hope and Harrison knew that an external campaign was only going to be effective after the new brand promise had been fully understood and integrated internally. Therefore, they hired an advertising agency to execute the external campaign "A Century in Motion" only once they were sure that employees and dealers were sufficiently on board with the new brand promise.

Project outcomes

Vauxhall managed to stabilise its market share and significantly improve sales revenue. Customer feedback signalled improvement of service quality provided and employees, in particular the sales force, began contributing tremendously to the alignment of internal and external brand perception by providing feedback through visiting their dealers and customers and reporting back observations.

Internal research indicated that employees were increasingly identifying with the new Vauxhall brand promise and with the identity of Vauxhall in general. The relationship between Vauxhall and its dealers improved, encouraging dealers to start believing again in the Vauxhall brand experience and reinforcing it.

By 2005, overall consideration levels of the Vauxhall brand had recovered to the level of 1997; an even greater lift was achieved in the under-35 market. In 2006, a new Corsa model was launched, but the positive impact could be established even for the old model. An uplift in retail sales overall and in particular in the younger market was further proof that the brand revitalisation programme had been successful. Harrison remarks: "In addition to the strong backing of our MD Kevin Wale, we also had the support of a fantastic team; without the help of Dean Barrett, marketing director at the time, and Sara Nicholson, brand manager Corsa, we would have never been able to pull this off."

Major challenges ahead

As with most branding initiatives, a key issue is to keep the excitement and momentum alive. Vauxhall needs to keep the new brand promise vibrant in order to avoid falling back into old habits. In order to address this issue, an internal brand manager was put in place with the sole task to look after employee brand engagement.

Another critical aspect concerns the interaction with dealers – there were still open questions around how to further optimise collaboration. But hey, this is all in the spirit of continuous improvement!

CONCLUSION

We have now discussed the major market forces that shape the current business and branding environment, demonstrated how companies have started to react to these market forces, proposed a model for building successful brands, and shared some practical insights in the form of critical success factors.

To recap connective branding is built on *brand engagement* and *brand alignment* as the two key drivers of brand equity and entails a number of shifts from traditional branding:

- *Broadening of audiences addressed* – moving beyond a sole focus on the customer to consider also the role of and build meaningful relationships with employees and other stakeholders
- *Networked collaboration* – moving beyond the notion that the marketing department is the sole owner of the brand by creating an approach that leverages brand enthusiasts within the organisation (role modelling) and coordinates all brand relevant functions
- *Living brand values from within* – moving beyond a brand paradigm that sees the brand as the creation of a favourable external image by placing greater emphasis on the willingness and ability of employees to enact the brand and deliver on the brand promise; this necessitates that the brand permeates the entire organisation, creating authenticity as a result
- *Building interactive relationships* – moving beyond one-way, disruptive and manipulative communication to new frontiers of brand engagement
- *Addressing CSR strategically* – moving beyond a paradigm that sees profitability and doing good at odds with each other, towards embracing CSR as a strategic opportunity that benefits both the company and society at large

EPILOGUE – THE LAW OF THE SEVENTH GENERATION?

> In our every deliberation we must consider the impact of our decisions on the next seven generations.
>
> *From the Great Law of the Iroquois Confederacy*

Traditional brand management saw the rise of the brand manager – a task that was focused on the short-term maximisation of product sales, the creation of an external image through advertising and other communicative measures, and the emphasis of functional product attributes.

Today the average brand manager stays in their job for less than two years – raising the question whether they are ill-equipped for the new challenges (unlikely) or whether the strategic time horizon is shortening (more likely).

We believe that the brands that will be successful going forward will be the ones that are embraced by the entire organisation, based on solid values that do not see profitability and doing good as mutually exclusive, take a long-term and holistic view with regards to nourishing the brand and consider that *how* you achieve success is as important as success itself.

This will require a new type of leader who understands the importance of value-based management, genuinely values her people, and can inspire and motivate employees, customers, and other key stakeholders alike. These leaders will carry the brand torch and successfully leverage a framework like connective branding.

Most importantly, they have a basic choice to treat their brand like a rainforest (extract and deplete) or a rice field (nourish and enrich). If they choose the rice field, connective branding will help them to achieve their goals. For this journey we wish them all the best.

INDEX

Aaker, David 140
Accenture 10
Adidas 7
advertising 3–4
Aer Lingus 288–94, 317–18, 321, 322
  advertising campaign 290
  challenges 291
  fate intervenes 292–3
Agassi, Andre 256
Ahrendts, Angela 254
Airtours 301
Alex Wilson & Company 336
alignment 279–348
Amazon 105–6
American Eagle Outfitters 109
Anheuser-Busche 109
animals, cruelty to 7
Apple 24, 36, 139, 144–5, 146
ARAL 197–200
Arthritis Ireland 172, 192
aspirational brand 137
Astra VXR 174

attributes 132
authenticity 50–69
  differentiation through 57
  dimensions of 55–7
  growth and 579
  ownership structure and 59–60
  through company life cycle 57–61
  transferability and 60–1
Aveda 14, 89–90, 200–1
Axe (Unilever) 28, 36, 107, 141

Baileys Original Irish cream 52
Bakan, Joel: *Corporation, The* 7
Barbie dolls 10, 12
Barnardo's 330
Bayer 7
Beastie Boys 103
Beiersdorf 36, 193
Ben & Jerry's 9, 14, 57, 60, 61, 62
Benetton 188
Blogbang 108
blogs 25, 96, 99, 100, 105, 185

INDEX

BMW 202–3
BMW Group Brand Academy 203
Body Shop 9, 14, 57, 60, 61
Bombay Sapphire 53
Bono 87
BP (British Petroleum) 54, 75–80, 197, 200
Brabeck-Letmathe, Peter 200–1
brand alignment 214–15
   brand building through 123, 126, 204–9
brand architecture 36, 139–40
   aligning brand vision and 298–305
brand building 148, 154–5
   through alignment 123, 126, 205–9
   through engagement 123, 126, 157–84
brand carriers 38–9
brand content 130–1, 214
brand creation 164
brand delivery 39
   aligning processes and structures for 318–20
brand dilution 142
brand, embracing 171–2
brand equity 143, 144, 151, 214
   key drivers of 124–5
brand essence 220
brand experience 154, 159, 214–15
   aligning brand delivery 318–20
   aligning brand promise and 314–17
   aligning with actual brand experience 324–7
   designing and enabling 314–20
   improving 324–7
   measurement of 320–3
brand expert 164
brand goals 321–2
brand launch 165–6
brand management 123, 126, 146–56
brand metrics 151–2, 155, 179, 321–2
brand ownership 146–7
brand principles 131–6
   differentiation 136
   hierarchy of 132–4
   on value level 134–6

brand promise 126, 137–8, 214, 222, 226, 249, 250
   aligning brand experience (design) and 314–17
   employee engagement programme and 161–2
   translating 265–8
Brand Relationship Spectrum 140
brand reminders and energisers 179–82
brand role models 162–3
brand strategy 123, 126, 128–45
   aligning brand architecture and brand vision 298–305
   aligning business strategy and 288–94
   aligning competing values 281–7
   aligning corporate culture and 295–7
   designing 281–305
   regular review of 327–35
   role in the organisation 129–30
brand training 182–3
brand values 44–6, 153
brand vision 126, 138, 220
   aligning brand architecture and 298–305
brand workshops 19
Branded House strategy 140, 142–5, 166
branding team 306–13
   aligning different brand perspectives 307–11
   aligning strategic role and power to act 306–7
   aligning strategic role and standing in the organisation 311–13
   structure of 147
Branson, Sir Richard 146, 174
British Airways 322
British Midland 322
Browne, Lord John 75, 79
Bruin, Jochem de 259
Burberry 253–4
Burton 150
Bush, George W. 6, 8
   administration 4
Bush family 8

INDEX 353

business strategy 128–9
　aligning brand strategy and 288–94
business-to-business (B2B) markets 142, 205, 306
business to customer (B2C) markets 205

Cadbury Schweppes 61
caring, brand value of 134, 135, 136
Cavalieri, Paolo 45, 49
challenger brands 58
Chanel 254
Chantelle 100
check-up 170
child labour 4, 7, 14, 18–19
Citigroup 7
Cliff Bar 73
Clinton, Hillary 8
Cluetrain Manifesto 26
ciao.com 106
Coca-Cola 83, 92, 110, 166
commoditisation 32
Companies Act 2006 16
company culture 138
connective branding 124–7
Conseil, Dominique 89–90
consistency 55
consumer fatigue 4
control issues 10–13
core team 147–9
　responsibilities 150–1
corporate culture, aligning brand strategy and 295–7
corporate branding 36, 37
corporate reputation 148–9
corporate scandals 4, 6
Corporate Social Investment (CSI) 48
corporate social responsibility (CSR) 9, 13–23, 70–94, 190
　environmental issues and concerns 72–80
　ethical behaviour 83–94
　quietly conscientious companies 93
　social responsibility 80–3
　strategic approach to 85–6
　strategy framework 73

corporate social responsibility entrepreneurs 86–9
corporate social responsibility leaders 89–90
country of origin tags 8
creation and brand carriers 38–9
credit cards 195
crowdsourcing 102–3
customer engagement 148, 184–204, 246–61
　authenticity 248–9
　brand online 252–3
　engaging different cultures 254–5
　finding ways to connect 257–61
　focusing on most important moments of truth 249–52
　paying attention to detail 256–8
　retaining relevancy to core users 253–4
customer satisfaction 173

Damon, Matt 83
Deneuve, Catherine 256
Deutsche Bank 7, 254–5
DHL 93
Diet Coke 107
discretionary commitment 56–7
distrust 6–9
Donna Karan 7
Dove (Unilever) 27–8, 36, 107, 141, 190
　Onslaught campaign 28
Ducati 199, 268, 269–77
Ducati Corners 276
Ducati Desmo Owners Club (DOC) 273–4
Ducati Museum 274
Ducati Stores 275–6
Ducati University/riding school 275

easyJet 294
eBay 106
Edelman 262
Edelman Trust barometer 6
EDUN 86–8
Egon Zehnder International 319

emotional benefits 4, 132
employee behaviour, desired 44–6
employee engagement 56–7, 159, 215–46
  across all phases of brand building 164–9
  brand building on simple and powerful ideas 226–8
  brand promise and 161–2
  demonstrating relevance to employees 231–5
  by employee type 163–4
  engaging role models 221–4
  first hand experience of brand values 228–31
  for connective brands 160–1
  maintaining 236–40
  networked collaboration 224–5
  translating the meaning of values 235–6
employee motivation and orientation 55–6
employee role 35
employee signature experience 183–4
empowerment 172
Enlightened Shareholder 16
Enron 4, 6
entrepreneurship 41
environment, work 43–4
environmental destruction 7
Environmental Protection Agency (EPA) 54
ESG (environmental, social and governance) issues 16
Estée Lauder 90
ethical behaviour 83–5
Ethos Water 82
evaluation portals 105–6
evolution of branding 3–4
EXCITE programme 175
exploitative practice 7

Faber Castell 72, 74
Facebook 95
Fahrenheit 9/11 8
Fair Trade 81, 223

fake authenticity 53–4
fake blogs (flogs) 119, 185
Federal Trade Commission (FTC) 54
financial community, engagement with 201
First Choice Holidays PLC 302
Fisher-Price toys 8, 10, 12
Flickr 117
focus 37
Ford 38
FOX media 8
France Telecom 218
Friedman, Milton 18
Fritidsresor 300
Frontier 241
functional benefits 132

Gap Inc. 4, 18–19, 20
  RugMark programme 19
Garnier 110
Garnier Fructis Style Bold 109
Gate Gourmet 309
GE 79
  Ecoimagination 91–2
Geldof, Sir Bob 59
General Motors (GM) 38, 336–40
  employee brand engagement 174–5
  employee incentivisation 176
  employee selling of brands 176–9
  EXCITE programme 176
  General Motors (GM) UK/Ireland 173–9
  Mates Rates programme 176
  pride in company 173–4
Genesis 56
GeoTrax 10
Global Demos 21, 22
Global March Against Child Labour 19
globalisation 32
Gmail 238
Gmeiner, Hermann 328
Goldman Sachs 78
Google 24, 33, 60, 111, 134, 187, 237–40, 297

Google News 238
Gorbachev, Mikhail 256
Gore, Al 14
Graf, Steffi 256
Green & Blacks 9, 60, 61
green movement 14
Green Partners 248
green products 74–5
Greenpeace 92, 249
greenwashing 53, 54, 74, 94
Gucci 254

Häagen Dazs 52
Hailwood, Mike 'the Bike' 272
Halliburton 6
Hapag Lloyd 298
Happy Digits 195
Harley-Davidson 271
Harrods 276
'Harry Situation, The' 109
Hayward, Tony 80
Helm, Sabrina 308
Hemetsberger, Andrea 103
Henkel 36, 141
henryjenkins.org 25
heritage 137
Hewson, Ali 86
Hirsch, Robert 235–6
holidaycheck.de 106
Hollard 40–56, 168, 229
Honda 74
House of Brands strategy 27, 36, 140–2, 166

IBM 81
incentive metrics 179
induction training 182–3
initial brand training 169–70
innocent 14, 62–9, 73, 129, 171–2, 194
innovation 41, 136
instore-engagement 192–4
insurance, corporate branding in 40–9
Intel 139
internal launch, timing of 166–9
internalmemos 26

Internet 4, 6, 24–9, 95–119
intimacy 289
intuition 289
iPod 145, 170
It's a Big World 10
iTunes 145

Jenkins, Henry 25
JetBlue 241
Jobs, Steve 146

Karan, Donna 276
Kerrygold 52
Kinderschutzbund 330
Klein, N: *No Logo* 7
Kneipp 180
KPGM 81
Kraft Foods 252–3
Kryptonite 25–6

Lacoste 221–3
Lauren, Ralph 254
leadership 55
LEGO 99, 113–19, 201, 252, 265–8
Lemon Tree Hotels 229–31
Linux 104
Litvinenko, Alexander 256
logos 3
LOHAS (Lifestyles of Health and Sustainability) 15
Lonsdale 191–2
L'Oréal 61, 109–10
louisvuitton.com 256
loyalty cards 195–6
loyalty pathway 186–96, 246–7
 awareness building phase 187–9
 consideration phase 190–2
 familiarity building phase 189–90
Lufthansa Credit Card 195
Lunn Poly 301

Macintosh 139
Mackey, John 84, 85
Macy's 276
Maggi 202, 232–5, 326

INDEX

Magic Life 301
Manner 180, 192–3
market forces 3–29
Marks & Spencer 72, 79, 92
Marriott Corporation 222
Mars bar 35
master brand strategy 36, 143–4
Masterfoods 35
Mattel 4, 8, 10, 11–12, 20
McDonald's 68
McKinsey & Company 262
measurement of brand experience 320–3
   aligning across the organisation 322–3
   aligning brand goals and metrics 321–2
   of synchronised brands 152–5
Melo, Fatima Moreira de 259
Mentos brand 107
Mercedes-Benz 112
Merck 222
Mero 181
MINI 202, 203
Moore, Michael 8
MPREIS 250–1
multi-stakeholder engagement 201–3
MySpace 26, 95

Nescafé Dolce Gusto 108
Nestlé 15, 36, 83, 108, 141, 200–1, 232
net promoter score 153
NetApp 183, 312–13, 322
netiquette 120
NGOs 3, 8, 9, 23, 33, 34, 38, 82, 137, 158, 200, 202
Nike 7, 18, 99
Nivea 166, 193
No-l-ita 188, 189, 190
Nostalgic 229
Nupedia 295

Old Mutual Group 224–5, 283, 286–7
oneworld alliance 293
online communities 100–2, 185

online customer interaction 95–119
   creative contributors 105–8
   engaging with customer-led communities 110–12
   entertainment seekers 108
   expert innovators 104–5
   individual customers 96–7
   information 97
   interaction 97
   involvement 100
   open source collaborators 102–4
   relationship 99–100
   transaction 97–8
   viral campaigns 108–9
   virtual worlds 110
online soap operas (webisodes) 109–10
Orange 218–19
organisational hierarchy 161–2
organisational level 39
outsourcing 12

Palazzo, Guido 21, 23
Panasonic 191
Parmalat 4, 6
partnerships 41
Passionata brand 100
Patagonia 14
Payback card 195
Pepsi 83
Philips 136
Philips, Sir Lionel 44
potmstudios 311
Preussag 298
price–earnings ratio 152
Procter & Gamble 36, 109, 141
product branding 36, 37
product life cycle 40
professionalism 299
Publicis Groupe 108
purchasing funnel 153

Quelle 191

Rabobank Group 257–61
Rasmussen, Torben Hangaard 114
Rechelbacher, Horst 89, 90

Red Bull 189
retailers, engagement with 201
Right Said Fred 118
risk management 10
RIU 301
roadshows 180
Robinson 301
rogue trader 12
Rolls-Royce 202–3
Rose, Stuart 92
RugMark 19
Ryanair 289, 290, 293, 294, 322

Saab 174
Sabo, Thomas 281, 316
Sainsbury's 67
SAP AG 152
Sarbanes–Oxley Act 150
Sarge 10, 12
Schultz, Howard 146, 325–6
Scott, Lee 262
September 11, 2001 4
shareholders, engagement with 201
Shell 7, 54, 76
Siemens 142, 143–4
  Answers campaign 223
Silicon Valley 239
Skandia 283
Snapple 61
Social Brand Capital 71, 73
social networking 26, 185
social responsibility 80–3
Société Général 12–13
Sony 185, 248–9
SOPI (Sequence–Oriented Problem Identification) 154
SOS Children's Villages 328–35
SouthWest 146
Southwest Airlines 241
Spitzer, Eliot 103
sponsorship 1899–90
Sportler 181
stakeholder engagement 213–78
stakeholder journey 205–9
Starbucks 81–3, 146, 325–6
Starwood Hotels & Resorts 112

stigma industries 14
Stonyfield Farm 73
story-telling 180
subprime-mortgage crisis 6
successes, early, celebrating 170
suppliers, engagement with 200–1
sweatshops 14

target 38
TD Ameritrade: *Power Book* 167
team
  branding 306–13
  core team 147–51
  extended 149–50
  structure 147
Technorati 26
Ted 241–5
TerraChoice Environmental Marketing 54
theharrysituation.com 110
Thomson Fly 301
Thomson Holidays 300
time horizon 40
Tivo 148
TNT 93
top management engagement 216–21
  brand decisions and projects 219–21
Toscani, Oliviero 188
Total 54
Toyota 38, 74
  Prius 16, 38, 74
transparency 55
tripadvisor.com 105, 106
Trust Barometer 9
trust, erosion of 6–9
TUI (Touristik Union International) AG 166–8, 298–305
  aligning brand vision and brand architecture 300–4
  basic holidays 301–2
  challenges ahead 304
  new brand architecture 299
  new brand vision, mission and values 299
  new logo 300

quality-volume brands 300–1
  specialist offers 301
TUI Travel PLC 303–4
TUIfly.com 301
Tyco 6

UBS 7, 182, 321
UNICEF 330
Unilever 27–8, 36, 107, 109, 141
United Airlines 241–5

value 31, 132, 134, 135
value chain 22
value congruency 135
value core 34, 51, 53, 130, 131–2
value-based branding 33–4
vault.com 26
Vauxhall 336–47
Vespa 52
Virgin Group 36, 142, 146
vocal corporate social responsibility
  converts 90–3
Volvo 246, 247
Vuitton, Louis 256–7

Waitrose 67
Wal-Mart 8, 185, 261–5
wall strategy 141
Walton, Sam 263
Web 1.0, 106
Web 2.0 6, 26, 95, 106

Web logs *see* blogs
webisodes 109–10
weforum.org 6
Wells Fargo 111
Whole Foods 85
Wikipedia 105, 295–7
Wild Oats 85
word-of-mouth marketing 173
World Ducati Weekend (WDW) 275
World Economic Forum 6
World of TUI 298–9, 302, 305
  logo 168
World Vision 330
WorldCom 6
Wrigley's 99

XXXLutz 227–8

Yale School of Management (SOM)
  16, 17, 18
YouBloom 59, 60
YouTube 26, 28, 95, 117

Zara 187
Zazzle.com 103
Zidane, Zinedine 108
Zotter Schokoladen Manufaktur
  GmbH 223
Zumwinkel, Klaus 171

Index compiled by Annette Musker